Rooted in the Body

Rooted in the Body

Arabic Metaphor and Morphology

Lisa J. White

Illustrated by Mahmoud Shaltout

The American University in Cairo Press

Cairo   New York

First published in 2021 by
The American University in Cairo Press
113 Sharia Kasr el Aini, Cairo, Egypt
One Rockefeller Plaza, 10th Floor, New York, NY 10020
www.aucpress.com

Dar el Kutub No. 19475/19
ISBN 978 977 416 977 9

Dar el Kutub Cataloging-in-Publication Data

White, Lisa
Rooted in the Body: Arabic Metaphor and Morphology by Lisa White, illustrator Mahmoud Shaltout.—Cairo: The American University in Cairo Press, 2021
p. cm.
ISBN 978 977 416 977 9
1. Arabic language_morphology
2. Linguistics
3. Metaphor
I. Shaltout, Mahmoud (ill.)
492.759

2 3 4 5 25 24 23 22 21

Designed by Rafik Abousoliman
Printed in the United States of America

Contents

Acknowledgments

Rooted in the Body has been years and years in the making, and along the way, many colleagues, friends, and students have contributed to it in ways large and small. Their questions, comments, and insights have made quite a difference to the end product. Although I cannot mention everyone, I am grateful to all for the inspiration and support they have provided.

I owe a special debt of gratitude to Professor Elsaid Badawi, Arabist and pedagogue par excellence, for having championed this project in its early years. When I told him I was creating a visual archive to show how the Arabic derivational system fleshes out body metaphor, his interest was immediate and intense. Over the years, he kept an enthusiastic eye on my progress, and made many substantive contributions to my understanding of the body, especially his elucidation of the link between the heel, العقب *al-'aqib*, and punishment, العقاب *al-'iqaab*. Dr. Badawi's sustained encouragement was a profound source of motivation.

What is now the textual component of this book was, for many years, presented orally and in small doses in the classroom. Its visual component consisted of illustrations scavenged piecemeal from the web, but thorny issues of attribution and copyright made publication impossible. Claude Audebert, professor emerita of Arabic at the University of Aix-en-Provence and at the American University in Cairo (AUC), was eager to help extricate me from this impasse, and briefly entertained thoughts of lending her talents as a watercolorist to the task. However, it soon became clear that completing her online Arabic–French dictionary of Egyptian Colloquial would preclude embarking on another major project. Nevertheless, in her biannual 'dictionary visits' to Cairo, we had many opportunities to discuss the fascinating topic of embodiment. Among her valuable insights was how much a careful look at poetry could enhance everyone's understanding of the ways in which the body is conceptualized in Arabic.

Still at a standstill on the copyright issue, I consulted the Center for Learning and Teaching (CLT) at AUC, where I made the acquaintance of Nadine Aboulmagd, who was familiar with the ingenious illustrations that Professor Mahmoud Shaltout had contributed to several CLT workshops. She advised me to contact him, and from that seed, a most fruitful collaboration soon sprouted. The present incarnation of *Rooted in the Body* would not have been possible without her fortuitous suggestion and without Mahmoud's inspired interpretations of the chapters.

Very special thanks go to Susan Spock, consummate reader and professional academic editor. In 2017, on a summer visit to the United States, I launched into a description of *Rooted in the Body* and the chapters that I had recently begun writing. Despite the fact that she has no background in Arabic, her curiosity was piqued. That enthusiasm made me wonder just how accessible the work might be to someone with an abundance of cultural and intellectual curiosity, but no acquaintance with the language. To find out, I sent her several chapters, and she was able to follow their logic quite well. In fact, between the summers of 2017 and 2018, she edited about fifteen of them. Thanks to her cogent observations, organizational savvy, and encouragement, I decided there was room for hope! A second experiment followed, this time with research librarian Ann Marie Breznay, who was also kind enough to read a handful of different chapters and offer some very clever comparative insights.

Arabists, too, from neophytes to full professors, were generous with their help. I thank Samira Khalil for her sustained interest in the project and, for her excellent suggestion to find a drawing of القَصّ *al-qaSS*, the sternum, as I searched for its elusive link to cutting. Hitomi Sakai also lent her Arabic talents to the project, and gave a particularly thoughtful reading to المحيّا *al-muHayyaa,* the face. Others dear to my heart, especially Mohammed El-Kawasmi, Azza Waked, Margaret Larkin, Laila Familiar, Marianne Petit, and Sandra McNabb offered information and encouragement of all sorts at just the right times. Dr. Mahmoud Rabei kindly shared his contacts at Magmaʿ al-Lugha, Cairo's Academy of the Arabic Language. He also volunteered insights of his own. When I found dictionaries to be contradictory on a point of gender, he immediately resolved my dilemma with a reference to some seventh-century anatomy, specifically that of Muʿawiya ibn Abi Sufyan, the first Umayyad caliph! For answers to a broad range of questions on usage, stylistics, classicisms, and jurisprudence that few single individuals can offer, I thank Dr. Mohammed Alaiwa of Cairo University's Dar al-Ulum. I am especially grateful to have learned from him that Arabic's nearly synonymous words for the eyelash, رمش *rimsh* and هدبة *hudba*, are temporally distinct. The latter is the only one of the pair with a classical pedigree. This issue of chronology could add another informative dimension to our understanding of body idiom, and especially of such semantic pairs and multiples.

Finally, I must mention Dr. Sylvie Denoix, CNRS historian and former director of research at l'Institut français d'archéologie orientale in Cairo. In 2013, this fellow traveler—*rafiiqat darbi*—on the long road to fluency in Arabic, was kind enough to introduce me to the very strange but intriguing theories of Georges Bohas. I remain a traditionalist in terms of root attribution, but his concepts also stem from a very basic sort of embodiment and deserve more attention. Sylvie was also instrumental in helping me overcome my reluctance to write, and I thank her from the bottom of my heart for her valuable remarks on the topic, delivered with such a light touch, but deeply felt.

As I reiterate my thanks to all who helped this project see the light of day, I apologize for any oversights or errors in it. In my heart of hearts, it will always be a work in progress.

Key to Body Parts

'Body' and Here, There, and Everywhere

Excrescences and the Ineffable

Front Upper Body (Shoulders and above) and Arm

30 Front / قبل
31 Head / رأس
32 Brain / مخّ
33 Brain / دماغ
34 Forehead / جبين
35 Face / وجه
36 Face (1) / محيّا
37 Face (2) / محيّا
38 Face (1) / طلعة
39 Face (2) / طلعة
40 Ear / أذن
41 Eyebrow / حاجب
42 Eyelid / جفن
43 Eyelash / هدبة
44 Eyelash / رمش
45 Eye / عين
46 Eye / مقلة
47 Pupil / حدقة
48 Cornea (1) / قرنيّة
49 Cornea (2) / قرنيّة
50 Dimple / غمّازة
51 Nose / أنف
52 Nostril / منخار
53 Mustache (1) / شارب
54 Mustache (2) / شارب
55 Lip / شفة
56 Mouth / فو، فم
57 Palate, Roof of the Mouth / حنك
58 Tongue /لسان
59 Tooth / سنّ
60 Throat, Larynx / حلق
61 Throat, Upper Chest / زور
62 Jaw / فكّ
63 Jawbone; Beard / لحْي، لحية
64 Neck / رقبة
65 Neck / عنق
66 Throat, Lower Front of the Neck / خناق، مخنق
67 Throat, Lower Front of the Neck / نحر، منحر
68 Shoulder / كتف
69 Shoulder, (Upper) Flank / منكب
70 Shoulder / عاتق
71 Arm, Forearm / ذراع
72 Forearm (1) / ساعد
73 Forearm (2) / ساعد
74 Elbow / كوع
75 Elbow / مرفق
76 Wrist / معصم
77 Hand (1) / يد
78 Hand (2) /يد
79 Palm / راحة

80 Palm / كفّ
81 Knuckle; Joint / عقلة
82 Digit: Finger, Toe / إصبع
83 Thumb; Big Toe / إبهام
84 Index Finger (1) / سبّابة
85 Index Finger (2) / سبّابة
86 Nail / ظفر
87 Fingertip / أنملة

Trunk and Lower Body, from the Front

88 Chest / صدر
89 Sternum / قصّ
90 Breast / ثدي
91 Breast / نهد
92 Bosom / حضن
93 Breast, Nipple / بزّ
94 Nipple / حلمة
95 Esophagus / مريء
96 Side / جنب
97 Rib / ضلع
98 Pulmonary Region, Lungs / سحر
99 Heart / قلب
100 Heart / فؤاد
101 Liver / كبد
102 Abdomen, Belly / بطن
103 Navel / سرّة
104 Genitalia; Vulva / فرج
105 Vulva / بضع
106 Womb / رحم
107 Penis (1) / ذكر
108 Penis (2) / ذكر
109 Leg / رجل
110 Leg / ساق
111 Knee / ركبة
112 Foot / قدم
113 Heel, Ankle; Breasts, Bosom / كَعب، كُعب

Back, Top to Bottom

114 Nape / قفا
115 Back (1) / ظهر
116 Back (2) / ظهر
117 Upper Back / كاهل
118 Back / متن
119 Back of the Body, Rear, Hindquarters / دبر
120 Seat, Rump / مقعدة
121 Butt, Bottom / عجيزة، عجز
122 Rump, Rear, Buttock / ردف
123 Backside, Hindquarters / كفل
124 Derrière, Behind / مؤخّرة
125 Heel / عقب

Introduction

Embodiment

We, as human beings, are always thinking about our bodies. It might even be more accurate to say that our bodies actually do our thinking. The act of thinking points to the presence of the abstract mind, but our bodies are right under our noses, so to speak, and they are well endowed with sensory receptors for heat and cold, hunger and thirst, pleasure and pain. It's not just that they are difficult to ignore. Take away the physical brain, and the intangible universe of the mind, conscious and unconscious, is gone, too. Because we simply cannot survive without it, the body has remarkable psychic weight, a fact borne out by its omnipresence in speech. The body has its own intelligence, and in language after language, however disparate, the body makes its voice heard. From everyday chitchat to formal discourse, speech is peppered with references to the body, even if individual *speakers* fail to notice it.

In ways simple and complex, straightforward and roundabout, the body determines how we conceive of the world, inserting itself in most every sphere of human endeavor. This phenomenon, dubbed 'embodiment' in modern scholarship, has important applications to a broad array of fields, including philosophy, cognitive psychology, ethnology, and cultural history, to name just a few. It also has obvious relevance to language studies and linguistics. Much has been said of this in George Lakoff and Mark Johnson's groundbreaking *Metaphors We Live By* and in Johnson's subsequent *The Body in the Mind: The Bodily Basis of Meaning, Imagination, and Reason.*[1] As they point out, embodiment is not only a question of the specific vocabulary of the body, although it starts there. Bodily processes, too, like eating and drinking—not to mention things we may be reluctant to mention in polite society—are aspects of embodiment.

The body profoundly influences our perspective as well. The proper physical orientation of the body, head held high, has insured that in many languages, up and down and high and low directly correlate with good and bad. Similarly, bodies are designed for movement. The commonplace metaphor of life as a journey would make no sense if humans were plant-like, with roots instead of feet. The countless long marches humans have taken to explore their worlds allowed them to conceptualize life, a grand abstraction, as a journey, something familiar. Pursuing such explicit and implicit references to bodily function, orientation, and shape in idiomatic usage is fascinating in any language, and especially so in Arabic. This is because, in Arabic, the body is the root, quite literally, of thousands of other vocabulary items.

On a much smaller scale, this is true of English, which can also modify a body part with a prefix or suffix to produce new and related vocabulary. 'Face' may be the most prolific example. Some words like interface and deface are quite obvious derivatives. Others, especially those that modify the original pronunciation, like surface, facet, and facetious may slip by under our conscious radar. A few other English body parts also accept minor morphological modifications. A suffixed '-le' or '-l' occasionally turns up. Can you *handle* that? I *sidled* up to him. He tried to *throttle* her. *Kneel!* English also has colorful compounds at its disposal. A tiny sample includes nouns like bloodbath, sidekick, and skinflint, adjectives like underhanded, pigheaded, and potbellied, and verbs like earmark, bad-mouth, and brownnose. It can also put adverbs and prepositions to work to add figurative 'oomph' to the original. Up and down are particularly versatile. The choice of one or the other may allow for a literal/figurative split, as in *backing down* the stairs and *backing down* in an argument. If one knows the meaning, the logic behind it is clear, but to the uninitiated, such expressions, especially when figurative, may be opaque.

Arabic uses prepositions in this same way to modify the sense of its vocabulary. But the derivational system (الاشتقاق *al-ishtiqaaq*), is the real jewel in Arabic's crown. This system takes a given source and adds not just prefixes and suffixes to it, but infixes as well, additions that modify the meaning of the source word in particular ways. As is the case in the change of pronunciation between face and surface, derived Arabic vocabulary is therefore quite prone to pronunciation changes. For this reason, vocabulary coming from one and the same source may seem unrelated. In fact, however, the overwhelming majority of elements produced from a given root or source word share important and ingenious semantic links. They may escape native and non-native speakers' notice, but they are *particularly* helpful to the latter in the otherwise arduous process of vocabulary building. These subtle links set me on this research path, and they are the inspiration for the title of this book. One can appreciate the derivational system for its compact, quasi-mathematical elegance and its prodigious semantic productivity with *any* root. The body, however, has a unique hold on human thought, and provides a unified, accessible, and intriguing semantic domain. All of this makes vocabulary of the body—and its rooted elements—a key to a larger slice of the linguistic and cultural pie.

Morphology and Multiplicity of Vocabulary

Some body idiom verges on the universal, but other expressions—like backing down in an argument—can be culturally specific and need careful 'unpacking.' Centuries of cultural and literary interactions surely add depth and specificity to the mix. Arabic has a long and impressive written history, over fifteen centuries' worth, and Arabic speakers since time immemorial have had a penchant for poetry. These are both significant issues when it comes to body idiom. At least two other features of the language combine to make it particularly rich in terms of embodiment. The first of these is morphology. Structurally speaking, Arabic is a language built on abstract roots, short sequences of single consonants that are systematically modified to produce actual vocabulary. Vowels of one variety or another *must* be added; some consonants may be called for, too. Depending on the vowels and consonants chosen, the same root may produce dozens of words, a constellation of vocabulary sonorously and semantically linked in subtle or obvious ways. Speakers can then get to work creating their message, contextualizing speech in ways as simple or complex, poetic or prosaic as their hearts desire. The theoretic beginning of it all, however, is the root, and learning to recognize and manipulate roots is an invaluable skill. This is especially true for non-native adult learners, because it lightens their memorization load significantly. Learning root meanings and the patterns of the derivational system teaches one how to make educated guesses, making Arabic's ocean of vocabulary much more navigable.

The second feature that contributes to Arabic's wealth in the field of embodiment is the multiplicity of names it often has for a single body part. A long tradition of writing and a vast territorial domain have surely added to Arabic's vocabulary. So must the innate inventiveness of its speakers, who created an impressive gallery of near-synonymous pairs or groups of words for the body. Arabic is not entirely unique in this. English, too, has some examples to offer, like side / flank, paunch / potbelly, and uterus / womb. It even has a few trios like guts / intestines / bowels and rare quadruples like face / visage / countenance / mien. Arabic, however, has *dozens* of such multiples (see appendix 1). In one exceptional case, speakers of both languages endowed a very dear bit of anatomy with a cornucopia of vocabulary. This is the posterior, whose polite English incarnations include backside / bottom / butt / derriere / hindquarters / rear-end / rump / seat. Arabic offerings are similarly inspired (and five of the Arabic words for the posterior are illustrated in this book).

Multiple vocabulary for the same body part offers the speaker attractive semantic leeway. Different tones and moods can emerge, from homey, to medical, to erotic, to euphemistic, to gendered, to derogatory, and beyond. In certain contexts, some of these multiple body parts are interchangeable, but this is not always the case. Figurative expressions and collocations may insist on one of these words as opposed to another. In English, for example, one may have a belly ache, or a stomach ache, but not an abdomen ache. English speakers sit on their haunches, but can only break their hips. There are bosom buddies, but no breast buddies. Arabic can be equally picky when choosing from its multiple word bank, but it does a lot more with this vocabulary, too, using the derivational system to add certain standard meanings. At the same time, the body roots' underlying attributes, especially those of shape, function, or orientation are subtly maintained or even amplified. Derivatives give the source word a new incarnation, choosing one or another of its aspects or qualities for elaboration and then adding a semantic plus. An example in English, sadly lacking in Arabic, is the wonderfully compact and convenient prefix re-. Presuming one understands the core word to which it has been added, the new meaning will be highly predictable. The basic semantic parameters of the derivational system have been very well studied, and they are outlined in table form on pages 6 to 7.

Nevertheless, it can prove challenging to discern the connection of a given Arabic body part to some of its derivatives. For instance, what do the legs have to do with context? The forehead with cowardice? The face with a snake? The nose with a judicial appeal? What could thumbs possibly have to do with obscurity? Riddles like these invite speculation, and I confess to indulging in it liberally as I tried to unravel these mysteries. Some issues are easily resolved; a logical thread linking vocabulary will reveal itself. In other cases, however, I remained stumped. Whatever the outcome of a particular search, it is hard to overstate the richness and variety of the results of the interaction between the Arabic derivative process and these psychically potent body parts. Metaphor and mood often combine with that framework in surprising, nuanced ways. Examples abound, but among my favorites are breath (النفس *an-nafas*), pupil (الحدقة *al-Hadaqa*), nipple (البزّ *al-bizz* and الحلمة *al-Halama*), and navel (السرّة *as-surra*). See the chapters and their illustrations to better understand how, over time, the derivational system ingeniously and quirkily fleshed out aspects of each source word.

Source versus Derivative

Many body parts serve as the source—morphologically and in terms of inspiration—of other 'derived' vocabulary. Like the shortest Arabic verbs and verbal nouns, they have only the most minimal additions to their root letters. There are also body parts that are themselves derived from other nouns or verbs. This is apparent in Arabic's duo for the elbow, كوع *kuu'* and مرفق *mirfaq / marfiq*. The first of these, very morphologically compact, gave rise to just three other words: one adjective, and two verbs. Shape is what unifies that minor constellation of vocabulary. All items in it play on the elbow's appearance, and in particular, its crookedness. The second word for the elbow is derived from ر – ف – ق, a verb meaning to be kind and friendly, or perhaps from the important noun associated with it, رفيق *rafiiq*, companion. The second version of the elbow has two pronunciations which allow for two interpretations. Voweled *mirfaq*, it follows one of Arabic's instrument patterns. As such, it suggests the habit of companions who stroll arm in arm, elbows linked. In this phonetic version, the elbow is specifically the physical instrument of friendly companionship. But an elbow—like a good friend—can also be leaned on. Besides, another derivative of the ر – ف – ق root, ارتفق, means to lean on one's elbows. When voweled *marfiq*, following the pattern of a noun of place, the elbow is presented as a 'place,' a convenient spot to lean on. In either case, body vocabulary of both varieties—source and derivative—is a great window onto Arab culture and society.

The Derivational System

Standard prefixes, infixes, and suffixes can be applied in systematic ways to any given root to create some of the many parts of speech available to Arabic. A concise but thorough description of this system was devised in the early days of Islam's rapid spread westward through North Africa into Europe and eastward into Asia as a pedagogic tool to help the burgeoning empire's many foreign subjects acquire the new language more efficiently. This pedagogical system is built around verbs because they are especially regular and productive. Most roots are triliteral, consisting of three consonants, but there are also plenty of four-letter and some rare two-letter roots. The table on pages 6 to 7 illustrates triliteral roots. In the triliteral verbal domain, there is one short, basic form (Form I) and nine others (II–X) that signal a variety of semantic permutations such as transitivity, causality, or reciprocity. In addition to these ten forms, there are a few additional rare ones. Arabic also has verbs based on four root letters. These quadriliteral verbs have a much more limited set of derivatives, not introduced here. The Roman numerals used to designate the forms are a more modern addition. Serious semanticists will find a detailed semantic analysis of classical Arabic verb forms in the venerable William Wright's *A Grammar of the Arabic Language*.[2]

Form I فعل, the shortest of all the forms, adds nothing to the root but vowels. These short verbs mean whatever they mean—they have no set semantic parameters at all. Form VIII, closely related to Form I, and sometimes identical in meaning to it, is also quite challenging to categorize. The table below spells out most of the categories of its potential meanings. Meaning in the other derived forms is not so arbitrary. Forms II, VI, and X tend to express three general semantic categories. Forms III, IV, V, and IX each tend to express two, and Form VII just one. Not every root has a Form I realization. Each verb form has a number of other patterns directly associated with it. The most important of these are مصادر *maSaadir* (verbal nouns, or, to English grammarians, gerunds). The primary meaning of the Arabic word مصدر *maSdar* is 'source.' Its choice as a technical term is an important clue to the power of this pattern in the language. Active and passive participles are two other important associated patterns. In addition, Form I has a wider array of options, including, among others, many adjectival patterns, a place noun, and an instrument pattern. Most roots occur in perhaps three to six of these forms. It is extremely rare for one root to occur in all ten forms. This table illustrates triliteral roots.

Form Number	Semantic Parameters	Pattern Word
I	Unspecified	فعل
II	Causative of Form I Intensive or Repetitive of Form I Denominative	فعّل
III	Associative (typically transitive, and involving someone else) Attempting to do Form I	فاعل
IV	Causative of Form I Unspecified but related transitive aspect of the root	أفْعل
V	Reflexive of Form II Similar to Form I, with added intentionality, effort, or duration	تفعّل
VI	Reciprocal of Form III (or I, if III doesn't exist) Progressive movement or change of Form I Pretense of Form I	تفاعل

VII	Compliant with Form I or, rarely, IV (pseudo-passive), without suggestion of one's own benefit	انْفعل
VIII	Synonymous with Form I Reflexive of Form I Compliant with Form I, often for one's own benefit Rarely, opposite of Form I Reciprocal of Form III, synonymous with Form VI Putting on a piece of clothing	افْتعل
IX	Having a bodily defect Turning a color	افْعلّ
X	Seeking or asking for Form I Estimative (comparative judgment, considering X to be Y) Reflexive of Form IV	اسْتفْعل

The Body in Language Pedagogy

When a single body part produces multiple derivatives,[3] a unifying metaphoric aura for that part can often be discerned. Even more intriguing, from a comparative point of view, are the body parts that have just one word in English, but two or three in Arabic. Ancient Arabic speakers were surprisingly creative on this front, spurred on, undoubtedly, by the psychic potency of the body. Considered as discrete vocabulary, multiple body-part terms might be just a curiosity, but each is usually the source of a thematic galaxy of derivatives. Learning to associate vocabulary from a root with its unifying theme or themes is an important skill to develop for Arabic vocabulary of any sort. With the body, though, it is innately enjoyable. This metaphoric garden is full of surprises. It stands to reason that sexuality should find metaphoric expression in body language. Sometimes, centuries of camouflage melt away, revealing truly profound body observations. Many less earthshaking observations are also quite enjoyable. How are throats and earrings alike? What links the sternum to scissors?

Native speakers of *any* language are mostly unaware of the body as a unified semantic field. Furthermore, native speakers of Arabic are, by and large, quite unaware of the amazing derivative system they use so naturally. For the most part, their manipulation of it is subliminal, only coming to conscious attention in old or challenging texts, or, perhaps, when exposed to unfamiliar dialects. As in any language, while speakers may consciously choose a particular body metaphor, the cohesiveness and amplitude of the body as a semantic domain often remains conceptually dormant. In Arabic, semantic domains have traditionally been the purview of literature and poetry more than language study. That may explain why Arabic pedagogy has not given the body much attention. Teachers of Arabic as a second language carefully highlight the importance of the derivative system as an essential element in the adult foreign learners' toolbox, and show how it can help them address the issue of vocabulary acquisition. That said, the exciting possibilities of semantic fields are rarely well exploited in teaching texts. The body may be the most powerful of these, but at least two other ancient and existentially important spheres—animals and the natural world—bear serious investigation.

This book focuses on body parts, themselves, and the constellations of vocabulary derived from them and their roots, with contextualized illustrations of its use. What is important to bear in mind is that this vocabulary is thematically related. Furthermore, body vocabulary, by its very nature, is ancient and primal, and carries a complex, often obscure history of associations. When applied to a body-part source word, Arabic's acrobatic morphology brings some of these deep associations to light. Many of these associations depend directly on physical aspects of the body part, and so a graphic presentation of the vocabulary is particularly warranted.

Arabic is challenging to pin down as a language. It has varieties within varieties, ancient, medieval and modern, urban and rural, written and oral. Like other languages, it is constantly evolving. Choices, however, must inevitably be made, and in this book, the Arabic being considered is primarily the standard, written form. Vocabulary and expressions are not limited to any given time frame, and are drawn from both the classical and contemporary idiom.

Objectives and Audience

As a native speaker of English, it took me decades of study to discover what a powerful semantic domain the body is in Arabic. The goal of this book is to shorten that learning curve for students of Arabic. First, the essential vocabulary of the body, itself, is presented as a unified semantic field, something curiously lacking in Arabic pedagogy to date. Each body part is the topic of a very concise chapter that identifies its root and highlights interesting and high-frequency expressions in which the word occurs. Second, each body root is used to introduce the mechanics of Arabic morphology, highlighting morphology's importance as a gateway to Arabic semantics. Third, a detailed illustration faces each chapter, offering a graphic interpretation of each body part and its derivatives, showing how semantically and metaphorically coherent they are. My stated goal is pedagogic, but what has sustained me on this long and winding research path is the surprise of discovery.

Arabic's semantic body domain is rich and mysterious, and I hope others will continue the intriguing process of exploring it.

Although my primary audience is the non-native intermediate and post-intermediate student of Arabic, this book has broader applications as well. Advanced students will certainly find some surprises in the metaphoric discussions. Graduate students intending to teach Arabic to non-native speakers may find this particularly useful.

Native speakers who rarely stop to think about the mechanics of the language they use may also enjoy considering familiar territory from a new perspective. For all of these readers, as well as for curious neophytes, comic artist Professor Mahmoud Shaltout has used his prodigious gifts to create the companion illustrations, bringing the body to visual life and adding an irrepressibly humorous dimension to the whole. He has also hidden some cultural 'cameos' in these drawings. Fans may be able to spot some famous faces, drawn especially, though not exclusively, from the archives of Egyptian cinema.

What Was Cut, Alas

The author faced a couple of practical challenges in putting this book together. First was the thorny issue of which body parts to include. Since exploring Arabic's morphological system was an important facet of the work, it was easy to ignore body vocabulary from minimally derivative families. On these grounds, short 'source' words like لثة gum, ذقن chin, رسغ wrist, ذهن mind, فخذ thigh, غدّة gland, and لغد double chin, as well as longer derivative orphans like مثانة bladder, and ظنبوب shinbone, were easily eliminated. However, beyond these, there remained quite a large number of body parts—in excess of 150—that were either the source of or elements in significant root constellations. Some 15 percent of these needed more than a single page of commentary. As each page of text has a facing illustration, including all of them would have produced an extremely bulky volume. Choosing which items to cut was quite difficult. In all, about 35 body parts had to be jettisoned. Among the most painful to cut, given their derivative amplitude, lexical piquancy, and cultural relevance were: بشرة complexion or skin, حسنة beauty mark, جوف abdomen, عطف side, شغف pericardium, and خلية cell.

Space constraints also meant that some of the chapters retained were deliberately truncated. Many body parts are extraordinarily rich in figurative associations, and some have derivatives galore. In a number of cases, it would have been easy to continue for a second page of text and an illustration. Among the more difficult chapters to trim in this way were عرق sweat/vein, وجه face, عين eye, صدر chest, and especially عقب heel, the final text of this collection.

Having decided which items to include, the second issue that had to be resolved was the order in which to present them. Several possibilities crossed my mind, none of them perfect, and I preferred to make the decision with help from my illustrator. Because the format of this work is much like a dictionary, one option was to list body parts in alphabetical order, thus allowing readers to immediately thumb to a given item of interest. The drawback to doing so is the fact of the body's natural and metaphoric coherence. People experience the body in meaningful ways and clusters (tongue in cheek; ear, nose, and throat; heart and soul) rather than alphabetically (abdomen, ankle, aorta, appendix, arm; back, bone, brain, breast). It seemed important not to go against this grain.

Another possibility was to present items in terms of frequency of use. Buckwalter and Parkinson's valuable reference, *A Frequency Dictionary of Arabic*,[4] subsequently referred to for convenience as the *FDA*, would have allowed this for sixty-two of our choices. After that, it would have been necessary to use some other criterion. In fact, the *FDA* has been used to provide frequency data for much of the vocabulary discussed here, but it seemed preferable to avoid blending criteria when it came to presentation order.

The idea we finally settled on was our innate sense of the body's orientation. Heads up! Thus, the items have been arranged from the top of the body to the bottom, and from the front to the back. That said, it was still surprisingly tricky to decide on a logical order. Certain elements of the body are essentially omnipresent (skin, pores, nerves) and others occur in many places (hair, limbs, bones, scars). Some are mobile (blood, drool). Yet others are whole regions (front, back, side) or occur at roughly the same level (ear and eye, elbow and navel). The abstractions (self, soul, mind) further clouded the waters.

In the end, my illustrator and I did the best we could, given the body's rather slippery nature and our own subjectivity. To impose a bit of order, we grouped elements in five general categories. These are: words for the body itself, and things found in multiple areas; excrescences and the ineffable; head, shoulders, and arms; trunk and lower body from the front; back, from top to bottom. To accommodate the reader who wishes to approach the work piecemeal and would like to find a particular entry quickly, an alphabetical index by root is provided (see page 279).

References

In addition to Lakoff and Johnson's *Metaphors We Live By*, which introduced me to embodiment as a grand multi-disciplinary concept, many Arabic language references came to my rescue over the dozen years in which this work gradually took shape. Always within hand's reach was the indispensable *Hans Wehr*,[5] and a number of other bilingual dictionaries of standard Arabic were consulted. These include *al-Mawrid* by Munir and Rohi

Baalbaki and *The Oxford English–Arabic Dictionary of Current Usage.*[6] Online dictionaries proved invaluable, too. The venerable two-volume *Le Kazimirski*, an Arabic–French behemoth first published in 1860, has been a fortuitous addition to the online archive. Arabic–Arabic dictionaries were crucial, too. Most important of these was *al-Ma'ani li-kull rasm ma'na*, a compendium that provides definitions from a smorgasbord of other Arabic–Arabic dictionaries including, but not limited to *al-Wasit*, *al-Ra'id*, and *al-Ghani*. Its citations of many of the search words in classical poetry were a bonus. Another invaluable source was the *Arabic–English Dictionary of Qur'anic Usage* by Elsaid Badawi and Muhammad Abdel Haleem.[7] Unless otherwise noted, Qur'anic translations are drawn from that volume. Frequency references were also essential, and I was glad to have *A Frequency Dictionary of Arabic*. To check both frequency and usage, the online arabiCorpus, maintained by Dilworth Parkinson at Brigham Young University, was extraordinarily convenient. Finally, for ideas from the spoken register and comparison to it, the *Dictionary of Egyptian Arabic* by El-Said Badawi and Martin Hinds was ideal.[8]

Early on in my research, I searched the databases for others writing in English on Arabic's lexical and metaphoric body. The only researcher I found was the prolific Zouheir Maalej.[9] Using Tunisian Arabic as his corpus, he has written on the heart and the eye, as well as on abstractions associated with the body, including anger and fear. The emphasis in his work seems to be on how an understanding of the way Tunisian Arabic refers to the body can contribute to cognitive embodiment theory and what the whole can add to a nuanced portrait of the psychosocial dimensions of Tunisian society.

I am gradually becoming familiar with the collaboration between Georges Bohas and Abderrahim Saguer, both of l'École normale supérieure of Lyon. One focus of their reѳsearch is the Arabic lexicon, explored by etymon (binary roots) and matrix (phonological area of articulation), rather than by root. This unconventional work suggests a dramatic intersection of sound and meaning, a kind of primitive manifestation of embodiment, relevant not only to Arabic but to a wide variety of languages. Their research also tantalizingly addresses the issue of Arabic etymology, a resource Arabists of all stripes ache for.

Summary and Conclusion

Being able to speak of the body is inherently important from a practical point of view. People needing to express themselves in a new language find it just as indispensable as its native speakers do. Besides the obvious abundance of specific body *vocabulary*, body *metaphor* is a significant feature of human languages, too. Computers can do wonders with numerical sequences, but human thinking is yoked to the physical brain, and the brain relies on the body for its data. This percolating body–brain–mind–brain–body continuum is like a grand petri dish. In it, thinking and feeling merge, simmer, and ferment. Then, when the time is right—or wrong—they bubble over into spontaneous acts of expression like dance and language. In language, echoes of the body crop up in countless inventive and idiosyncratic ways. As a unified semantic field, body language, in all senses of the term, offers broad horizons for linguistic, psycholinguistic, and literary exploration. It is colorful, sometimes quirky, and packed with cultural references. That alone is sufficient justification for its study, but in Arabic, this same lyrical semantic field offers a further pedagogic windfall: it is a catchy and logical way to learn to navigate the morphological system. Furthermore, given Arabic's large pool of nearly synonymous body parts, metaphoric meanings are exponentially multiplied.

The terms embody and embodiment offer a convenient example of how this is so. English and Arabic both begin with the word 'body' to produce the verb 'to embody.' In Arabic, though, there are three words for the (living) body: بدن / جسد / جسم. First, one must know which 'body' to choose and second, how to transform that noun into a transitive verb. That, however, is not necessarily enough. Collocations, the affinity of certain words for each other, may also have a bearing on the best choice. In the case at hand, the noun بدن *badan* has no transitive verbal elaboration. The only verb based on it means 'to be stout.' *Badan* and its derivatives suggest a bodily physique of substance and girth. Both of the other nouns make transitive verbs that can be translated 'to embody' (جسّد and جسّم), but they are not quite interchangeable. Instead, they offer a contrast between the concrete or tangible and the abstract. Of them, جسّم *jassama* is the more concrete. It can suggest, for example, how tight clothing recreates its wearer's body, revealing its most intimate details, or how a 3-D model of a chemical compound gives it discernible material substance. On the other hand, for notions of how an actor embodies a character trait, bringing it to life on stage, جسّد *jassada* is the verb to use. Arabic's *multiple* body lexemes have a charm all their own.

Throughout, this is a work that approaches Arabic from a comparative perspective. Having chosen to write in English for an audience that is primarily—though not exclusively—composed of non-native learners of Arabic, the comparative approach is a natural one. This is a perspective I did not really wish to escape, if, indeed, that were a possibility. It is exceedingly difficult to ignore one's native-language body perspectives, and in my opinion not desirable to do so. Instead, allowing each perspective to inform the other draws one deeply into language, a process that is infinitely intriguing and unbounded.

For an adult, non-native learner, an apprenticeship to Arabic is a complex affair, an evolving process with a multitude of aspects, some mundane and mechanical, others poetic. As one acquires a rudimentary working vocabulary and masters the basics of meeting and greeting, glimpses of the culture in which the language is embedded appear. Elementary students must juggle the cognitive load of a strange new alphabet, one written from right to left without short vowels, an impressive new phonology, and the basics of grammar in order to communicate. In the process, though, they gradually get a sense that something else is at work in the language. Even in the early months of study, novices are likely to notice that root sequences keep recurring. Before long, a straightforward presentation of morphology is warranted. Here again, mechanics and poetry overlap. Arabic's derivational system hinges on the basic distinction between short vowels and single consonants and their long and doubled counterparts. Educating the ear to these *systemic* phonological distinctions is therefore essential to oral proficiency in Arabic. For this reason, *Rooted in the Body* uses side-by-side transliteration, emphasizing the semantic power embedded in such minimal differences. For advanced students, phonology holds other surprises, too, as a look at the theories of Bohas and Saguer demonstrates.

A truly successful apprenticeship in Arabic requires one to venture ever deeper into phonology, semantics, and metaphor, the big picture. The body's many figurative threads, with all their humor, hyperbole, and innuendo, are to be enjoyed in and of themselves, at face value, as English likes to say. But as the apprentice's focus shifts and evolves, little by little, cultural terrain that could otherwise hardly have been guessed at comes into view.

By way of morphology, *Rooted in the Body* conceptually and graphically investigates the body, one of Arabic's most cherished and coherent semantic domains. In the process, it highlights new connections and suggests further avenues of research. It is our hope that this book will provide a tantalizing glimpse into Arabic's beating heart and soul.

Body Parts

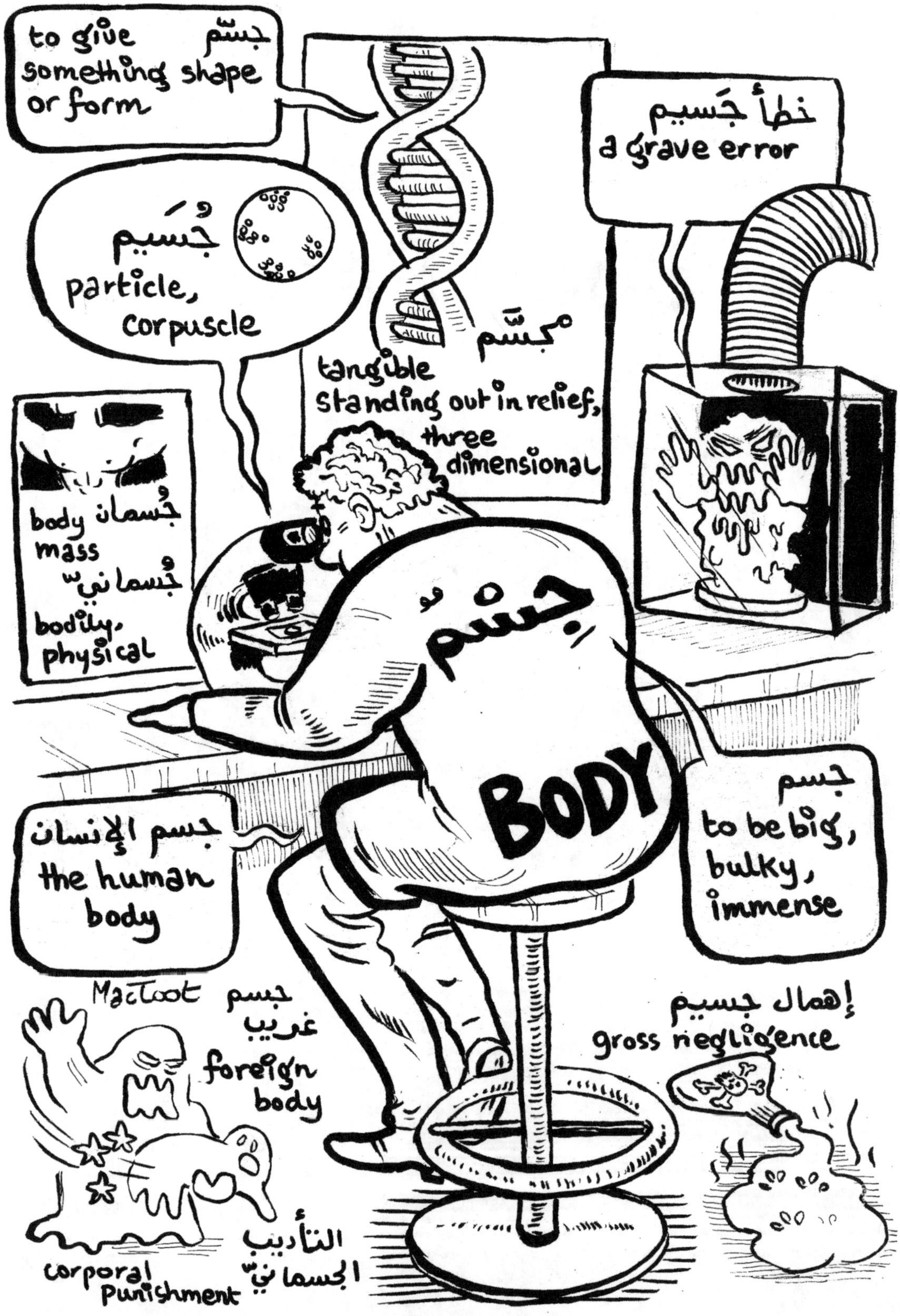

جسّم to give something shape or form
جُسَيم particle, corpuscle
مجسّم tangible standing out in relief, three dimensional
خطأ جَسيم a grave error
جُسمان body mass
جُسمانيّ bodily, physical
جِسْم
BODY
جسم الإنسان the human body
جسم to be big, bulky, immense
MacToot
جسم غريب foreign body
إهمال جسيم gross negligence
التأديب الجسمانيّ corporal punishment

1
Body جِسْم - أَجْسام
Mass; Substance

Considering the living body from various points of view, Arab forebears gave it a trio of names, each with its own metaphoric amplitude. This word for the body explores aspects of volume and shape, facilitating the expression of observations on the physical world. It lends itself very well to physics and medicine, among other fields, and also allows for the expression of abstractions. Furthermore, certain derivatives have something of an attitude.

The word جِسم *jism*, itself, is quite versatile. It is a generic body, not specifically human unless so specified, as in the *iDaafa* construction جسم الإنسان *jism al-'insaan.* It is not necessarily animate, either, and may describe concrete things (a dam) or even complete abstractions (a nation). It can also be what English calls 'a foreign body,' جسم غريب *jism ghariib*, such as one might have the misfortune to discover in one's eye. In such contexts, it is sometimes translated as organism. This wide range of meanings is what gives جسم its high frequency ranking of *FDA* 745. This body also has a diminutive, جُسَيم *jusaym*, a particle, in physics, and a corpuscle, in biology. Just as it can be made tiny, جسم can be augmented, producing جُسمان *jusmaan*, body or mass. Diminutive excluded, of course, the derivatives of الجسم suggest bulk and dimensionality.

The Form I verb جَسُم – يجسُم *jasuma* is to be big and bulky. Closely related vocabulary includes the *maSdar*, الجسامة *al-jasaama*, volume, massivity, and the adjective جسيم *jasiim*, massive. These Form I derivatives come with an important figurative association, negativity. Rendering them into English can be tricky, though, as usage may be idiomatic. Examples of expressions that collocate with جسم derivatives, rather than those of جسد *jasad* and بدن *badan*, discussed in the next two chapters, include جسامة الأضرار *jasaamat al-'aDraar,* the massive scope of the damage(s), جسامة الجرم *jasaamat al-jurm*, the gravity of the offense, and جسامة المجازفة *jasaamat al-mujaazafa*, the magnitude of the risk. Notable examples from the adjective domain are خطأ جسيم, *khaTa' jasiim*, a grave error, and إهمال جسيم, *'ihmaal jasiim*, gross negligence. It is also possible to use the adjective in comparative form, أجْسم *'ajsam*, more massive, even greater.

Form II جسّم and its *maSdar* التجسيم *at-tajsiim* mean to endow something with a body and, therefore, with bodily dimensions. By extension, the *maSdar* may mean enlargement or magnification. The verb can also mean to reveal bodily contours, as tight clothing may do. Something with a body is three-dimensional, an adjective conveyed by the passive participle, مُجَسَّم *mujassam*. Form V تجسّم is the reflexive equivalent of Form II, and means to acquire a body or shape. Thus it may be translated to materialize, and take shape, to grow in size, and, more figuratively, to become tangible.

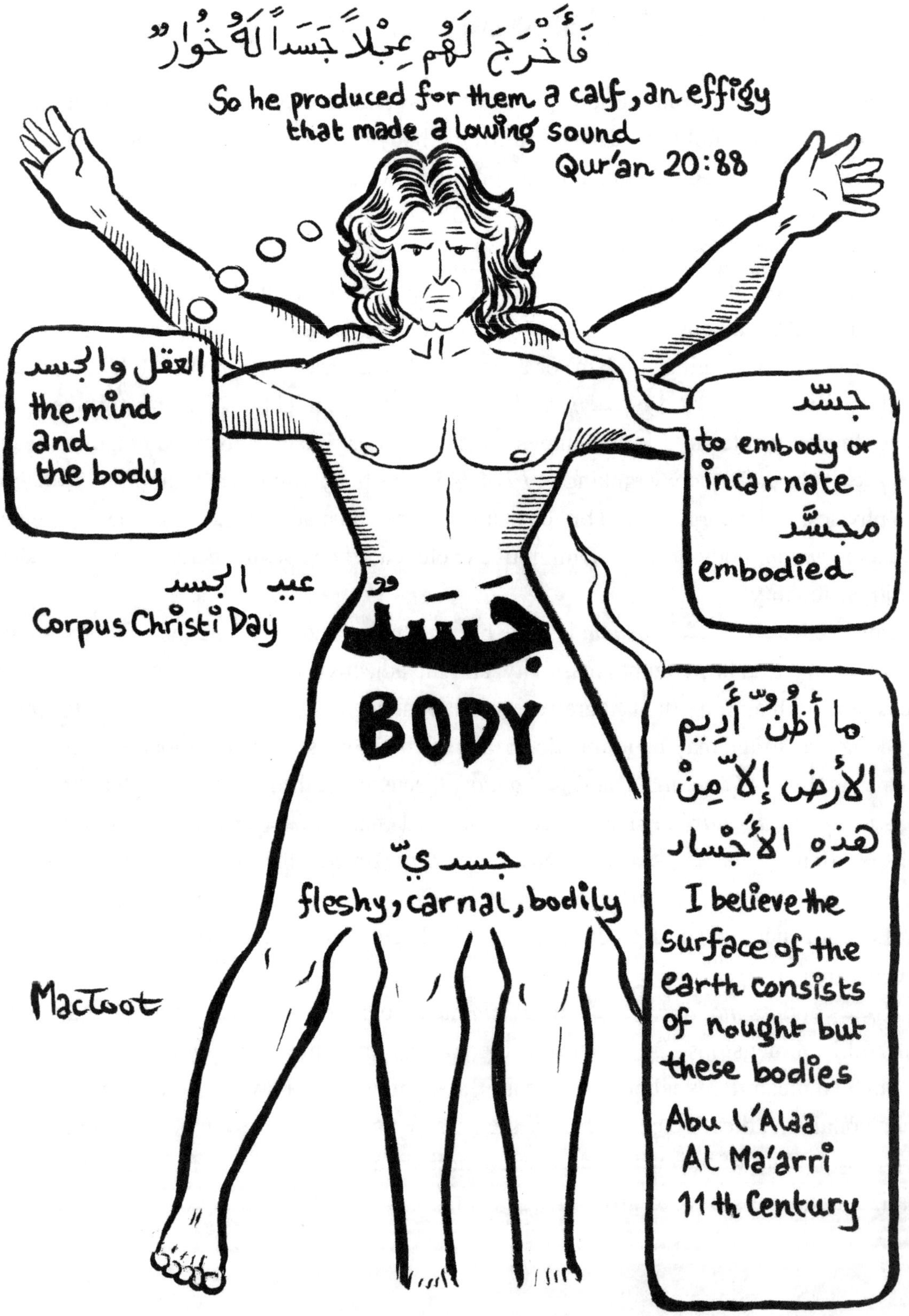
فَأَخْرَجَ لَهُمْ عِجْلًا جَسَدًا لَهُ خُوَارٌ
So he produced for them a calf, an effigy that made a lowing sound
Qur'an 20:88
العقل والجسد
the mind and the body
جسّد
to embody or incarnate
مجسّد
embodied
عيد الجسد
Corpus Christi Day
جسد
BODY
جسديّ
fleshy, carnal, bodily
ما أظنّ أديم الأرض إلّا مِنْ هذهِ الأجْساد
I believe the surface of the earth consists of nought but these bodies
Abu l'Alaa Al Ma'arri 11th Century
MacToot

2
Body جَسَد – أَجْساد
Fleshy, Corporeal

In Arabic's body gallery, الجسد *al-jasad* is the necessary choice in the important collocation العقل والجسد *al-'aql wa-l-jasad*, the mind and the body. But, language apprentices, beware. Usage can be fickle, and in the expression 'a sound mind in a sound body,' Arabic insists on *al-jism*, discussed in the first chapter: العقل السليم في الجسم السليم *al-'aql as-saliim fi-l-jism as-saliim.* The noun *al-jasad* almost always refers to a living body, but can describe something which resembles one. It is used like this at 20:88 of the Qur'an in the story of Moses and the Israelites: فَأَخْرَجَ لَهُمْ عِجْلاً جَسَدًا لَهُ خُوارٌ *fa 'akhraja lahum 'ijlan jasadan lahu khuwaarun, so he produced for them a calf, an effigy that made a lowing sound.*

It is almost as high in the *FDA* ranking ranking as جسم, coming in at 963. Given the singular pattern it is built on, فَعَل, *jasad* has a very predictable plural, أجساد *'ajsaad.* The great eleventh-century philosopher–poet Abul Alaa al-Ma'arri uses this plural in addressing one of the grim realities of existence. He orders his listeners to tread lightly as they walk. Countless generations, he says, have died and been buried; their remains are the very dust and dirt on which we step. ما أظنّ أديم الأرض إلّا من هذه الأجسادِ *maa 'aZunnu 'adiim al-'arDi 'illaa min haadhihi al-'ajsaadi.*

This ج – س – د root is behind a crucial concept of Christianity. Most significantly, rather than using the word for flesh (لحم *laHm*), Arabic expresses the gospel doctrine of Christ's incarnation (And the Word was made flesh; John 1:14) using this word for the body: وصار الكلمة جسدا, *wa Saara al-kalima jasadan.* In the Christian calendar, we find Corpus Christi Day, عيد الجسد *'iid al-jasad.* Neither of Arabic's other words for the body are used in this Christian doctrinal sense. However, the word جسد is by no means specific to Christianity. It is also used four times in the Qur'an, where it describes the human body, as well as, in one instance, an effigy or figurine, in the famous story of the Golden Calf, 20:88, cited above. The most common non-verbal derivative of *jasad* is the workhorse *nisba* adjective جسديّ *jasadiyy*, which has translations ranging from physical, corporal, and bodily to carnal and sensual, and ranks 3,765 in the *FDA*. One of these uses is in the phrase عقوبة جسديّة *'uquuba jasadiyya*, corporal punishment. This same adjective can also act as a contrast to spiritual, (in which case English sometimes prefers corporeal,) as in احتياجات جسديّة *iHtiyaajaat jasadiyya*, corporeal or bodily needs.

This word for the body has only two associated verb forms. Form II جسّد means to embody or incarnate, as in acting or a work of literature, when the actor or main character embodies one or another trait, and it ranks 3,756 in the *FDA*. Being the incarnation or embodiment of something is the *maSdar* التجسيد *at-tajsiid.* The passive participle مجسَّد *mujassad* means embodied, given corporeal form.

Form V تجسّد, the only other verbal derivative, means to be made corporeal, to be invested with a body. This is a verb of paramount importance in Christian thought, and it figures in the vital Nicene Creed.

بَدَنة ج بُدْن
fat camel or cow fit for the Eid Al-Adha sacrifice in Mecca
مُبدَّن
a fatted calf, camel
bodily Corporal
بَدَنيّ
بدُن
to be or become fat, corpulent
بادِن ، بدين
stout, fat, obese
بَدانة ، بُدونة
obesity
بَدَنٌ
BODY TRUNK TORSO
to be/become fat; بدّن
to dress in a coat of armor;
to fatten up (an animal)
MacToot

3
Body; Torso , Trunk بَدَن – أبْدان / أَبْدُن
Fat

In the live body gallery, البـدن *al-badan* emphasizes fatty bulk. In ordinary use, it refers to the body as a whole, but torso and trunk are sometimes correct translations for this word, too, because, technically, البدن excludes both the head and the extremities. The more common of its plurals, أبـدان *'abdaan*, figures in a famous and colorful collocation describing physical revulsion: أمرٌ تقشـعرّ له الأبدان, *'amrun taqsha'ir-ru lahu al-'abdaan*, something that bodies shudder at. English has evolved similar embodied expressions depicting the distress that dreadful sights and events provoke: something spine-chilling; something that gives you goosebumps; something that makes your skin crawl.

The *nisba* adjective بدنـيّ *badaniyy* is typically translated as physical or bodily. Expressions include أذى بدنـيّ *'adha badaniyy*, bodily harm, and التربيّـة البدنيّـة *at-tarbiyya al-badaniyya*, physical education. Like جسـديّ, discussed in the previous chapter, بدنـيّ is also used to convey 'corporal' punishment, عقوبـة بدنيّـة, *'uquuba badaniyya*. The *nisba* adjective is the most common derivative of the ب – د – ن root and the only one to figure in the *FDA*. That said, most of its other derivatives are familiar vocabulary; only a couple of classicisms derived from this root are especially uncommon.

The Form I verb, بـدن - يبـدُن, to become fat or corpulent, has two past tense vowelings, *baduna* / *badana*. Getting fat is the *maSdar* البـدن *al-badn*. Corpulence or obesity is expressed by either البدانـة *al-badaana* or البدونـة *al-baduuna*. There are two corresponding adjectives in ordinary usage, بـادِن *baadin* and بديـن *badiin*. Classically, the masculine form of فعيـل adjectives could be used for all numbers and genders, but in modern writing full agreement is typically applied. The plural of بديـن is بُـدُن *budun*.

Like Form I, the Form II verb بـدّن can be intransitive, to become fat. However, it also has transitive uses. One such classicism is to dress a warrior in his coat of mail, a process that would have made him appear fatter. Another is to fatten up an animal. This last meaning provides the link to the only other word from the ب – د – ن root found in the Qur'an besides بـدن, itself. This is البُـدن *al-budn*, and it only figures once. Neither this plural nor its singular is familiar in modern usage. As a singular, the form is بَدَنة *badana*, and it means a fleshy camel or cow. From ancient times, such animals were made available for sacrifice in Mecca, a practice continued after Islam at عيـد الأضحـى *'iid al-'aDHaa,* the Feast of Immolation. In 22:36, the Qur'an says: والبُـدْنَ جَعَلْناهـا لَكُـم مِـن شَـعاعِرِ الله, *Fat camels and cows have We given you as part of God's sacred rites*. This classical term brings to mind the biblical fatted calf, an expression that can be conveyed by the Form II passive participle مُبـدَّن *mubaddan.*

to tear Someone/Something limb from limb
مزّقه إرباً إرباً
to tear to pieces
أرّب
to be tight-fisted
to be skillful, proficient أرِب
to best someone, cleverly outdo آربه
المؤاربة
outdoing
11
MacToot
مأرَب
wish, desire need; purpose, aim, goal
to win آرب عليه
إرب
LIMB
Knot أُربة - أُرَب

4

Limb إرْب - آراب

Adroitness; Self-Interest

This word for a limb is not sufficiently common to rank in the *FDA*, nor does it occur in the Qur'an. Nevertheless, we find it in a familiar collocation, مزّقه إربًا إربًا *mazzaqahu 'irban 'irban*, to tear someone limb from limb. In this grisly expression, repetition serves Arabic and English equally well for rhetorical emphasis. Two derivatives of the أ – ر – ب root, however, do figure in the Qur'an. In a reference to prepubescent male dependents or, potentially, to eunuchs, the noun إربة, *'irba*, sexual potency or desire, occurs in 24:31: وَلا يُبْدِينَ زِينَتَهُنَّ إلّا لِبُعولَتِهِنَّ . . . أوِ التّابعينَ غَيْرِ أُولي الإرْبَةِ مِنَ الرِّجالِ, *And they (should) only reveal their charms to their husbands . . . or such men as attend them who have no sexual desire.* Limbs, it need hardly be said, are long appendages of the body, and one might speculate that this connection to the notion of sexual desire and potency is also a veiled reference to male anatomy.

One meaning of the classical Form I verb, variously voweled أرُب – يأرُب *'aruba* and أرِب – يأرَب *'ariba* is to be skillful, probably inspired by the noun أُربة *'urba*, a knot or a bow. Knot tying requires a measure of dexterous skill, and the adjective أريب *'ariib*, means skillful and resourceful. Furthermore, to tie and untie a knot, the use of the upper limbs is essential. In the colloquial Egyptian register, *'ariib* gets a vowel change and a new gender slant: the adjective أروبة *'aruuba* is used exclusively for females. In either register, the word no longer has any associations with knots, but it does suggest admirable problem solving in new or challenging situations. Such adroitness might well come in handy in an effort to obtain المأرب *al-ma'rab* or المأربة *al-ma'ruba*, one's desire, purpose, or goal, and their plural المآرب *al- ma'aarib*. Once again, Qu'ranic usage is apropos. In 20:18, we find: هِيَ عَصايَ أتَوَكَّأُ عَلَيْها وَأهُشُّ بِها عَلى غَنَمِي وَلِي فِيها مَآرِبُ أُخْرَى, *It is my staff, I lean on it; I beat down leaves with it for my sheep (or, I restrain my sheep with it) and I have other uses for it.* With just a minimal vowel change, مأرب, a goal, becomes Ma'rib, a city in Yemen to the east of the present-day capital Sanaa (صنعاء). Ma'rib is a city with a long history; it may well have been the capital of the ancient kingdom of Sheba (سبأ). A city of such significance would have been the goal of many a traveler.

Prepositions often significantly modify the meaning of a verb, something observable in an alternative sense of the Form I verb. The expression ارب بماله *'ariba bimaalihi* means to be or become stingy with one's money. This sense is augmented in Form II أرّب, to be tight-fisted. Here, the hand, rather than being open and generous as a hand should ideally be, is metaphorically clenched as tightly as a knot. This limb adroitly puts one's own مآرب ahead of others'. Form III آرب and its *maSdar* المؤاربة *al-mu'aaraba* mean to outdo someone. Form IV forms a verb–preposition idiom آرب على, to win. This verb is indistinguishable from Form III in the third person masculine singular of the past tense, but its derivatives allow identification of it as distinct. Both of these verbs suggest how the resourcefulness and self-interest of الأريب, the clever, resourceful fellow, can be put into action.

جارحة ج جَوارِح
predatory animal;
bird of prey
بكلّ جوارحِهِ with all his might
جَوارِح
LIMBS
جرح to wound;
to earn (classical)
مجروح
wounded
جُرح wound, injury
جريح ج جَرحى
wounded person
جرّاح
surgeon
سكّين جارحة
broad-bladed knife
Mactoot
DR AMR
جراحيّ
surgical
الجراحة
surgery

5

Limbs; Body Parts That Can Do Harm جَوارِح

Wounds

Some body parts have the potential to inflict grievous harm; this functional metaphor led to their naming based on the ج – ر – ح root. The plural form جوارح *jawaariH* is derived from جارحة *jaariHa*, used frequently in reference to predatory animals and birds of prey. Literally 'a wounder,' جارحة is in turn derived from the Form I verb جرح – يجرَح *jaraHa*, to wound. Eagles, hawks, and owls are also جوارح, so named for their tactical use of powerful beaks and deadly talons. They are mentioned in 5:4 of the Qur'an: أُحِلَّ لَكُمُ الطَّيِّبَاتُ وَمَا عَلَّمْتُم مِنَ الجَوارِحِ مُكَلِّبِينَ, *Permitted to you (for food) are all good things and (the catch of) such predatory creatures as you train to hunt.*

By analogy to avian predator anatomy, human limbs were also dubbed جوارح. Wounding, الجرح *al-jarH*, is normally physical, but injuries may be figurative, too. It is not just talons and powerful limbs that can wound. That is why eyes and ears, which may see and hear what others wish to conceal, share this same designation. Arabic also recognizes the particular power of speech to hurt and so does not subscribe to the dictum 'Sticks and stones . . .' that depicts name-calling as harmless. Hurtful words are كلام جارح *kalaam jaariH*. Using all of one's limbs requires great physical effort, and so بكلّ جوارحه *bi kulli jawaariHihi* means with all his might. Even more figuratively, جوارح is a synonym of مشاعر *mashaa'ir* feelings. Given its root, it suggests overpowering, even painful emotions.

The noun جُرح *jurH* and its multiple broken plurals designate wounds. A wounded person is جريح *jariiH*; many are جرحى *jarHaa*. The plural pattern on which it is based, فَعْلَى, packs a real semantic punch, as it refers exclusively to those deemed very unfortunate. Examples include السكرى, the drunk, المرضى, the sick, الأسرى, prisoners, الموتى, the deceased, and even الحمقى, the foolish. Another pattern with relevance to this root is فَعّال, used to designate professions. Applied to this root it creates the only term for a surgeon: جرّاح *jarraaH*. Perhaps the name evolved from the distressing wounds that resulted from الجِراحة *al-jiraaHa*, surgery. Still, whatever perils surgery suggested to those about to endure it, there may also be a link to a broad-bladed knife, سكين جارحة, *sikkiin jaariHa.*

In classical usage, the Form I verb جرح *jaraHa* could mean to endeavor, to gain, or to earn. In 6:60 of the Qur'an, we find: وَهُوَ الَّذِي يَتَوَفَّاكُم بِاللَّيْلِ وَيَعْلَمُ مَا جَرَحْتُم بِالنَّهارِ, *It is He who recalls you to Him by night, and knows what you have earned by day.* This use of جرح directly links it to birds of prey: they, too, were essentially earners, providing for their young by hunting. With its intensive associations, the Form II verb جرّح can mean to inflict many wounds. On a figurative level, though, it means to invalidate something. Beneath the dry, practical veneer of that word is the shadow of grievous 'bodily' harm. The Form VIII verb اجترح is the last of the verbal derivations of this root. It means to abuse, to commit (an outrage, for example). Like the verb commit, in English, اجترح collocates with the pejorative to produce blameworthy actions.

In modern usage, five derivatives of this root figure in the *FDA*. All are confined to the semantic domain of wounds and surgery. No predators, limbs, or emotions are among them.

وَمَن يُعَظِّمْ شَعَائِرَ اللّه
Whoever honors God's rites
Qur'an 22:30
عظمة
majesty; pride; augustness
والله العظيم
by Almighty God!
مُعظم
most of
the great majority (of the people)
الغالبيّة العظمى
السواد الأعظم
BONE عَظْم
تعظّم
to be arrogant, presumptuous
تعظّم بـ ...
to vaunt, be proud of, boast of
تعاظم على
to be proud, arrogant, haughty
استعظم
to be arrogant, presumptuous; to regard as significant or important
MacToot

6
Bone عَظْم - عِظام / أَعْظُم
Colossality, Greatness

Using just a few bones, عظام *'iZaam*, forensic anthropologists can tell us all sorts of things about our ancestors, even the most remote of them. Bones are the most sizable solid component of the body, and a bone, عظم *'aZm*, lasts longer than anything. Such basic observations of nature are easily made by those living close to it, and the Arabs of old were extraordinarily dependent on and observant of their natural world. Logic nevertheless suggests that the adjective عظيم *'aZiim*, great, immense, weighty, appropriate in such a variety of contexts, would have been the starting point for vocabulary of this prolific family. This adjective is among the most common words in modern Arabic, ranking 570 in the *FDA*, and its impressive range of meanings is connected, one way or another, to prodigiousness, whether in a positive or negative sense. From عظيم comes a plural specifically for great people, العظماء *al-'uZamaa'*. Even one of God's 'most beautiful names' is العظيم, *The Almighty*.

Verbal derivations extend the semantic reach of the ع – ظ – م root. Form I عظم – يعظُم *'aZuma* can mean to be or become great, magnificent, imposing, vast, or weighty. On the other hand, in negative contexts, it can mean to be distressing, painful, or agonizing. Form II عظّم introduces the standard causative sense to the root, to make something grand or grandiose, or, conversely, (more) distressing. Form IV أعظم carries these same causative meanings, as well as the alternative of considering (something or someone) to be عظيم. It may thus mean to extol, or, on the contrary, to deem oppressive. Form V تعظّم articulates another semantic possibility: to be haughty, or to boast and flaunt. Synonymous with تعظّم is Form VI تعاظم. Context allows for various interpretations of greatness: being haughty, or weighty and grave. Since the semantic parameters of Form VI include reciprocal interaction, تعاظم may also mean to be equal in weight, significance, or importance. Form X استعظم can express most of the meanings of Forms IV, V, and VI: to be excessively proud, or to regard as great, significant, or important.

Six nominal derivatives of the ع – ظ – م root appear in the *FDA*. The second most common of them, ranking 841, is مُعْظَم *mu'Zam*, a passive participle of Form IV. Used as the first term of an *iDaafa* construction, it means most (of), the majority of, as in معظم أعضاء الجسم *mu'Zam 'a'Daa' al-jism*, most body parts. Another is عظمة *'aZama*, grandeur, magnificence. As might be expected, this noun tends to collocate with other references to eminence and majesty, such as God, the empire, and our history: عظمة الله / عظمة الإمبراطورية / عظمة تاريخنا. Of particular interest is a noun based very directly on عظيم, the adjective discussed at the outset of this chapter. This noun is exclusively feminine: *'aZiima* is specifically a terrible thing, a great misfortune, a calamity. The use of the feminine gender for disasater hardly seems accidental. The same is true for the largely synonymous trio for catastrophe: فاجعة *faaji'a*, مصيبة *muSiiba*, and كارثة *kaaritha*. This brings to mind the penchant for designating disasters as feminine that held sway for a quarter century in the United States. Beginning in 1953, the National Weather Service began giving hurricanes female names. However, in 1979, the burgeoning feminist movement forced a more egalitarian approach on the institution, and from then on, hurricanes have been named after men in alternating years.

JOINT
فصل
فصيلة ج فصائل
genus, species, family
فصل
season
الفصول الأربعة
the four seasons
فاصِلة
comma
فاصل
pause, interval, like in a news program
فصّل to arrange something in sections; to classify, to categorize something; to tailor
فصل
class, classroom
فصل act (in a play)
تفصيل detail
بالتفصيل in detail
-Macloot-

7

Joint (1) مَفصِل - مَفاصِل

Division, Separation; Detail

The Form I verb يفصِل – فصل *faSala* means to separate two or more things, and a dizzying array of derivatives can be traced to it. These include مَفصِل *mafSil*, a joint, and its plural مفاصل *mafaaSil*. The مَفْعِل pattern is used to identify places, and so المفصل actually depicts the joint as a site of separation between two segments of the body, rather than the converse English view as one of junction.

Used with the preposition في, this verb means to make a final decision or render a decisive judgment on something, thus effectively separating the desired option from any others. A most unusual pattern, فَيعَل, elaborates on this meaning: فيصل *faySal*, a decisive criterion. The same word can also designate someone capable of applying decisive criteria, an arbiter or arbitrator. Such an impressive talent turned into a proper name, commonly spelled Faisal, but worthy of a king!

The *maSdar*, الفَصل, the same form with the common meanings cited, is one of the names of Judgment Day, يَوْمُ الْفَصْلِ *yawm al-faSl*, so named in 77:38 of the Qur'an. With the preposition عن, the meaning is to set something apart from something or someone else, or to segregate one group from another. With no preposition at all, Form I means to isolate, sever, cut, or separate something. In modern employment contexts, it means to fire someone.

Derivatives of the productive ف – ص – ل root figure an impressive nine times in the *FDA*. As for Qur'anic usages, ten different forms are used forty-three times. Form I is used transitively and with a variety of prepositions, to depict all sorts of separations, including that of weaning a young animal from its mother's milk, a noteworthy breaking of that most fundamental of attachments. As a pattern, فعيل may refer to an adjective or a noun. With this root, فصيل *faSiil* specifically designates a weaned calf or camel.

A small modification to this noun, the addition of the feminine gender marker ة, yields فصيلة *faSiila*. This minimal change produces a noteworthy new word that was adapted for the biological and zoological sciences: فصيلة and its plural فصائل *faSaa'il* are used with some latitude to describe the divisions of family, genus, or species. In genetics, فصيلة دم *faSiilat dam* is a blood type. However, this is a very old word, and in ancient times, before such academic designations were made, it was used to mark distinctions in kinship. Members of the clan or sub-tribe could be so designated, as in 70:13 of the Qur'an: وَفَصِيلَتِهِ الَّتِي تُؤْوِيهِ, *And his kinfolk who give him shelter.*

مَفصِل
JOINT
فصل (في)
to wean; to sack, fire someone
فصيل
weaned camel
انفصل من
to be sacked, fired
تمّ فصله
he was fired
الإنفصال
separation firing
انفصل عن
to dissociate oneself; to be separated, divorced
فصل في
to make a decision about; to render a judgement on
فاصل
to part ways with to bargain with to haggle with over...
MacToot

8
Joint (2) مَفصِل - مَفاصِل
Division, Separation; Detail

The Form I verb يفصِل – فصل *faSala* means to separate, and Arabic's multiple morphological patterns come in handy in the expression of its many real-world aspects. The noun فاصِل, *faaSil*, this verb's active participle, signifies a pause or interval, such as a short break in a news program. A gender change yields فاصِلة *faaSila*, a comma, which Arabic uses mathematically, in place of a decimal point. For example, the equivalent of the English 4.3 would be written with a comma rather than a period, and would be pronounced, if read aloud, *'arba'a faaSila thalaatha*. The same term can be used for the comma of punctuation, or one may use فصلة *faSla*. A classroom—and by association the class held in it—is called فصل *faSl*, because a classroom is understood as a smaller section or division of a department, institute, or the like. The plural is فصول *fuSuul*, which can also designate seasons, the largest divisions of the year, as well as acts, the major segments of a play.

Form II فصّل, with its morphological suggestion of repetition, means to divide into sections or arrange by groups. From there, it is just a small step to the idea of presenting something in detail and making it clear. The plural of the *maSdar* pattern is used to convey the root's most common derivative of all, 1,112 in the *FDA*, تفاصيل, *tafaaSiil*, details. The Form II verb is also used in the fashion world, where it means to create clothing with great attention to detail. The *maSdar* is التفصيل *at-tafSiil*, tailoring.

Form III typically implies another person, and فاصل means to part ways with someone, thus creating a separation. It also has a very common transactional sense, to haggle with someone or to bargain. The *maSdar* الفصال *al-fiSaal*, is bargaining. This form suggests the incremental price distinctions offered in the process of bringing the transaction to a successful conclusion. Finally, the Form VII verb انفصل, used with the preposition عن, means to dissociate oneself from someone else, and especially to be separated from a spouse, a separation of consequence.

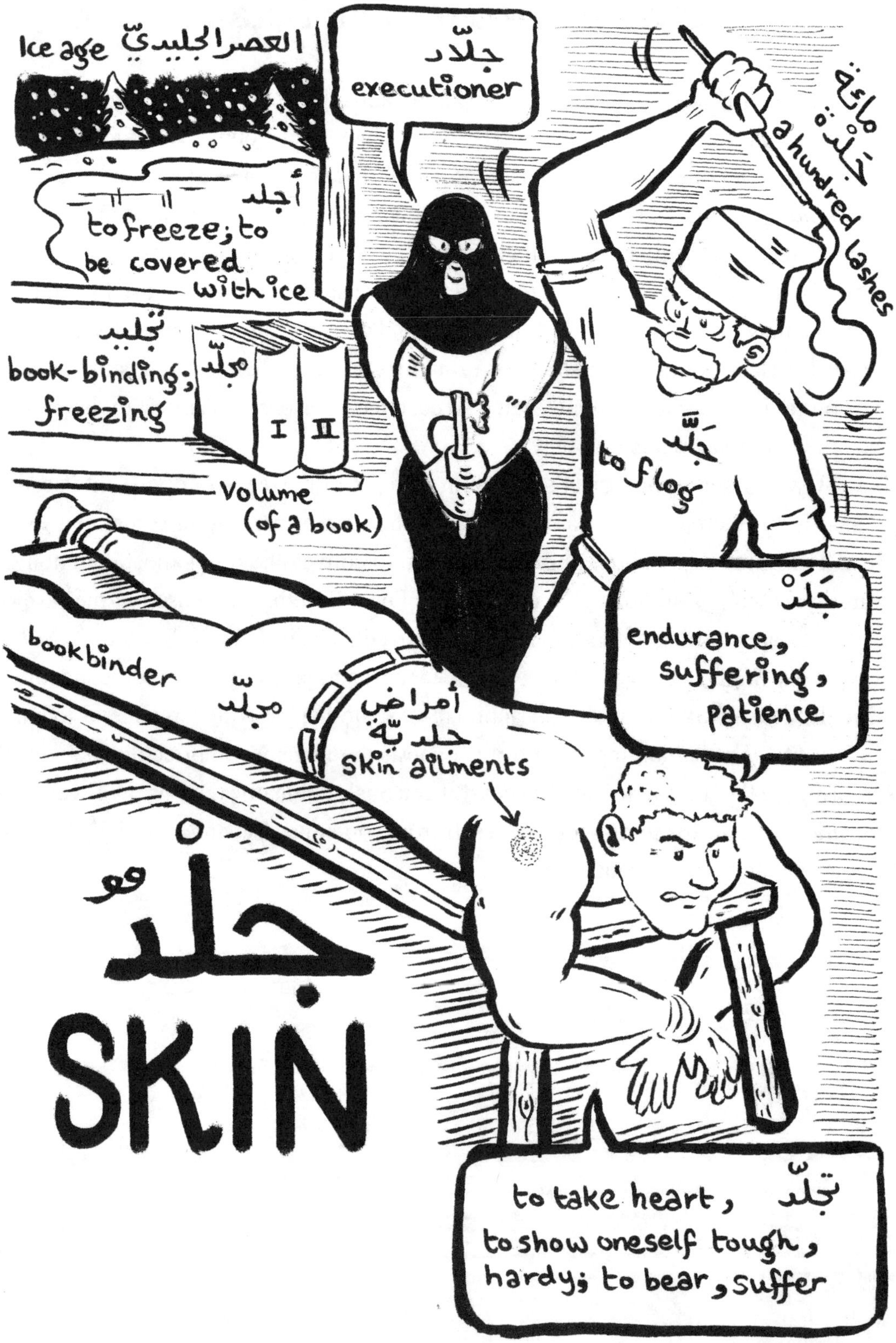

جلد
SKIN
Ice age العصر الجليديّ
أجلد to freeze; to be covered with ice
تجليد book-binding; freezing
مجلّد Volume (of a book)
جلّاد executioner
مائة جَلْدة a hundred lashes
جَلَّد to flog
جَلَدْ endurance, suffering, patience
bookbinder مجلّد
أمراض جلديّة skin ailments
تجلّد to take heart, to show oneself tough, hardy; to bear, suffer

9

Skin جِلْد - جُلود

Endurance; Long-suffering

One of Arabic's words for the skin, الجلد *al-jild* designates an extremely slender membrane. As such, it inspired the word for another thin coating, الجليد *al-jaliid*, ice. In addition to human skin, جِلد may also mean an animal's skin or hide, as well as hide treated for preservation, leather. It is in this sense that the plural جلود *juluud* might be used. These two words both make the *FDA*. By adding a *taa marbuuta* to skin, Arabic produces جِلدة *jilda*, which may mean a skin or a piece of leather. Classically, this word figures in a designation of ethnic belonging: ابن جلدتنا *ibn jildatina*, the son of our skin, literally, is our fellow tribesman, one of our clan.

The relative adjective derived from جلد is not skinny, as an elementary learner has a right to expect, but rather the erudite 'cutaneous' or perhaps 'dermal.' Fortunately for Arabists, *nisba* adjectives like this one, جلديّ *jildiyy*, are delightfully easy to form.

The Arabs put animal hide to various uses, including to make a whip. A more common word for whip is سوط *sawT*, but Arabic's instrument pattern can also be used to produce مِجلدة *mijlada*. This designation astutely links the instrument to the skin in terms of substance *and* purpose, since the real intent of a whipping is excoriation. One lash with a whip is جَلْدة *jalda*. Whipping was a brutal punishment, and the professional who carried it out, الجلّاد *al-jallaad*, grew to be viewed as a hangman or executioner, by whatever method. The Form I verb to whip يجلِد – جلد *jalada* is used twice in the Qur'an, as is the word for a lash.

The past and present tenses of the Form I verb derived from this body part can be voweled in three different ways, each time with a specific meaning يجْلِد – جلَد *jalada*, to whip, to flog; يجلَد – جلِد *jalida*, to freeze, be frozen; and يجْلُد – جلُد *jaluda*, to be tough, hardy, or steadfast in the face of adversity. This last sense animates three derived verb forms, too. Form III جالد means to fight someone, and مجالد *mujaalid* is a particular one who does so, a gladiator. Form VI تجالد conveys the mutuality of the fighting process, to engage (each other) in a sword fight. Form V, تجلّد, is largely synonymous with Form I, to bear, suffer; to take heart, show oneself to be tough. Form IV أجلد, however, takes its inspiration from الجليد, and thus means to freeze, be covered with a layer of ice.

Animals' hides can be put to use, too, and the Arabs used a Form II verb from this root to create 'to bind,' literally putting the skin back on. In Cairo, in the 2020s, it is still possible to visit the workshop of a مجلّد *mujallid*, a bookbinder, and order a binding, تجليد كتاب *tajliid kitaab*, for under US$30.

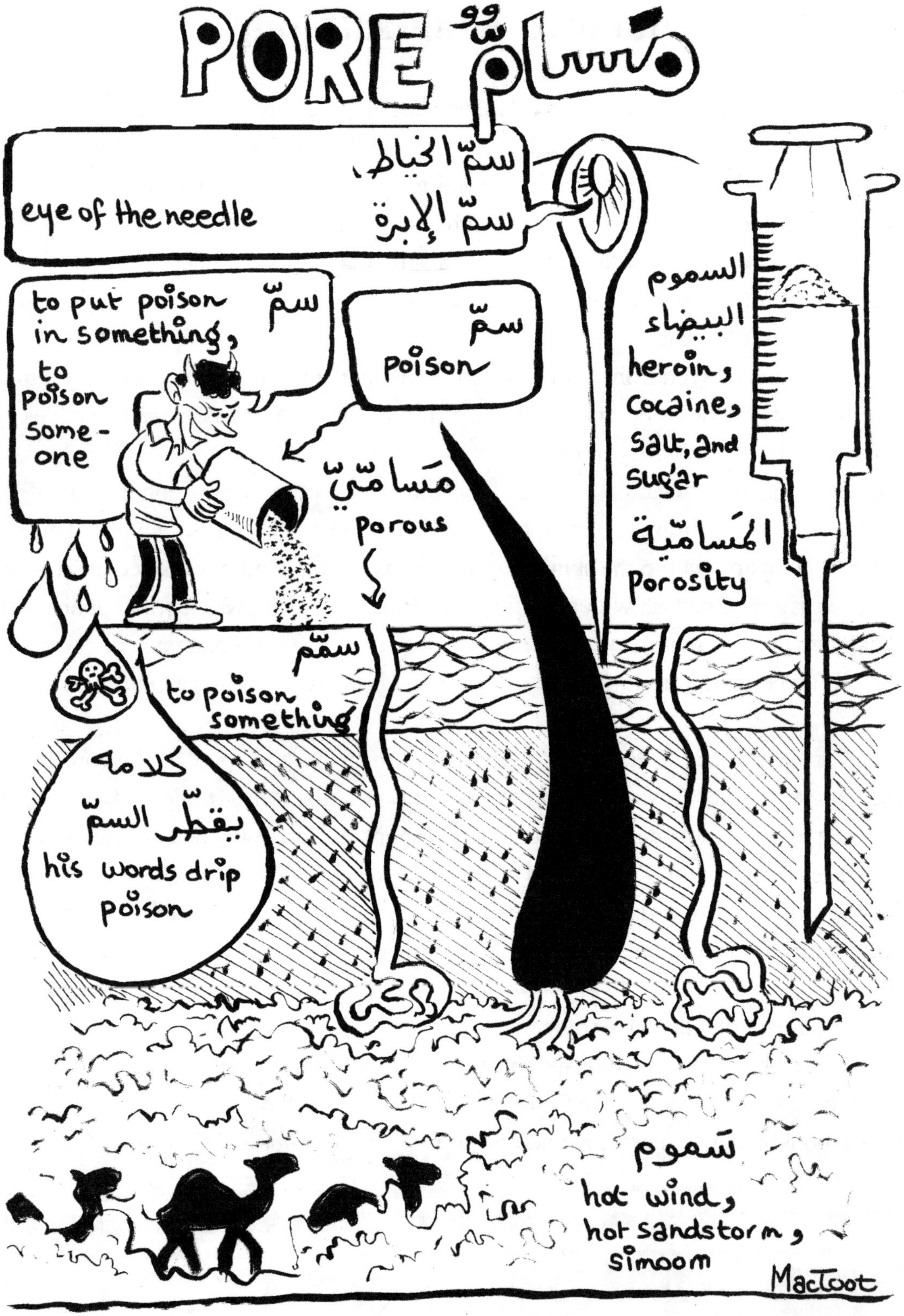
PORE مَسامّ
سمّ الخياط،
سمّ الإبرة
eye of the needle
سمّ
to put poison in something,
to poison some-one
سمّ
poison
السموم البيضاء
heroin, cocaine, salt, and sugar
مَسامّيّ
porous
المَسامّيّة
porosity
سمّم
to poison something
كلامه بيقطّر السمّ
his words drip poison
سموم
hot wind, hot sandstorm, simoom
MacToot

10

Pore مَسامّ – مَسامّات

Poison; Penetration

The connection of المَسامّات *al-masaammaat*, pores, to the س – م – م root seems quite strange at first glance. What could pores and poison, السُّم *as-summ*, the most common vocabulary item based on this root and the only one to figure in the *FDA*, have to do with each other? But perhaps such a connection is not so farfetched after all. Poisoning, السَّم *as-samm*, is one of the dark arts, and many poisons, سُموم *sumuum,* have been developed and refined over the ages. Originally, السموم البيضاء *as-sumuum al-bayDaa',* literally the white poisons, meant cocaine and heroin, but in modern, health-conscious times, the expression has come to be applied to sugar and salt. The diabolical nerve agents one reads of in the news are the product of advanced technology, but the general premise they are based on is not new. Toxic agents that attack through the skin are common in nature, both in flora and fauna, and the skin's vulnerability was well known in the ancient world. The very word toxic is derived from *toxon*, the Greek word for a bow. Poisoning in hunting, warfare, and beyond has been exploited in diverse societies and cultures, east and west, north and south. To take an example from the culture under consideration, reports of poisoning are extant from the first century of Islam. Al-Hasan, Ali's son and the Prophet's grandson, is presumed to have died of poisoning in 670. The exact method, however, is a matter of speculation.

There are three verbs based on this root, Form I سمّ – يسُمّ *samma*, to put poison into something or to poison someone, Form II سمّم to poison someone, and Form V تسمّم to be poisoned. The participles of Form I are in common use: سامّ *saamm*, poisonous, toxic, and مسموم *masmuum*, poisonous, poisoned. The Form V *maSdar* التسمّم *at-tasammum*, poisoning or sepsis, is also in common use.

In a figurative sense, the Form I verb is used intransitively: سمّ اليوم *samma al-yawmu* means the day turned into a hot sand storm. The Arabs had plenty of experience with السَّموم *as-samuum*, hot and violent dust-laden winds. The name they chose for the phenomenon speaks volumes on their aversion to it, and it has even worked its way into English as 'simoom.' The grit in these winds makes breathing difficult and stings exposed skin as though it were being pierced. In another connection to porosity, المسامّية *al-masaammiyya*, the expression سَمّ الخياط *samm al-khiyaaT* or سَمّ الإبرة *samm al-'ibra* means the eye of a needle. From here comes an interesting take on the *function* of a needle, sewing: سمّ الثوب *samma ath-thawb* means to repair or darn a garment, while سمّ بين الناس *samma bayna n-naas*, is to repair a metaphorical tear in relations among people. The plural of this sense of سمّ is used in the *iDaafa* construction سُموم الإنسان *sumuum al-'insaan*, the orifices of a human being.[10] It refers specifically to the mouth, nostrils, and ears. Pores were not included in that list, and we must therefore recall that مَسامّ is actually a place noun by form. This suggests that one must consider the pore a place where something noxious can pierce the skin, a place for poisoning.

نَدَبٌ | نَدَبَةٌ
SCAR
باب المندب
Straits of Mandab
to give... انتدب لـ
(a country) a mandate over another's territory
مندوب
representative
wailing, weeping نَدْب
dirge نُدْبَة
مَنْدَب
lamentation
to mourn, lament, bewail; نَدَب
to appoint, delegate, deputize
MacToot

11

Scar نَدَب / نَدْبة – أَنْداب / نُدوب

Lamentation; Delegation

In a dramatic flourish, the Arabs linked scars الأنداب *al-'andaab* / الندوب *an-nuduub* to lamentation, النَّدْب *an-nadb*, perhaps suggesting all the pain associated with a wound serious enough to leave a scar *nadab / nadba*. With another grand metaphoric leap, they associated scars and the action of delegating *an-nadb*. A first glance, the two seem to have nothing in common, but actually, a scar does just that, taking the place of the wound that caused it and forever reminding one of it! The Form I verb has two vowelings, ندب – يندب *nadiba – yandabu*, to scar over, and *nadaba – yandubu*, to lament or to delegate.

Ceremonies of mourning were of cultural significance, and a second *maSdar* المَنْدَب *al-mandab* came into use, amplifying this idea of lamentation. This is a *maSdar miimi*, one of a rather small group of Form I verbal nouns labeled as such because of the initial letter *miim* (always voweled with a *fatha*). This common prefix *ma-* can create a degree of derivative ambiguity. It's worth noting that occasionally a *maSdar miimi* can be made plural. Here, it produces منادب *manaadib*, wails of lamentation. In its singular, this same *maSdar miimi* is also famous in the geographical domain. The narrow strait between the Gulf of Aden and the Red Sea that separates Yemen from Djibouti on the Horn of Africa is called باب المندب Bab al-Mandab, sometimes translated the Gate of Tears, rather than the more literal Door of Lamentation. One might postulate that many ships have foundered in these waters. Furthermore, the ancient geological record shows that there have been major tectonic shifts in this area, and a land bridge connecting Africa and Asia has appeared and disappeared over the course of the last 100,000 years. Perhaps this strait's name preserves a cultural memory of those ancient upheavals, as in the Qur'anic and Biblical accounts of Noah. In any case, as it does today, life in antiquity presented many occasions for tears. Mourning was serious business, and specific vocabulary evolved for it. Further linking the basic meaning of lamentation and delegation, hired mourners, especially female ones, ندّابات *naddaabaat* / نادبات *naadibaat*, might be delegated to lament the deceased, reciting or singing a funereal dirge or نُدبة *nudba*.

As we have seen, النَّدْب could also mean authorization or delegation, from which comes the common word, 2,972 in the *FDA*, مندوب *manduub*, someone delegated, a deputy. This is used in the commercial domain, where it means a company representative or an authorized agent. In a further extrapolation on this idea, the Form VIII verb انتدب لـ means to authorize (to do something), and in the geopolitical domain, with the preposition على, to give a country a mandate over (the territory of another). The *maSdar* الانتداب *al-intidaab* is such a territorial mandate, like the one claimed by Great Britain in 1799 over the Island of Perim in the Bab al-Mandab Strait. The British objective was strategic security: their valuable sea trade with territories in India had to navigate the dangerous waters of this southern gateway to the Red Sea. In October 2015, that same island returned to the headlines, when loyalist Yemeni forces and their powerful Gulf allies seized it from Houthi control, one small battle in a protracted civil war giving twenty-first-century Yemenis caught in the middle much cause for lamentation.

وَلْيَتَلَطَّفْ وَلا
يُشْعِرَنَّ بِكُمْ أَحَدُ
and let him be unobtrusive and not cause anyone to become aware of you
Qur'an 18:19
Hair
شعر
قرون
الاستشعار
feelers
أشعرَ...
to inform, to make someone feel
to perceive,
شعرَ...
to feel, know
شُعيرات دَمَويّة
capillaries
poetry
knowledge
شِعر
poet
شاعِر
MacToot

12
Hair شَعْر – أَشْعار / شُعور
Sensing, Sensitivity

Observe the lowly caterpillar and wonder. Its brain may be the size of a pinhead, but its antennae and the hairs on its body allow it to sense its surroundings with uncanny precision. Similarly, a cat's whiskers increase its ability to navigate gracefully in the dark. We humans have devised a host of elaborate rituals and fashions for our hair, and yet can't agree on what should be done with it. Depending on the culture and the fashion of the times, we spend fortunes curling hair or straightening it, implanting it or pulling it out by the roots. Despite the various enhancements, our ability to detect the environment with our hair is ever so limited, allowing for little more than the detection of a mosquito as it lands on our arm. Hair is a lot of work, but of little practical value in the day-to-day lives of humans. The Arabs, as mesmerized by hair as the next culture, must have observed the valuable role hair played in other species and appropriated it as a metaphor. To designate a single hair, one must add a ة to the collective شعر *sha'r*. Counting hairs uses this feminine singular as a point of departure: شعرتان *sha'rataani*, two hairs, ثلاث شعرات *thalaath sha'raat*. English inventively describes making unnecessary and trivial distinctions as splitting hairs, noting, as does Arabic, the minute dimensions of a shaft of hair: قيد شعرة *qayd sha'ra*, a hair's breadth. The sleek, slender nature of a single hair inspired another metaphor that describes escaping easily from a difficult situation, or, in cricket terms, a sticky wicket: كما تُسل الشعرة من العجين *kamaa tusallu ash-sha'ra min al-'agiin*, as a hair is gently drawn out of dough.

The Form I verb شعر – يشعُر *sha'ara* means to feel. Form IV أشعر is to make someone feel, and Form X استشعر is to be cognizant of something, to be filled with a sense or feeling. This last is a reflexive version of the transitive Form IV, one of the less common semantic derivations of Form X. The term for an insect's antennae or feelers, based on the Form X *maSdar*, is, literally, 'the horns of trying to sense,' قرون الاستشعار *quruun al-istish'aar*.

Now return to Form I, شعر, to feel, and its *maSdar* is الشعور feeling(s). Can you guess which field it is linked to? What sort of work requires the ability to feel deeply? The Arabs did not hesitate long to answer this question. Their verdict was poetry. Prose writers need to write clearly and convincingly, but before one can write poetry, الشِعر *ash-shi'r*, and call oneself a poet, شاعِر *shaa'ir*, one must feel. Feelings are based on knowledge, but it is a particular type of emotional knowledge, also called الشِعر, the very same word as poetry. The master of old Arabic songs, Sabah Fakhri sings a gorgeous مُوَشَّحة *muwashshaHa*, a post-classical ballad, recounting the heartbreaking separation of Bedouin lovers who have pledged fidelity to each other. Watching the caravan as it moves off into the predawn gloom, the lover who must remain behind torments himself by wondering: يا ليت شِعري بطول العهد ما فعلوا, If only I knew—*yaa layta shi'ri*—what they would do over the span of the pledge!

لحّم
to weld, solder
شِعْر ملحميّ
heroic poetry
welding لِحام
to stick together, fit closely; التحم
to be in immediate contact, grapple
لحّام
welder; butcher
FLESH
لَحْم
من لحم ودم
(made of) flesh and blood; having feelings
تلاحم
to engage in a mutual massacre
MacToot
لحم
to mend, patch
يأكُل لحْم أخيه
he speaks ill of his brother behind his back
massacre, مَلحَمة
fierce battle

13
Flesh لَحْم
Holding Together

English likes to say that *eating* helps keep body and soul together. Derivatives of the Arabic word اللحم *al-laHm*, flesh, seem to echo that sentiment. Flesh is the product of what we eat, and in Arabic it is also the word for meat, itself. Bread may be the staff of life, but meats, اللحوم *al-luHuum*, are high on the list of favorites in Arab cuisine. In English it is possible to use flesh as a substitute for the whole physical person, as in the famous phrase 'The spirit is willing, but the flesh is weak.' Both Arabic and English emphasize this point when they say that people are of flesh and blood, من لحم ودم *min laHm wa dam*, with all the conditions, good and bad, that apply to the medium. Flesh is a substantial part of the body, and English says 'to show up in the flesh,' meaning to come in person. In one instance, Qur'anic usage also portrays the flesh as the whole person in 49:12: أن يَـأْكُل لَحْـمَ أخِيـه, *to speak ill of his brother behind his back (lit., to eat the flesh of his brother)*. This is remarkably like the English backbiting. Unlike bone and cartilage, flesh is soft and pliant. In fact, those soft but sometimes troublesome fleshy lymph tissues in the pharynx known as the adenoids are descriptively called اللحميّة *al-laHmiyya.*

A term from the field of weaving adds to our understanding of the extended meanings of اللحم. As opposed to السَّداة *as-sadaa*, the warp or lengthwise threads or yarn of a fabric, the crosswise *weft* is called اللحِمة *al-laHima*. The choice of this word suggests that the weft is what holds fabric together. The Form I verb has two vowelings, each with a distinct meaning: لحم – يلحُم *laHama* means to mend, patch, weld, or solder. A welder is therefore called لحّام *laHHaam*. In its other voweling, Form I لحِم – يلحَم *laHima* means to get stuck. The Form II verb لحّم also means to weld and solder. All convey the idea of adhesion. Since weaving is an age-old art, one that predates welding, it may be that اللحِمة, the weft, is the nominal source of those verbs. When clothes had to last and last, mending and patching would have been an essential practice, and terms created for it were presumably transferred to later metal-working endeavors.

Two other nouns are also at work in animating the verbal derivatives. A person who deals with meat may be called لحّام *laHHaam*, a butcher. The other is ملحمة *malHama*, a bloody fight, fierce battle, slaughter. Such battles sometimes figured in الشعر الملحميّ *ash-shi'r al-malHamiyy*, epic poetry, preserving heroic battles as tribal history. Two verbal derivatives incorporate these ideas into their family of meanings. Form VI تلاحم adds its typical sense of mutuality to the root. It may mean to hold firmly together, be joined, or stick together, as two pieces of patched clothing or soldered metal might, but it also has the particular sense of doing battle, engaging in a mutual massacre. In this second sense, the idea of bodily contact is front and center, each combatant at the other's throat, so to speak, bent on butchery. Of all the derivatives of this root, the only two that figure in the *FDA* are لحم, meat, and ملحمة, epic poetry. Form VIII التحم may also depict battle in which the parties fiercely grapple with each other. Its other common meaning is to intermesh, or stick together, and here it offers an altogether positive approach to the flesh: the healing and scarring over of a wound. In this case, the flesh comes together and patches itself.

MUSCLE عَضَلة
MacToot
muscular, brawny عَضِل
to prevent (a woman) from getting married عَضَل
related to muscles عضلي
difficult, puzzling مُعضِل
dilemma مُعْضِلة
أعضل الداء الأطباء
the disease stumped doctors
chronic; incurable عُضال

14
Muscle عَضَلة – عَضَلات
Difficult; Prevent

Muscles are metaphors for strength in English, whereas in Arabic, if the connection is not one of physical appearance or resemblance, the image is one of difficulty, suggesting a muscular opponent of sorts with the power to prevent one from doing something, or to baffle one with difficulty.

The English verb to flex collocates very closely with muscle and can be understood literally or figuratively. In Arabic, however, the two senses are separated. To cause a muscle to contract by flexing it is ثَنَى العضلة, *thanaa al-'aDala.* To flex one's muscles in the figurative sense of letting others understand the full degree of one's power is rendered as to put them on display, استعرض عضلاته *ista'raDa 'aDalaatahu*. The muscle as a unit, as noted, is عضلة *'aDala*. Arabic views muscles tending to occur in multiples, and so removing this ة suffix produces عضل *'aDal*, the collective designation, muscles. For further examples of singular versus collective nouns, see chapter 12 on شعر, hair, and chapter 43 on هدب, eyelashes. A muscular person may be described with the adjective عضِل *'aDil*. However, the *nisba* adjective عَضَليّ *'aDaliyy* is reserved to describe conditions rather than people, as in الضمور العضلي *aD-Dumuur al-'aDaliyy*, muscular dystrophy. The diagnosis one hopes not to get is that a disease is chronic and incurable, عُضال *'uDaal*.

The Form I verb has different vowelings, each with its own variation on the theme. To simply be muscular is عضِل – يعْضَل *'aDila*, whereas عضَل – يعْضِل / يعْضُل *'aDala* means to prevent a woman from marrying, using one's brawn, as it were, to preclude her choice. This verb is used twice in the Qur'an, as in 2:232: فَلا تَعْضُلوهُنَّ أَنْ يَنْكِحْنَ أَزْواجَهُنَّ, *Do not prevent them from remarrying their husbands.*

Forms IV أعضل and V تعضّل are essentially synonymous, to be or become puzzling, intractable, or problematic. They are commonly used in the medical domain, where a disease is said to baffle doctors or to be baffling, مُعضِل *mu'Dil*. A feminine noun derived from this same participle means a dilemma, مُعْضِلة *mu'Dila*. Other than muscle, itself, this is the only item from the ع - ض – ل root to make the *FDA*.

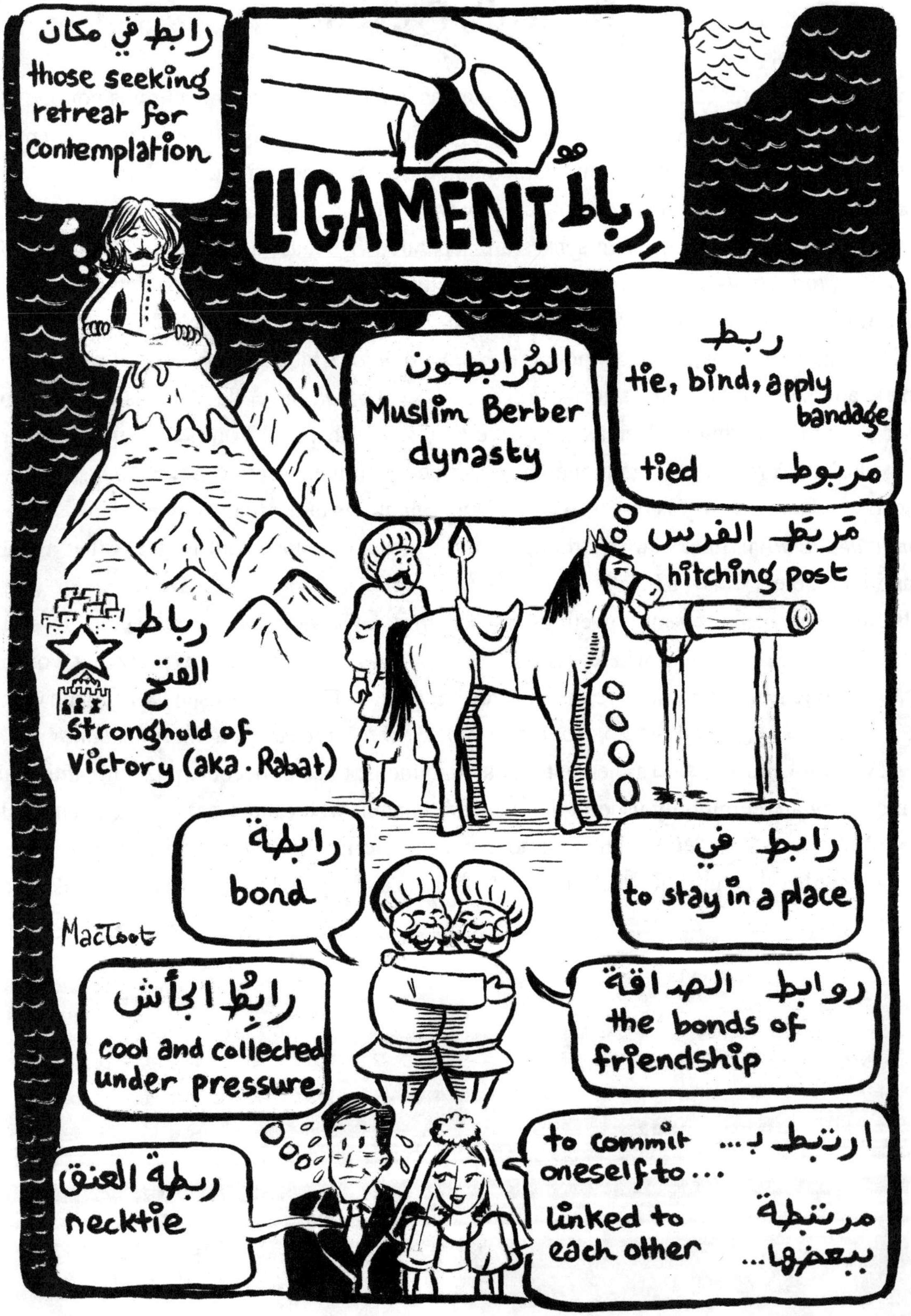

LIGAMENT رباط
رابط في مكان
those seeking retreat for contemplation
ربط
tie, bind, apply bandage
tied مَربوط
المُرابطون
Muslim Berber dynasty
مَربَط الفرس
hitching post
رباط الفتح
Stronghold of Victory (aka. Rabat)
رابطة
bond
رابط في
to stay in a place
MacToot
رابِط الجأش
cool and collected under pressure
روابط الصداقة
the bonds of friendship
ربطة العنق
necktie
ارتبط بـ...
to commit oneself to...
مرتبطة ببعضها...
linked to each other

15
Ligament رِباط – أَرْبِطة
Tie, Bind

The Form I verb يربِط / ربـط – يربُـط *rabaTa* means to physically tie or bind something, as well as to apply a bandage to a wound or injury, thus binding it up. This verb is the source of a large family of vocabulary including الأربطة *al-'arbiTa*, anatomical ligaments that bind bones together and hold organs safely in place. The verb ربـط has abstract and concrete applications. In the temporal domain, ربـط pins an event down, tying it to time. The same verb ties up a horse, ensuring it will not run off. A horse so tied is مَربـوط *mar-buuT*. Horses can still be tied up at مَربَط الفرس *marbaT / marbiT al-faras*, the hitching post. Modern urban dwellers, and even many of their rural confrères, have little contact with hitching posts. Even so, the term has survived as a figure of speech, meaning the moral of the story, the crux of the matter.

In both Arabic and English, agitated emotions are sometimes likened to skittish horses; English reins them in, while Arabic ties them down. This is the classic collocation ربط جأشَه *rabaTa ja'shahu*, which can be used as a particple, رابِـطُ الجـأشِ, to mean cool and collected (under pressure). There are other nominal derivatives, too, such as ربطـة العنـق *rabTat al-'unuq* the formal word for a necktie. The noun رابطة *raabiTa* is a bond or link, with various translations in the sociopolitical domain: confederation, league, guild. Its plural figures in the collocation روابـط الصداقـة *rawaabiT aS-Sadaaqa*, the ties or bonds of friendship.

The ر – ب – ط root has two verbal derivatives. Form III, رابـط has both religious and military associations. In Sufism, someone seeking a retreat for contemplation can be said to رابـط فـي المكـان *raabaTa fi-l-makaan*. From 1061 to 1147, a Muslim Berber dynasty known as المُرابِطـون *al-muraabiTuun*, rendered into English as the Almoravids, ruled over territory in North Africa and Andalusia. The name of the dynasty stems from its founders' Sufi leanings. Larousse calls them *moines guerriers*, warrior monks. The Almoravids gave way to another Berber empire, also preserved in the historical record with an imprecise transliteration, the Almohads (المُوحِّـدون). In the mid-twelfth century, the Caliph Ya'qub al-Mansur, the dynasty's founder, moved the Almohad capital to the site of Morocco's modern capital, which had come to have strategic importance. It was given the auspicious name ربـاط الفتـح, *ribaaT al-FatH*, the garrison or stronghold of victory. Over time the word victory became superfluous, and the modern city is simply called Rabat الربـاط, Morocco's capital. This same noun is the *maSdar* of the Form III verb رابـط فـي, to stay in a place, something said of troops stationed in a garrison, for example. Being tied to a place is the key image, and consequently, in the maritime domain, this same verb means to moor a ship. Also derived from this Form III verb is *marabout*, better known in modern French than in English. In parts of Muslim North and West Africa, it designates the tomb of a man revered during his life and posthumously for what are considered to be his special, even magical powers. This tomb/shrine was typically placed near where the man resided رابط فيـه. By extension, *marabout* also refers to the man himself.

The Form VIII verb–preposition idiom ارتبـط بـ means to commit oneself to someone else or to an organization. Having done so, one is linked, perhaps even romantically, in an alliance. Things may also be مرتبطـة ببعضهـا *murtabiTa biba'Dihaa*, linked to each other.

NERVE عَصَبٌ
عِصابة
gang
to form a league, coalition; اعتصب
to gang up on
عصب
to wind, fold, tie, bind, bandage; to wrap the head with a turban
عصيب
critical; stressful; trying
تعصّب
..مع.. على
to take sides with... against...
عَصَبيّ
short-tempered, high-strung
عُصبة
a group, a clique, male relations in the male line
تعصّب
to wind a turban round one's head; to bandage over something; to be bigoted; to cling to fanatically
MacToot

16
Nerve عَصَب – أَعْصاب
Binding; Temper

So microscopic a filament as a nerve cannot have been a primitive discovery, and nerves shared the same designation as sinews and tendons. This shared label is a revealing analogy to pursue. In both Arabic and English, nerves are negatively associated with how one comports oneself, but the interpretations are different. Rather than meaning anxious and jittery, Arabic's workhorse *nisba* adjective produces عصبيّ *'aSabiyy*, meaning short-tempered, high-strung, temperamental. Changing the adjective into a noun yields العصبيّة *al-'aSabiyya*, irritability. However, when speaking of a nerve-racking experience, a different word from this root, عصيب *'aSiib*, is the appropriate choice. The collocation وقت عصيب *waqt 'aSiib* succinctly expresses a difficult, tension-filled time.

The word عِصاب *'iSaab* means a bandage, and Form II عصّب, a denominative derivation of it, means to wind a bandage around an injured limb, or wrap a headband or other cloth around the head. Protectively binding an injured limb is an age-old practice as common now as then. Binding the head, the location of English's headstrong temper, may have been seen as treatment for it. Form V تعصّب is its reflexive counterpart, and means to bandage oneself, or wrap one's own head with a cord or a turban. Bandages and turbans are tightly wound and do not come off easily. They cling. This explains how Form V took on the figurative sense of to cling (too) tightly to one's position. One who does so is a fanatic, a zealot, مُتعصّب *muta'aSSib*. The Form VIII verb اعتصب also took a denominative tack, using as its source عِصابة *'iSaaba*, a gang. The verb means to form a tightly wound clique, all the better to gang up on one's adversaries with.

A very old derivative of عَصَب is عُصْبة, *'uSba*, a band of male relatives. Choosing this term for a group of related men may suggest that the Arabs who coined the term considered a band of male relatives to be naturally prone to act temperamentally. The noun عُصْبة appears four times in the Qur'an, including in the story of the Prophet Joseph, whose nine older brothers were jealous of their father's preference for him. The band of brothers hatches a nefarious plot to take Joseph out into remote pastures and dispose of him. First, they disingenuously ask their father, who is suspicious of their intentions, to trust the strength of their numbers, using this term (12:14): لَئِنْ أَكَلَهُ الذِّئْبُ وَنَحْنُ عُصْبَةٌ, *(What a shame it would be) were the wolf to eat him, when we are (such) a large band.* In jurisprudence, paternal relatives can also be called عَصَبة *'aSaba*. This term contrasts with ذوو الأرحام *dhawuu al-'arHaam*, maternal blood relatives, discussed in chapter 106.

As one moves from nerve, to high-strung, to a tightly bound head, to tight bands of men, the morphologically mobile عصب *'aSab* flashes like an aggravated neural circuit: temper, temper!

ثقيل الدم
bad company, unpleasant to be around
خفيف الدم
good company, pleasant to be around
دَم
BLOOD
دمّي = أدمى
to bloody, to make bleed
دَمِيَ
to bleed
مصّاص الدماء
Vampire
دمّ
to daub, smear, color, tint, dye
bloody دمويّ
rouge الدمّ
دامي الشفتين
red-lipped
دمّم
to rub, anoint
MacToot

17
Blood (1) دَم – دِماء
Red

It is hardly surprising that something as colorful and precious as blood would have a significant presence in speech, and the nominal duo of الدم *ad-dam* and its plural الدماء *ad-dimaa'* are, in fact, a metaphoric powerhouse. From the English point of view, blood doesn't need a plural. But Arabic sometimes avails itself of the plural option as a less literal, less tangible alternative to الدم. That literal singular is nicely illustrated in the expression من لحم ودم *min laHm wa dam*, of flesh and blood, an especially literal depiction of a sentient person. Similarly, in evoking the psychosomatic torment of waiting, Umm Kulthum sings: والثواني جمرات في دمي, and the seconds are hot coals in my blood. The contrast between الدم and الدماء is not unlike the contrast in English between water and waters, although this plural is more common.

Let's examine some of the idiomatic and metaphoric expressions associated with blood. Color, weight, and temperature are all of relevance. Linking blood to its red color, we find a collocation involving the lips, دامي الشفتين *daami ash-shafatayni*, red-lipped. Literal blood is red, but Arabic and English agree that figurative blood may be blue. Using that less literal plural form, Arabic identifies nobility as الدماء الزرقاء *ad-dimaa' az-zarqaa'*, literally, blue-bloods. Blood also has weight, and in this domain, the Arabs made positive associations with lightness. He has light blood, دمه خفيف *damuhu khafiif*, means he is pleasant, good-humored, and easy to be around; attributively, such a person is said to be خفيف الدم *khafiif ad-dam*. Heavy blood, on the other hand, is pejorative: دمه ثقيل *damuhu thaqiil* refers to someone who has no sense of humor, with whom it is unpleasant to spend time. In terms of heat, English and Arabic agree that premeditated crimes are committed بدم بارد *bidam baarid*, in cold blood. Similarly, a hot-blooded, excitable person, or creature, is حارّ الدم *Haarr ad-dam*, a term that may also apply to mammals, as explained in the reference to science in the next chapter.

Despite these similarities, Arabic and English often diverge on the topic of blood. In terms of the eyes, English usually describes red eyes as being bloodshot. Arabic, however, conveys this through the word محتقنة *muHtaqana*, with no reference to blood at all. Comparatively speaking, it is tempting to posit that religious dogma is responsible for blood's highly charged sacred/profane aura in English. Christ's blood is the central symbol of Christian ritual, and perhaps as a result, the word has a wealth of grisly associations. Bloodthirsty and blood-curdling come to mind. Bloody has even transformed itself into a swear word in British English. Arabic uses its workhorse *nisba* adjective to produce bloody, دموي *damawiyy.* This adjective may convey something blood-soaked, like عهد دمويّ *ahd damawiyy* a brutal or savage era, but can also be utterly devoid of gore, as in the phrase أوعية دموية *'aw'iyya damawiyya*, blood vessels.

BLOOD دَمٌ

دميم
ugly
بدم بارد
in cold blood
دمه لن يضيع هدراً
His blood will not be shed in vain/ with impunity
أراق دمه
to shed someone's blood, to kill
أهدر دمه
to declare someone fair game and kill him
-MacToot-

18
Blood (2) دَم – دِماء
Red

Strangely, from a morphological perspective, the singular form of blood suggests one root source, while its plural suggests another. Without considering both, the range of derivatives would be smaller than expected for such an important element of anatomy. The plural form الدماء *dimaa'* appears to be based on a weak root د – م – ي. This root has three verbal derivations, all with straightforward functional meanings. The Form I verb دمي – يدمَى *damiya* means to bleed, while Form II دمّى is causative and means to make something bleed. Its passive participle مُدَمًّى *mudamman* means bloodied. Form IV أدمى is synonymous with Form II. One famous usage is in the poem "al-Atlal" (the ruins) by Ibrahim Nagy, interpreted by the inimitable Umm Kulthum. Depicting the torments of thwarted love, she sings: آهٍ من قيدك أدمى مِعصمي, Aah, your bond! It has bloodied my wrist.

When it comes to determining the root of two letter words like دم, Arabists get a bit nervous. Why aren't there three? The answer is that the word is a borrowing from Hebrew, in which the pronunciation is also *dam*, and even from Ugaritic,[11] an ancient Semitic cousin, whose word for blood was *dm*. Spoken Egyptian Arabic uses the base of the standard word for blood, but regularizes it by doubling the final letter, *damm*. Such a doubling, however, produces a root that already exists in standard Arabic, د – م – م, one with two verbal derivatives. Form I دمّ – يدُمّ *damma*, means to coat, daub, or smear something with color or dye or an ointment. The noun دمّ *damm* means ointment or salve, as well as paint, pigment, dye, and even rouge. Adding a bit of intensity, Form II دمّم means to rub or anoint with such a salve. A tie-in with blood is suggested, however, by a classical description of military combat: it may be said دمّ الجيش عدوّه *damma al-jaysh 'aduuwahu*, the army obliterated its enemy. The few other derivatives of this root all have to do with ugliness and repulsiveness, not necessarily linked to blood. The most common of them is probably دميم *damiim*, ugly. However, the د – م – م root's core meaning of tinting something red offers one of blood's inherent associations not otherwise available in the د – م – ي mix and helps round out the metaphoric picture of this crucial bodily element.

In Arabic, blood seems most common in references to life (ما دام دمي يسيل في عروقي, as long as my blood flows through my veins), death (إراقة الدماء / إهدار الدماء, bloodshed), and science (مشتقات الدم, blood derivatives, حار الدم, warm-blooded, الدورة الدموية, blood circulation or the circulatory system). Fear is another domain in which one might expect to find it. Arabic has a number of one-word terms for fearsome creatures (غول / عفريت / جنّي), but vampires are not among them. This concept seems to be a cultural import. Arabic simply identifies a vampire as a bloodsucker, مصّاص الدماء *maSSaaS ad-dimaa'*. Ultimate origins are disputed, but English seems to have borrowed the concept and the term from the Hungarian *vampir*. This word makes no direct reference to blood, although it is impossible to conceive of vampires without it. One might wonder if the English adjective bloodthirsty has vampiric origins.

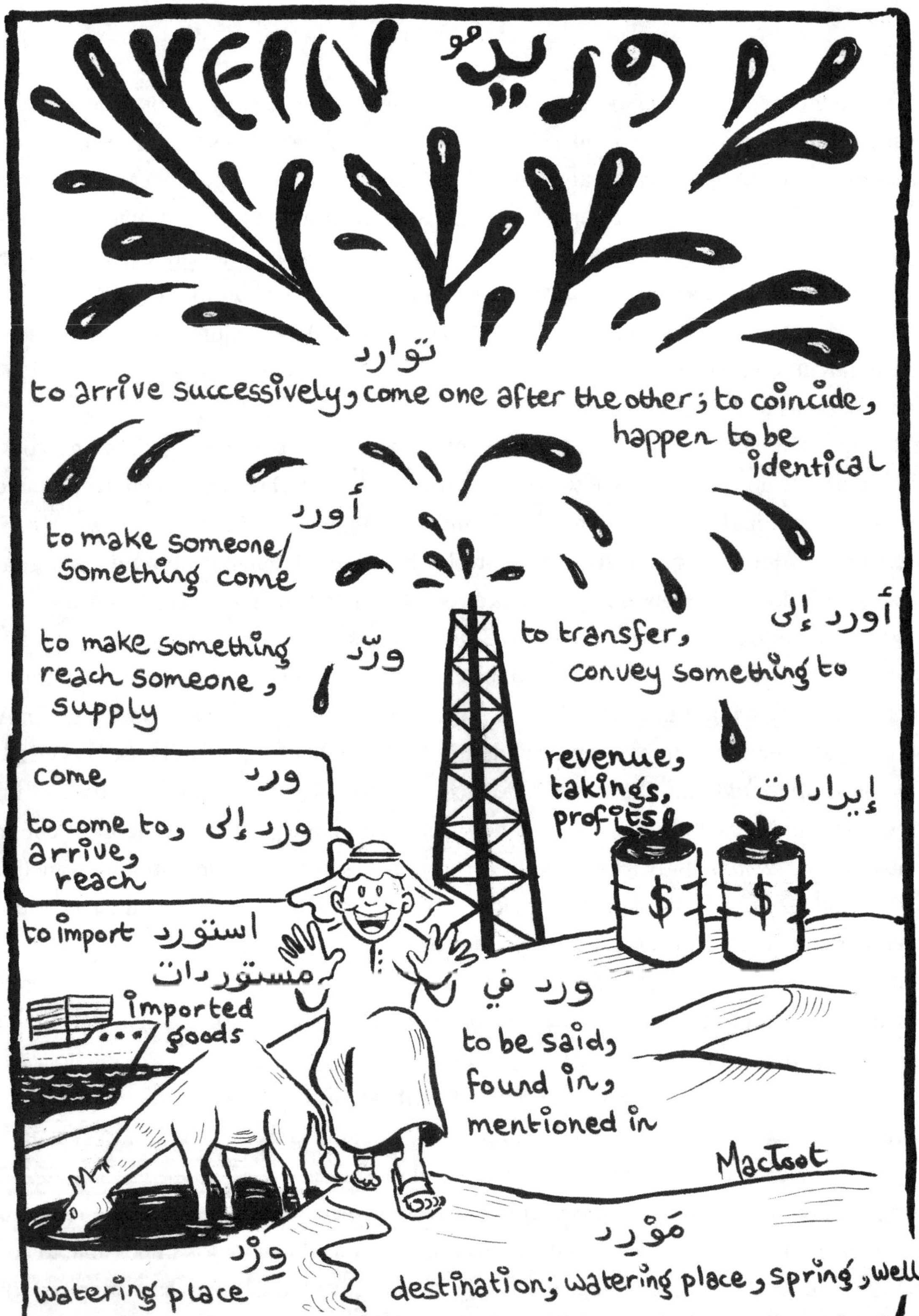
VEIN وريد
توارد
to arrive successively, come one after the other; to coincide, happen to be identical
أورد
to make someone/something come
ورّد
to make something reach someone, supply
أورد إلى
to transfer, convey something to
ورد
come
ورد إلى
to come to, arrive, reach
revenue, takings, profits
إيرادات
استورد
to import
مستوردات
imported goods
ورد في
to be said, found in, mentioned in
MacToot
وِرد
watering place
مَوْرِد
destination; watering place, spring, well

19
Vein وَريد – أَوْرِدة
Source

One vein, the jugular, is singled out in the Qur'an, at 50:16, to metaphorically encapsulate God's proximity to mankind: وَنَحْنُ أَقْرَبُ إِلَيْهِ مِنْ حَبْلِ الْوَرِيدِ, *And We are closer to him than his jugular vein.* In addition to this noun, seven other derivatives of the و – ر – د root occur ten times in the Qur'an. In the modern idiom, the root has five verbal elaborations, making it a very productive one. The word وريد *wariid*, itself, ranks 1,839 in the *FDA*. Given the crucial importance of water sources in nomadic life, the origin of this whole family of vocabulary, including vein, must be ورد *wird*, a watering place.

Directly related to the watering place is the Form I verb وَرَدَ - يرِد *warada*, to arrive or show up at a place. The Arabs then coined a place noun based on it, مَورِد *mawrid*, literally, wherever one arrives. In pastoral society, one's destination was often a spring or water source, and مورد designates that source as well as access to it. By extension, this same word acquired an abstract meaning: resource, revenue, income. The authors of one of classical Arabic's important dictionaries even chose this name for it, المورد *al-Mawrid*, encouraging scholars of the language to consult it as an indispensable source. Returning to life on the Arabian peninsula, this same place noun, along with its plural, could not suffice for all the destinations associated with water, and a second place pattern emerged, مَورِدة *mawrida*. This could designate a water source, but had the added meaning of a landing place or wharf. Finally, the important Form I verb went on to acquire two figurative meanings: to come into one's hands (of money), and to be mentioned (in a text).

Form II ورّد means to take something to a source, as well as to supply. Form IV أورد - يُوْرِد means to deliver or transfer someone or something to a place. Both are causative articulations of ورد. With the obvious commercial implications of traffic to and from water sources, this vocabulary often refers to financial transactions. For example, the word for a supplier is مورِّد *muwarrid*, while أورد can also mean to deposit funds into an account. The *maSdar* الإيراد *al-'iiraad* and its plural الإيرادات *al-'iiraadat* mean revenue.

In this root, Form VI adds a successive notion to the idea of coming: توارد means to come one after the other, an image of animals flocking to a source. This concise encapsulation of ancient pastoral experience produced two related meanings: to happen to be identical (like all those camels at the watering hole), and to coincide, a temporal abstraction of flocking.

Form X استورد is one momentous side of trade, importing, and it plays on the sense of seeking built into this form. In this case, one seeks out the source along with what it has to offer. Interestingly, export التصدير *at-taSdiir*, is also the outgrowth of a body root, الصدر *aS-Sadr*, the chest.

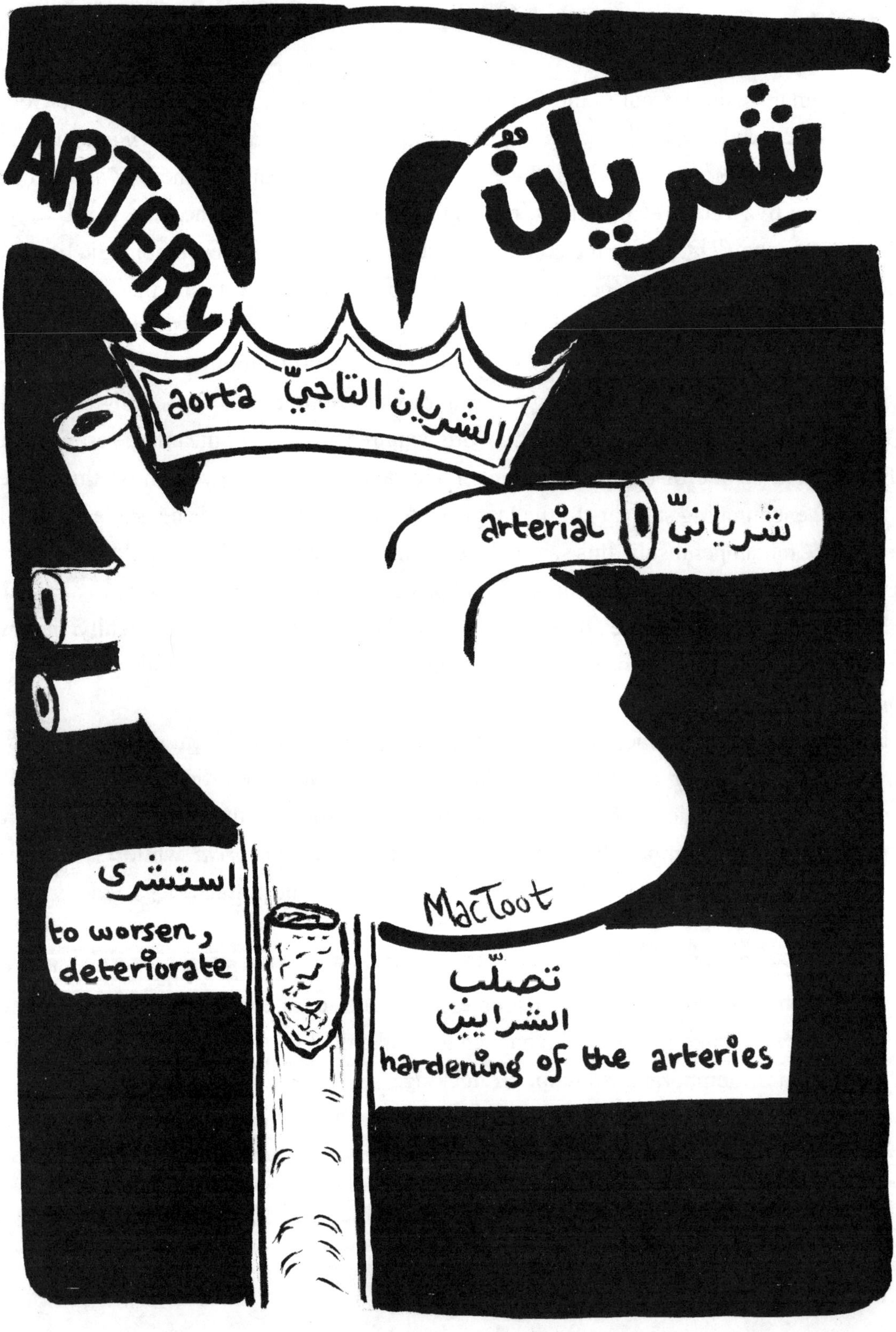

ARTERY
شِريانٌ
aorta
الشريان التاجيّ
arterial
شريانيّ
استشرى
to worsen, deteriorate
MacToot
تصلّب
الشرايين
hardening of the arteries

20

Artery (1) شِرْيان – شَرايِين
Trade; Spreading

The most common derivatives of the ش – ر – ي root, whether ancient or modern, are words related to selling and buying, and at first sight, there seems to be no semantic connection between those activities and الشـرايين *ash-sharaayiin*, the arteries. Over the past few thousand years, purchasing has become fundamentally associated with money in those regions originally governed by empires. However, if we think back to more ancient times, before the advent of the currency systems that centralized societies developed, the age-old system of trading and bartering, with its associated *spread* of goods along physical paths suggests how such an association might have developed. The arteries are an essential element of the circulatory system, physical pathways that allow the transport of blood. Trade also moves along physical pathways, as buyers and sellers transport their goods to and from the market.

The essential role of arteries and veins is partly visible to the naked eye. Clamping down on a vein عـرق *'irq*, painfully shuts off circulation; deep wounds may show blood spurting from an artery, شـريان *shiryaan,* a rather surprisingly high 3,642 in the *FDA*. Nomadic dependence on animals and subsequent slaughtering rituals would have contributed significantly to early insights into anatomy and perhaps gradually to the dual nature of the circulatory system. The term الشريان التاجي *ash-shiryaan at-taajiyy*, the aorta, is an interesting case in point. This English word is derived from a Greek root, where it was associated with the verb to lift. However, the Arabs dubbed it 'the crown-like artery,' using a simile based on its appearance that also suggests its importance. English uses the intimidatingly erudite arteriosclerosis to describe تصلُّـب الشـرايين *taSallub ash-sharaayiin*, an easily understandable term in Arabic that is also popular in less formal English, hardening of the arteries. In both languages, arteries, but *not* veins, can be used to describe vital metaphoric pathways. One may say, for example, شـرايين الحيـاة الاقتصاديـة / الثقافيـة *sharayiin al-Hayaat al-iqtiSaadiyya / ath-thaqaafiyya*, the arteries of economic / cultural life.

ARTERY
شِريانٌ
شارٍ / الشاري
buyer
a purchase
شَرْوة
شرى - يشري
to sell
الشِراء
buying
المُشتَري
Jupiter
اشترى
to buy
مُشْتَرٍ
المُشْتَري
purchaser
N
MacToot

21

Artery (2) شِرْيان – شَرايين

Trade; Spreading

The classical Form I verb شـرى – يشـري *sharaa* means to sell or, in some contexts, to buy. In modern usage, باع *baa'a*, to sell, has entirely supplanted شـرى, and the Form VIII verb اشـترى, to buy, has supplanted Form I شرى. The *derivatives* of the Form I verb remain in common usage, and are exclusively associated with purchasing. First among these is the *maSdar* الشِّـراء *ash-shiraa'*, buying, which ranks 1,210 in the *FDA*. This word appears in the important collocation البيـع والشـراء *al-bay' wa-sh-shiraa'*, selling and buying, an expression that interestingly reverses the order common in English. Also worth noting is قـوّة الشـراء *quwwat ash-shiraa'*, purchasing power. Another common derivative is the active participle شـارٍ *shaarin*, a buyer. (Weak roots can produce 'defective' nouns like شارٍ, whose final ي disappears in certain indefinite forms. In the colloquial domain, this word is always pronounced *shaari*.)

In a popular song of the 1970s, sung by Egypt's heartthrob Abd al-Halim Hafiz, selling and buying are contrasted in the realm of romantic attachment: بيـع قلبـك، بيـع حبّـك، شـوف الشـاري ميـن, Sell your heart, sell your love, see who the buyer is. In this context, a buyer is a committed suitor, one willing, in a crass English expression *not* normally applied to romance, to put his money where his mouth is. A third noun from Form I still in use is شـرْوة *sharwa*, a purchase.

The Form VIII verb اشـترى is extremely common, ranking 1,265 in the *FDA*, which puts it within the most common 200 verbs in the modern spoken and written media corpus. The Form I *maSdar* الشراء tends to be used instead of الاشـتراء, but the Form VIII active participle مُشـترٍ *mushtarin* is preferred in writing to شارٍ. The plural of the passive participle is مشتروات *mushtarawaat*, purchases. Both Form I and Form VIII occur in the Qur'an, although there, too, the latter is much more common, used twenty-one times as opposed to just four. Of these four, however, one very famous use is in the story of Joseph, 12:20, وَشَـرَوهُ بِثَمَنٍ بَخْسٍ دَراهِمَ مَعْـدودَةٍ, *And they sold him for a meager price, just a few dirhams*. In a very different domain, astronomers mysteriously gave the name المشـتري *al-mushtari* to Jupiter, something historians of science may be able to comment on more knowledgeably.

The strangest and most intriguing derivation of this root is Form X استشرى, to spread dangerously, to become aggravated. The most common of the Form X semantic parameters, seeking, is at work with this root. Since استشـرى collocates exclusively with the noxious and pernicious, especially المـرض *al-maraD* and الـداء *ad-daa'*, illness, and الفسـاد *al-fasaad*, corruption, it is these things which are portrayed as seekers. Rather than buying and selling, they are seeking the literal *arteries* along which to spread.

عِرْق سوس
liquorice
عرِق
to sweat
عرّق
to make sweat; to dilute a drink; to take root, be deeply rooted; to vein, marble
sweat; arak (alcohol distilled from liquorice)
عَرَق
عِرْق
VEIN
عِرْق النساء
Sciatica
عِرقيّ
ethnic
العروق الضوارب
the arteries
العراق
Iraq
عَريق
deep-rooted
عَراقة
deep-rootedness
MacToot

22
Sweat / Vein عَرَق / عِرق – عُروق
Deep Root

The ع – ر – ق root has four verbal derivatives. The first of these is the denominative Form I verb, عـرِق – يعـرَق *'ariqa*, to sweat, based on the noun العَـرَق *al-'araq,* sweat. Modern science has taught us that there are sweat glands, but as ancient desert dwellers تفصّـدوا عرقـا *tafaSSaduu 'araqan*, dripped with sweat, imagine their speculation on its mysterious interior pathways. The name of that liquid was later lent to a similarly colorless alcoholic drink flavored with aniseed, famous in rough transliteration as arak.

Anatomically, عِرق *'irq* is a blood vessel, whether vein or artery, but it has other meanings, too. Most generally, العرق *al-'irq* is the source or origin or root of anything. This word has important metaphoric and idiomatic usages, too. As anthropology teaches us, kinship is an integral underpinning of human society. In Arab culture, lineage was (and is) of paramount importance. In English, both 'line' and 'lineage' are commonly used in speaking of kinship. These very terms declare that family is eminently traceable. Furthermore, blood is especially associated with kinship, as in the expression 'Blood will out!' Arabic has a very similar saying, العرق دسّاس, *al-'irq dassaas*. Both suggest that ancestry and breeding—and especially the lack of it—are powerful factors in comportment that, even if disguised, will sooner or later surface. Visually, العرق functions nicely as a simile for a traceable path, and in fact, in addition to the literal sense of blood vessel and root, it signifies the abstract race, stock, or descent. The one word العَراقة *al-'araaqa* means old ancestral line, venerable old family. The adjectives عرقـيّ *'irqiyy*, ethnic, and عريـق *'ariiq*, deep-rooted, ancient, take the ancestral line concept as their starting point. A comparative/superlative adjective is also used: أعرق *'a'raq* means even more deep-rooted, and thus more distinguished in lineage.

Medicine and botany also make use of العـرق. Arabic gives sciatica (a painful condition originating in the hip joint) a gendered slant by using an *iDaafa* construction عِـرق النسـاء, *'irq an-nisaa'*, literally women's vein. In botany, the Greek designation 'glycyrrhiza' means sweet root, a word English mimicks in 'licorice.' This plant is native to southern Europe, the Middle East, and parts of Asia and South Asia, and it would be difficult to say that one name or another is 'original.' In any case, Arabic dubbed it 'the root of the suus plant', عـرق السـوس *'irq as-suus*.

Returning to the verbal domain, we find the Form II verb عـرّق. It has several meanings associated with root and vein: to take root, or to be deeply rooted, both intransitive, and to marble, a transitive verb, which can be used, for example, for veins of fat running through a cut of meat. Finally, this verb has two meanings associated with sweat and its homonym arak. In the first instance, it means to make someone sweat, or to promote perspiration. In the second, it means to add water to a drink or dilute it, as one must do in proper preparation of arak.

Form IV and Form V are, quite unusually, synonymous: both أعرق and تعرّق mean to take root. This is also a second meaning of the Form I verb. The Form II passive participle 'having prominent veins' or 'firmly rooted' is مُعـرَّق *mu'arraq*. Finally, and most interestingly of all, which country name comes from this root? Which Arab country is the cradle of civilization? Of course, it is that ancient land العـراق *al-'iraaq*—Iraq!

لُعاب
DROOL
لعَب
to drool, slobber
تلعّب
to play with; act playfully
to play لعِب
to play with; to trifle with لاعب
game لَعْبة
playground; court (tennis) مَلعَب
his mouth watered for سال لعابُه على
لُعْبة
toy, doll
أُلعوبة
toy; trick, stratagem
تلاعب
to make fun of; to toy with; to act fraudulently
مَلعوب
ملعوب في
altered (as a bogus check)
MacToot

23

Drool لُعاب

Play

Associations between play and childhood are obvious, and the Form I verb لعِب – يلعَب *la'iba*, to play, must be the ultimate source of اللعاب *al-lu'aab*, drool, saliva. The proximate source, I would argue, is لُعبة *lu'ba*, a toy, plaything. Phonetically speaking, *lu'ba* is temptingly similar to *lu'aab*. Together, they effectively call to mind the primordial image of babies chewing on toys and drooling.

The Form I verb is typically literal, but it has figurative possibilities, too. For instance, one may say لعبت بهم الهموم *la'ibat bihim al-humuum*, worries beset them, gave them no rest. The verb gave birth to a variety of nouns and adjectives, including the active participle لاعِب *laa'ib*, a player, and its passive counterpart, ملعوب, *mal'uub*, literally something which has been played, a prank or a ruse. One can also add a preposition to this participle, yielding ملعوب فيه *mal'uub fiihi*, to describe something that has been improperly altered and is therefore bogus. The noun أُلعوبة *'ul'uuba* is similar to the first sense of ملعوب, plaything, dalliance, trick. The former is an example of a very remarkable pattern, أُفْعولة *'uf'uula*, typically associated with speech, in the broadest sense. Other significant examples, though not derived from body parts, include أغنية *'ughniyya*, song; أطروحة *'uTruuHa*, thesis; أملوحة *'umluuHa*, anecdote, and أنشودة *'unshuuda*, anthem. Among the adjectives derived from the ل – ع – ب root is لِعّيب *li''iib*, extremely playful. This unusual form, فِعّيل *fi''iil*, always signals a very emphatic meaning. One may also use لَعوب *la'uub* in this sense, but when describing a woman, its sense is pejorative: loose, wanton.

Given that it is a function of the mouth, drooling is likely to appear in the context of food. English speakers drool over appetizing dishes just as well as anyone else, but may be shy to admit it. However, they are happy to confess to the fact that their mouths water, a slightly euphemistic alternative with its exclusively positive connotations. Arabic is not squeamish about this age-old human response to the impulse to eat, and says سال لعابه *saala lu'aabuhu*, he salivated, literally, his drool flowed.

Back in the verbal domain, there are five more forms. Forms II لعّب and IV ألعب mean to make someone play, or to set something in motion, making it play. The transitive Form III لاعب means to play with. One must therefore not use the preposition مع before its object. Like Form I, the Form V verb تلعّب means to play, but with an emphasis on repetition. Form VI تلاعب بـ means to trifle with. This is an example of the least common and most fascinating semantic parameter of Form VI, to pretend to do Form I. In this case, one makes a show of playing, a friendly, harmless activity, but the true intent is quite different. Translations must be contextualized, as English has many words for such activities. In romance, there is an almost perfect intersection between the two languages, to toy with (someone's affections). In a work situation, it can mean to manipulate or doctor figures, to cook the books.

مَرْيُول
مَرْيَلة
apron; bib
to drool رال
drooling الرِّيال
رِيال
DROOL
رُوال - رِيالة
راوُول
Slobber (of animals, and especially of horses)
to drool ريّل
ريّل على
to drool over
MacToot

24

Dribble رِيال / رِيالة

Slobber

Dribbling and drooling are among the endearing markers of babyhood. Having plenty of saliva is also a sign of good health. While saliva, الريق *ar-riiq*, normally stays in the mouth, what leaves it may be called اللعاب *al-lu'aab*, as described in the previous entry, or الريال *ar-riyaal* / الريالة *ar-riyaala* / الروال *ar-ruwaal*. Teething babies whose salivary glands are in high gear, and healthy ones, absorbed by everything but their appearances, get distracted from efficient swallowing. The result is that they drool, يريل – رال *raala*, dribbling down their chins and onto their shirts. Weary mothers everywhere have battled these hyperactive salivary glands. In efforts to keep good clothes dry, they have designed purpose-suited defenses to add to babies' wardrobes. English, perhaps inspired by the word imbibe and its drinking associations, called it a bib. Arabic created the logical مريول *maryuul*, dribbled on (thing). As an alternative, there is the even more common مريلة *maryala*, literally 'a dribbling place.' This last word may also be used to mean an apron. The Form II verb ريّل, with its suggestion of more intensive or abundant activity, also means to drool, and is the more common of the two verbs. The addition of the preposition على yields to salivate over, with its figurative implication of overly avid desire.

Dribbling is not the exclusive province of humans. Animals slobber, too. The words ريال / ريالة may be used, but the classical *Lisan al-'arab*, citing the eleventh-century Andalusian lexicographer Ibn Sidah, also gives روال *ruwaal*, a pattern which matches the very familiar لعاب *lu'aab*. It also cites an unusual alternative pattern, راوول *raawuul*. Nouns constructed on this pattern are quite limited in number, and all of them indicate a very special permutation of the associated root meaning. Examples include صاروخ *Saaruukh*, missile or rocket (scream) خازوق *khaazuuq*, stake used for impalement (pierce), and ثالوث *thaaluuth*, trinity (three). The word راوول, according to some old sources, was to be used exclusively with horses, and given its form, one must imagine some very dramatic slobbering, indeed.

Of course, the very common word ريال, riyal / rial, the currency of Saudi Arabia and several other Gulf countries, ranked 1,074 in the *FDA*, is not derived from this root at all. Instead, it comes from a Spanish source, *real*. Etymologically related to the English word regal, its very name marked it as the official royal currency.

راق-يريق على
to surpass, prove superior to, outshine
راق - يروق
to be clear, pure; to surpass, excel, to please
A+
لا يَجِفُّ له الريق
he talks incessantly
ريق
SALIVA
راق - يريق
to be pure; to glisten
على الريق
on an empty stomach
إراقة الدماء
bloodshed
في رَيِّق الشباب
in the full bloom of youth
بلع ريقه
he paused to collect his thoughts
جفّ ريقه
his mouth was dry; he exerted great effort; he talked and talked in vain
MacToot

25

Saliva رِيق

Shining Vitality

English speakers can be reticent when it comes to talking about saliva. Bodily secretions, and especially the acts of secreting them, are regarded as vaguely off-color, better avoided in polite conversation. Nevertheless, there is no lack of vocabulary devoted to these processes. With its liquid consonants around a long vowel, drool even sounds wet and babyish. Saliva and salivate, however, have an entirely adult and slightly clinical ring to them. Alternatives to these two are even less palatable. Spit suggests insults, or the spittoons of the Wild West. Slaver, rather bookish and dated, brings rabid dogs and hungry predators to mind. Slobber is hardly an improvement, with its sloppy and uncouth associations. None of these items has an ounce of appeal. Arabic, however, has a beautiful word for saliva with many positive associations. This is الريق *ar-riiq*.

It is useful to consider the ر – ي – ق and ر – و – ق roots together, as there is some overlap between their derivatives. Saliva is, of course, essential to proper chewing and swallowing, and as might be expected, vocabulary based on these roots will show some functional connections to the food domain. Hunger is behind one such expression, and the context is deprivation: على الريق *'alaa ar-riiq*, on an (utterly) empty stomach. Another of the mouth's essential functions is speech. In Arabic, pausing to collect one's thoughts or to calm oneself gets condensed into the image of swallowing, thus postponing what might be an ill-considered, off-the-cuff remark. Someone who can't stop talking is imagined to have an inexhaustible supply of saliva, never running out of steam, as it were: لا يجف له الريق *laa yajiff lahu ar-riiq*. Conversely, جفّ ريقه *jaffa riiquhu*, in addition to the literal sense of having a dry mouth, suggests expending all one's energies. The phrase is often used in the speaking domain to convey that despite sustained efforts to convince someone of something, the attempt has been in vain.

For a people with an intimate knowledge of the rigors of thirst, the idea of water in the mouth is an exceedingly attractive one. The Form I verb راق – يريق *raaqa, yariiq* means to be pure, limpid; to glisten; to pour forth. This puts an altogether positive sheen on the properties of saliva. An alluring metaphor based on this root is في ريّق الشباب *fii rayyiq ash-shabaab*, in the prime of youth, where youth is depicted as something succulent, full of the sap of life. On the other hand, راق – يروق *raaqa, yaruuq* means to be pleased by something as well as to excel, surpass. When describing something we like with this verb, its grammatical object (or the object of the preposition لـ) is the person who is pleased, as in يروق له المنظر *yaruuqu lahu l-manZar*, the view appeals to him. Salivating over something suggests pleasant anticipation, something that may also link the two roots.

The derived forms of the ر – و – ق root are directly linked to fluids. Form II روّق means to purify or filter a liquid. In the figurative expression روّق دمَه *rawwaqa damahu*, a drink is said to refresh someone, literally to purify one's blood. The same expression also has the figurative sense of placating, whereby the blood—hence the person—is cooled and calmed. The Form IV verb أراق means to make something flow, and once again, the liquid referred to is blood. Its common *maSdar*, إراقة الدماء *'iraaqat ad-dimaa'*, is bloodshed. *Very* rare but related verbs are the ecclesiastical هراق *haraaqa* and أهراق *'ahraaqa*, and their derivatives, which refer to the metaphor embodied in the Christian mass, in which Christ's blood is shed for mankind.

BREATH
نَفَس
مُتنفَّس
a place in which to breathe freely
تنفَّس
inhale and exhale
نفَّس
to get a load off one's chest, to air one's feelings
to compete with, try to outdo
نافس
تنافس
to compete with each other
new mother
نُفَساء
نَفِست تنفَس
to be in childbed delivering or having just done so...
Mactoot

26
Breath نَفَس – أَنْفاس
Spirit

The breath, النفس *an-nafas*, is the most easily detected physical sign that we are alive and well. The Old Testament's Book of Genesis immortalized this ancient observation in the collocation 'the breath of life.' In its King James edition, we read: "*And the Lord God formed man of the dust of the ground, and breathed into his nostrils the breath of life; and man became a living soul.*" Arabic equates breath and life in the phrase لآخِر نفس *li 'aakhir nafas*, an expression with a perfect echo in English, until the last breath.

Breathing is a process easily felt, but the breath itself is typically unseen, unless another medium like water, or very cold air, renders it visible. Its effects beyond the body, however, are easily seen, as when one blows out a match or a candle, or inflates a balloon. Not surprisingly, the most common derivative of النَفَس (*FDA* 2,164) is Form V, تنفّس, and its *maSdar* التنفّس *at-tanaffus* (*FDA* 3,753) the straightforward activity of breathing in and out. In derived verbs, the passive participle can also function as a place noun. In this instance, مُتنفّس *mutanaffas* can be translated in a variety of ways that describe a place in which to breathe freely, such as breathing room.

Arabic morphology elaborates on the breath in some other less predictable ways. The Form I verb نفِست – تنفَس *nafisat* means to be in childbed, delivering or having just done so. This process can be designated by the *maSdar*, النِفاس *an-nifaas*. The new mother is said to be a نَفْساء *nafsaa'*. What is the connection to the breath? It seems to be saying that she has, as it were, just exhaled this new life out of her body and into the visible world. In the process, her body also becomes visibly deflated. With inflatable things like balloons and tires, this process of deflating is expressed by the Form II verb نفّس. Figuratively speaking, feelings that we hold inside ourselves can also weigh very heavily on us—not unlike a full-term baby—and this same verb نفّس can also mean to get a load off one's chest, to *air* one's feelings. Using the ordinary place pattern, an opening from which air may escape is called مَنْفَس *manfas*.

The Form III نافس means to compete with someone. Verbs of this pattern typically imply the existence of another person. Here, that person is a rival, a competitor. As might happen in a tight race, the hard breathing of المنافس *al-munaafis* (*FDA* 2,504) would be easily audible. Form VI تنافس makes this competition, in which one might become *winded*, mutual.

بِشِقِّ الأَنْفُسِ
Qur'an 16:7
extreme hardship
"splitting of souls"
نفس
SOUL
جِهاد النفس
Combatting one's selfish inclinations, taming the ego
نفيس
Costly, precious
النفاسة
Costliness, preciousness
نفيسة
a gem or precious object
MacToot

27
Self; Psyche نَفْس – نُفوس / أَنْفُس
Ego, Id

By deriving the words for the breath and the self from one root, and making them near homophones, at that, Arabic invites us to consider what essential attribute(s) they might share, as well as how they differ. *Unlike* the breath, the self النفس *an-nafs*—with its various contextualized translations in English, including soul and ego—cannot be perceived by touch or hearing. Housed in the body, it is conceived of as part of the mental or metaphysical or emotional landscape. On the other hand, *like* the breath, but even more so, it is linked to interiority, tied to the internal body or the hidden, internal life. In this way, both breath and self retain an air of ethereality, and hence of mystery. In a further similarity to the breath, the *effects* of the invisible self are visible. While a person's actions may be the direct results of immediate bodily needs, they may also be spurred by other less tangible and perhaps more problematic desires. When the powerful psychic self takes charge, it may dictate one course of action or another, actions that impinge on other people and consequently have moral or ethical implications.

Hence, in more than one instance, the Qur'an suggests that the psyche is a dangerous entity. The story of Joseph provides more than one example of this view, including 12:53, in which the wife of the powerful Egyptian who owns him admits that she has succumbed to her selfish desires and tried to seduce him. In another chapter, God is said to have a self, and in 3:30 we find: وَيُحَذِّرُكُمُ اللهُ نَفْسَهُ, *God warns you (to beware) of Himself.* But as the self or the soul may transgress or cause harm, it may also suffer, as in 16:7 بِشِقِّ الأَنْفُسِ *bishiqq al-'anfus*, with extreme difficulty. In more modern contexts, these same concerns resurface in the collocation جهاد النفس *jihaad an-nafs*, combating one's selfish inclinations, taming the ego. This also reveals the real sense of الجهاد, jihad, a sustained struggle to solve a problem.

The other feature of the self that derivatives of this root spell out clearly is how valuable it is. In the nominal domain, we find the noun النفاسة *an-nafaasa*, costliness, preciousness, and the adjective نفيس *nafiis*, precious, priceless. From this comes نفيسة *nafiisa*, a gem, a precious object. Finally, as in English, 'self' has an impersonal use: same, self-same. This is an extraordinarily common word, ranking 44 in the *FDA*. The same word, but in the sense of soul or spirit, is the second most common usage, at 805.

راح
to go away, leave; to begin; to set out to do
روح
soul, spirit
الروح القُدُس
the Holy Spirit
صلاة التراويح
additional evening prayers (only in Ramadan)
روحانيّ
spiritual
MacToot
SOUL رُوح

28
Soul رُوح – أَرْواح
Volatility

One of Arabic's more prolific body roots serves as the foundation for two words with dramatic import to the body–mind continuum. This is the hollow root ر – و – ح. However, there is considerable overlap between it and the root ر – ي – ح, so it makes sense to consider their combined derivatives. This chapter focuses on the words more closely linked to the soul, الروح *ar-ruuH*. Another derivative of these roots designating a body part is الراحة *ar-raaHa*, the palm, discussed in chapter 79.

The common nouns derived from these roots have an interesting semantic coherence, echoed, to a degree, in English. In both languages, they point to an underlying metaphor of the soul, volatility. The most chemically volatile of things is an odor, and رائحة *raa'iHa* and its plural روائح *rawaa'iH* mean scent, odor, and perfume. Air and spirit are closely associated in both languages: الريح *ar-riiH* is the wind and الروح *ar-ruuH* is the soul. It is worth noting that الريح, the wind, is feminine, even though it lacks the typical marker of feminine gender, the ة suffix. The Christian term الروح القدس *ar-ruuH al-qudus* is English's The Holy Ghost / Holy Spirit, evidence that the link between air and spirit is age-old, and a reminder of Christianity's Semitic origins. Popular (but not obligatory) Islamic evening prayers during Ramadan, التراويح, *at-taraawiiH*, also make use of this root. Among other things, this word for prayers suggests the spiritual comfort sought in الروحانيّات *ar-ruuHaaniyyaat*, matters of the soul.

Classically, some verbs of motion were associated with particular times of the day or night, and Form I راح – يروح *raaHa*, to go, is one. This verb could also mean to go home, and its *maSdar* الرَّواح *ar-rawaaH*, with this directional sense, occurs in the Qur'an at 34:12, with a mention of the wind in the very same verse: وَلِسُلَيمانَ الرِّيحَ غُدوُّها شَهْرًا وَرَواحُها شَهْرًا, *And to Solomon (We subjected) the wind; its outward journey (took) a month, and its return journey (took) a month*. The classical noun روحة *rawHa* is an evening journey and مراح *maraaH* is a place visited in the evening. In modern usage, this association with time has been lost, and the Form I verb راح usually just means to go, to set out, or to begin to do. The same association is made in colloquial English combinations of 'to go and do,' as in "Why did you have to go and do that?" The verb راح is extremely frequent in many spoken varieties of Arabic, where more formal synonyms are largely ignored. The spoken Form II روّح preserves this directional sense of going home.

معقول
rational reasonable idea
عقّل تعقّل
to be rational
MIND
عقل
العقليّة mentality
عاقِل
rational, prudent, reasonable
أعْقَل
even more rational, prudent, reasonable
العقيلة
the best, choice
part or element of something; formal polite form of wife
عقيلة
السيّد فلان
Mrs So-and-So
MacToot

29
Mind, Reason عَقْل – عُقول
Rational Restraint

Two body parts are derived from the ع – ق – ل root, العقل *al-'aql*, the mind, and العقلة *al-'uqla*, the knuckle, discussed in chapter 81. Determining how two such unrelated things stem from one and the same root requires some real sleuthing. First, one must identify the source word. Generally speaking, the shorter word is the better candidate, and this is backed up by semantics. Surely mind and reason, though abstractions, are more important than the knuckle, or any other joint. One might also argue that the verb is the source, and that all meanings stem from it. The first sense of the Form I verb عقل – يعقِل *'aqala* is to hobble (an animal). However, quite significantly, it also means to be endowed with reason, to be rational. In this sense, it is used an eye-catching forty-nine times in the Qur'an. The overarching sense associated with rationality is using reason to make informed assessments and *restrain* one's impulses. This idea of the rational mind is a metaphor for the physical restraint imposed on the hobbled animal.

The rational mind, العقل *al-'aql*, is a very high frequency word (*FDA* 646) and it occurs in proverbs and collocations. One of these is equally familiar in English: العقل السليم في الجسم السليم *al-'aql as-saliim fi-l-jism as-saliim*, a sound mind in a sound body. There is also the admiring العقل الراجح *al-'aql ar-raajiH*, composure or sangfroid, essential characteristics of the eminently rational mind. In an expression that embodies top-notch planning or scheming, the mind stands in metonymically for the strategist, العقل المدبّر, the mastermind. Presumably because it is amorphous, the *FDA* chooses not to list العقل as a body part, but if so listed, it would figure as the eighth most frequent one, after heart, eye, hand, face, head, blood, and foot. There are a number of important words derived directly from العقل, including the more abstract العقليّة *al-'aqliyya*, mentality. Of particular historical and cultural interest is the rather uncommon noun, عقيلة *'aqiila*, which means the choice part or element of something, and is a female given name as well. In fact, a likeness of the famous Egyptian actress Aqila Ratib animates the facing page. This same noun is also used as a formal and polite word for wife, an alternative to حرم *Haram*, as in عقيلة السيّد فلان Mrs. So-and-So. The suggestion is that the better part of something is its more rational part, an implicit admission that the wife is the rational half of a couple. The Arabic term is not jocular, and yet it suggests the English phrase (Mr. So-and-So's) better half. In the adjectival domain, a person can be reasonable, rational, or prudent عاقِل *'aaqil*, a Form I active participle, and comparatively, even more so, أعْقَل *'a'qal*. Things, however, have no powers of reasoning, and so to describe a thing, like a plan or an idea, as reasonable, the proper term is necessarily the passive participle معقول *ma'quul* (*FDA* 1,348).

Form II عقّل and Form V تعقّل elaborate on the concept of being rational. Form II is causative, to bring someone to reason, while Form V تعقّل means to become reasonable, or sensible, to grasp or understand something. As elsewhere, where Form I and Form V are near synonyms, the latter suggests a greater degree of effort or intention.

FRONT OF THE BODY قُبُل
أقبل الليل يا حبيبي وناداني حنيني
Night has come, my love, and my longing has summoned me
Umm Kulthum
قُبلة
a kiss
قبّل
to kiss
قبِل
to accept
مُقابلة صَحَفية
a press interview
قابل
to meet
تقبّل
to accept (sometimes with a bit of resignation)
تقابل
to meet each other
N
E
S
قبلي
facing al-qibla; southwards
THU
8
الأسبوع المُقبل
next week
استقبل
to receive (someone or something); to apply oneself gladly (to a task)
MacToot

30
Front قُبُل
Forward Orientation

With seven verbal derivatives, القبل *al-qubul* is a very well endowed body part. It is also quite semantically cohesive. Each of the verb forms based on it depicts an action to be undertaken *facing forward.* Form IVأقبل approaches from the front. Acts of meeting and receiving Forms III قابل, VI تقابل, and X استقبل are never done sideways or in opposite directions. Accepting, Forms I قبِل *qabila* and V تقبّل, must also be done facing forward. Were there still any room for doubt, kissing, Form II قبّل, clinches the argument. The whole family, then, is built on a directional metaphor, forward orientation. The word قُبُل the front of the body, appears three times in the Qur'an, but fourteen other of the root's many derivatives are used 310 more times. This ancient root family has had remarkable staying power, too. A stunning twenty-four items from the ق – ب – ل galaxy rank in the *FDA*.

Reams of vocabulary are derived just from قُبُل and the Form I verb قبِل – يقبَل *qabila.* At the top of the list is قَبْل, before, and its adverbial sense, voweled *qablu*, previously, which rank 68 in the *FDA*. (Such a ranking makes it almost as common as كبير big, and even more common than أب father.) Arabic embroiders deliciously on قَبْل *qabla* by modifying its vowel sequence. The future, المستقبل *al-mustaqbal*, is always before us, but to convey just moments before, Arabic makes use of its diminutive infix. Inserting 'u-ay' into the root transforms قَبْل into the more precise, and yet more poetic قُبَيْل, *qubayl.* A very common adjective that may refer to time or to sequence is the Form IV active participle المُقْبِل *al-muqbil*, the next.

The specific positional sense of 'before' can also be conveyed by قُبالة *qubaala,* across from, facing, vis-à-vis. Perhaps this says something about how we should understand the crucial social unit, القبيلة *al-qabiila*, the tribe. Was it not their own tribe that the ancient Arabs saw before them on a daily basis?

Using the preposition مِن *min*, Arabic adds to the directionality of the front. The phrase مِن قُبُل, *min qubul*, 'from the front,' is an expression of crucial significance in the Qur'anic story of the attempted seduction of the Prophet Joseph by the wife of his Egyptian guardian. Changing both internal vowels of this noun creates a new word also closely associated with that preposition: مِن قِبَل, *min qibal*, 'on the part of.' Another minor change produces Islam's essential orientation القِبلة *al-qibla*, the direction in which believers face in ritual prayer. In Egypt, this is a generally southward orientation, and the phrase الوجه القِبليّ *al-wajh al-qibliyy*, which uses the *nisba* adjective derived from *al-qibla*, is even a common alternative to the more topographically exact Upper Egypt.

From the Form I verb, Arabic derives the word for the midwife, القابلة *al-qaabila.* The midwife must, of course, face forward as she exercises her occupation, midwifery, القِبالة *al-qibaala*, that most important of receptions. To express being receptive to something, often rendered into English with the suffixes -able/-ible, Arabic uses قابل لِـ *qaabil li-*, as in قابل للشفاء *qaabil li-shshifaa'*, curable, or قابل للكسر *qaabil li-l-kasr*, breakable.

HEAD رَأْسٌ
رأّس
to appoint as chief or head; to entrust with the management
president رئيس
رأس = ترأّس
to head, chair, run, be in charge
رئاسة
leadership, presidency
مرؤوس
subordinate
على رؤوس الأشهاد
publicly, for all to see
رأساً على عقب
upside down, head over heels
الرأسمالية
Capitalism
من الرأس إلى أخمَص القدم
from top to toe, from head to foot
MacToot

31
Head رَأْس – رُؤُوس
Leadership

The head's position at the top of the body is an anatomical clue to the key role it plays in life and in language. In Arabic, English, and so many other languages, the head is a symbol of leadership and importance. As far as English etymology is concerned, a president is one who sits or presides over government. Arabic sticks with the metaphor of the head and turns it into a verb, رأس – يرأس *ra'asa*, to head, manage. It uses the ر – أ – س root to form رئيس *ra'iis*, analogous to English's head of state, and French's *chef d'état*, but more succinct than either. Politics is a big part of modern life, and this word and its plural, رؤساء *ru'asaa'*, rank 47 in the *FDA*. One reason for this very high ranking, of course, is that the *FDA* is a media-based corpus. Head, itself, lags behind at 215. Even the office of the presidency, الرئاسة *ar-ri'aasa* figures in the *FDA*'s top 1,000. Both presidency and president have common *nisba* adjectives: رئاسيّ *ri'aasiyy* is the one meaning presidential. The *nisba* formed from president, رئيسيّ *ra'iisiyy* has a variety of possible translations: main, chief, principal, or leading. For example, in a theatrical performance, one might play a leading role, دور رئيسيّ. Just as one can be رئيس, it is possible to be مرؤوس *mar'uus*, presided over, a subordinate.

The Form I verb is nearly synonymous with Form V ترأّس to preside over or to head a meeting or organization. Form II رأّس, in its standard causative sense, means to appoint someone to the position of manager, leader, or president.

The head, itself, occurs in many important collocations and idiomatic expressions. One such idiom is مسقط الرأس *masqaT ar-ra's*, birthplace. This phrase paints a verbal picture of birth: the place the head falls. Another idiom particularly rich in anatomy is من الرأس حتّى أخمص القدم *min ar-ra's Hattaa 'akhmaS al-qadam*, from head to toe, top to bottom, totally. (The second body part it mentions, أخمص القدم, is not the toe, but rather a wonderfully specific bit of anatomy, the hollow of the sole of the foot.) Another idiom which plays on the upsetting of proper spatial orientation, رأسًا على عقب *ra'san 'alaa 'aqib*, has what looks like a direct equivalent in English, head over heels. However, this is not a metaphor for topsy-turvy love, but rather for a disturbing physical or mental upset, a fall such as Humpty Dumpty had. The plural of head, رؤوس *ru'uus*, also occurs in numerous expressions. Worth noting is the idiom على رؤوس الأشهاد *'alaa ru'uus al-'ashhaad*, literally, on the heads of the witnesses, that is, for all to see, brazenly, in plain sight.

Finally, in the economic domain, one tends to think of Karl Marx when speaking of capital رأس المال *ra's al-maal* and its derivative, capitalism الرأسمالية *ar-ra'smaaliyya*. The word 'head' is clearly visible in the Arabic term. In English, it takes some background in Latin to recognize capital as a derivative of *caput*, head. According to *Merriam-Webster's Collegiate Dictionary*, the English word 'capital,' in the sense of the value of one's accumulated goods, has been in use since the seventeeth century. A thousand years earlier, in seventh century Arabia, business terminology was already well-developed. The plural form of capital, رؤوس الأموال *ru'uus al-'amwaal*, is actually to be found at 2:279 of the Qur'an, where questions of property and ownership were nothing to be shy about.

BRAIN
مُخّ
ارتجاج في المخ
stroke
مُخيخ
cerebellum
مُخّ
essence
MacToot
brains (culinary)
مُخّ
(Personal) prayer is the essence of worship - Hadith
الدعاء مُخّ العبادة
- MacToot -

32
Brain مُخّ – أَمْخاخ / مِخاخ / مِخَخة
Astute Judgment; Essence

Written Arabic commonly uses two words for the brain: الدماغ *ad-dimaagh* (see chapter 33) and المُخّ *al-mukhkh*. The two are loosely synonymous, but المخ is slightly more restricted anatomically. It encompasses most of the gray matter, but not the diminutive المُخَيخ *al-mukhaykh*, the cerebellum, itself a diminutive form of the Latin cerebrum. That small organ, located in the lower back part of the skull, is mainly responsible for coordinating movement.

Both الدماغ and المُخّ are depicted as the seat of judgment and complex problem-solving, and Arabic has many idioms that highlight their importance in that process. A popular command offered as advice in the Egyptian spoken register is شغّل مخّك *shaghghal mukhkhak*, which finds a close equivalent in English: Use your head! Still in the colloquial register, المخّ collocates with awake and clean: مخّه صاحي *mukhkhu SaaHi*, he is capable and on the qui vive, or مخّه نضيف *mukhkhu nDiif,* he is clever, he's a good problem-solver. On the other hand, in a very negative vein, those who, having taken a position on a topic, refuse to consider any other points of view are critiqued with a reference to standard home security: مخّه قفل وترباس *mukhkhu 'ifl wi tirbaas*, his brain is a lock and a dead bolt. In a different and quite formal register that offers a gauge of its crucial importance, المخ is used to mean the essence of a thing, or what is best in it. A noteworthy Hadith says: الدعاء مخ العبادة *ad-du'aa' mukhkh al-'ibaada*, Prayer (personal, as opposed to ritual) is the essence of worship.[12] Mental powers and quintessence aside, مخّ is a culinary designation as well and when making one's selection at the butcher's shop or the meat counter دماغ cannot be substituted for it. The links of المخّ to food as well as to intelligent action, or a lack thereof, are probably behind its *FDA* ranking of 3,818.

Injuries may be described with either of these two major designations of the brain. Probably most common is ارتجاج في المخ *irtijaaj fi-l-mukhkh*, a concussion. A potentially fatal brain event can be identified with either word for the brain: جلطة في المخ *jalTa fi-l-mukhkh*, or alternatively, سكتة دماغية *sakta dimaaghiyya*, a stroke. The English term is opaque, but the Arabic, 'blood clot in the brain' and 'brain silence,' provide much clearer pictures of what actually comes to pass.

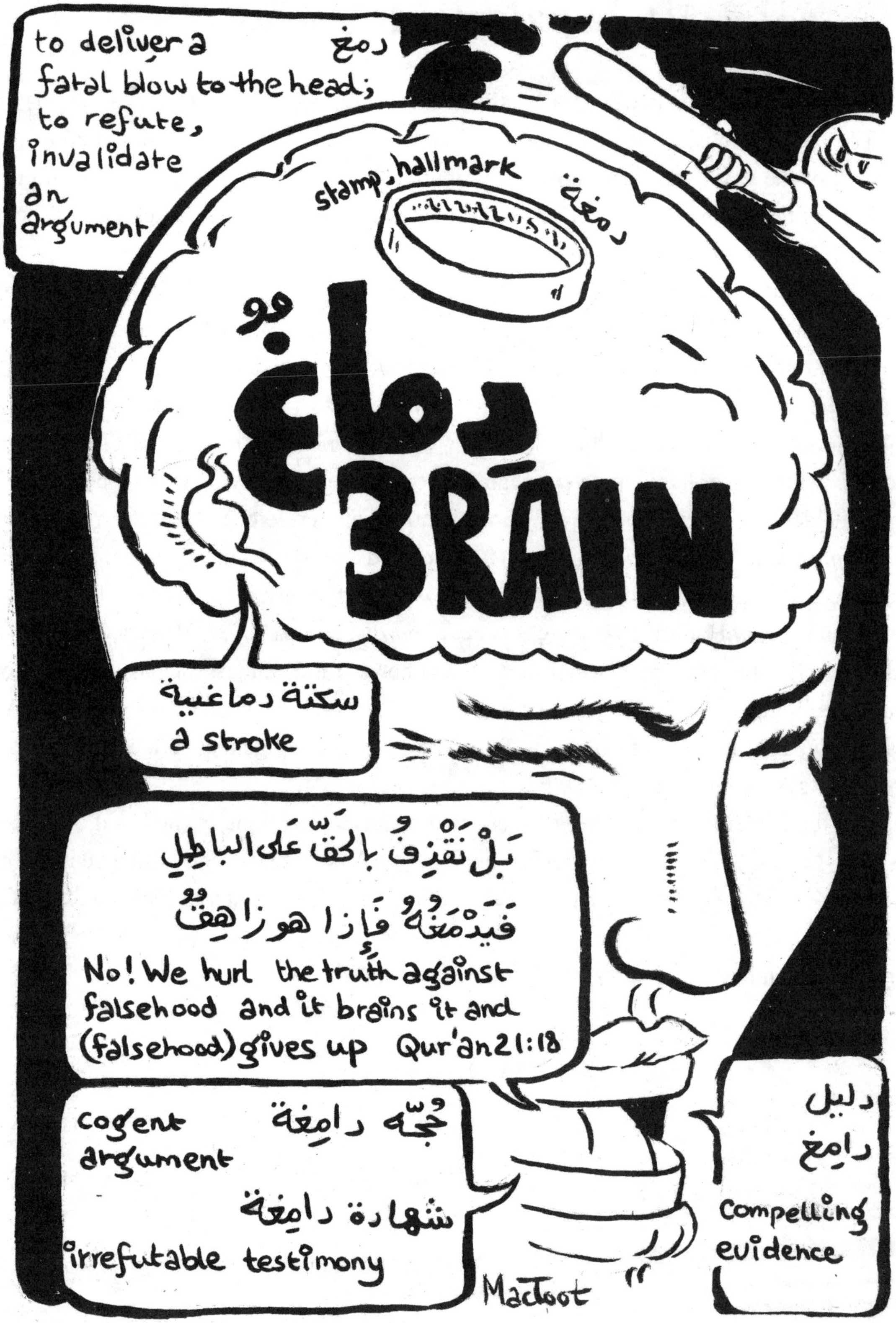
دمغ
to deliver a fatal blow to the head; to refute, invalidate an argument
دمغة
stamp, hallmark
دِماغٌ
BRAIN
سكتة دماغية
a stroke
بَلْ نَقْذِفُ بِالْحَقِّ عَلَى الْبَاطِلِ
فَيَدْمَغُهُ فَإِذَا هُوَ زَاهِقٌ
No! We hurl the truth against falsehood and it brains it and (falsehood) gives up Qur'an 21:18
حُجّة دامغة
cogent argument
شهادة دامغة
irrefutable testimony
دليل دامغ
compelling evidence
MacToot

33
Brain دِماغ – أَدْمِغة
Cogency; Imprint

Expressions based on مـخ *mukhkh* and دمـاغ *dimaagh* tend to comment on the critical role of the brain in matters of life and death. Identifying its quintessential powers of judgment, they highlight its consequent connection to validity and credibility. Since الدمـاغ is slightly more abstruse than المـخ, it seems to have more applications to issues of faith and legality.

The brain as الدمـاغ has a number of nominal uses. Egyptians like to say of a stubbornly inflexible person: دماغه ناشفة *dimaaghu nashfa*, his brain is hard (as a rock, English might add). The د – م – غ root is the only one of these two roots with verbal derivations in the standard language. The Form I verb دمـغ – يدمَغ *damagha* means to refute or invalidate (a false claim). Surprisingly, Qur'anic Arabic and colloquial English see eye to eye in describing a potentially deadly assault directed at the head. In 21:18 we find: بَـلْ نَقْذِفُ بِالحَـقِّ عَلـى الباطِـلِ فَيَدْمَغُـهُ فَـإِذا هُـوَ زاهِـقٌ, *No! We hurl the truth against falsehood and it brains it and (falsehood) gives up the ghost.*

Less poetically, delivering a mortal blow to something abstract like falsehood means invalidating it, and the Form I verb's active participle دامِـغ *daamigh* is directly associated with validity. Examples include the collocations حجّـة دامغـة *hujja daamigha*, a cogent argument, شـهادة دامغـة *shahaada daamigha*, irrefutable testimony, and دليـل دامـغ *daliil daamigh*, compelling evidence. Although *Hans Wehr* treats the verb دمـغ – يدمُـغ *damagha* to brand or to mark with a stamp as a separate entry, I think the two verbs and their derivatives can be better understood together. Branding an animal marks ownership clearly, obviating false claims. This age-old practice must have preceded another important commercial application, that of stamping silver and gold with a دمغـة *damgha*, a hallmark, detering unscrupulous merchants from passing off valuables of undocumented purity and giving consumers a guarantee of value.

جَبين
BROW, FOREHEAD
عرق الجبين
the sweat of one's brow
جبّانة
cemetery
جَبان coward
جَبُنَ
to be a coward
جبّن
to accuse of cowardice, call a coward
MacToot
جبّان
cheese-maker
تجبّن
to curdle (of milk)
turning into cheese
جُبْن/جُبْنة
cheese
جبّن
to cause to curdle; to make into cheese

34

Forehead جَبين – جُبُن / أَجْبِنة / أَجْبُن

Sweating; Curdling

As a prominent, highly visible area of the face, the forehead's appearance is at the root of a variety of expressions. In modern day usage, الجبين *al-jabiin* ranks 3,327 in the *FDA*. Arabic does not use the English highbrow/lowbrow dichotomy, which suggests that intelligence and sophistication correlate with a high forehead. However, it does take into account the forehead's orientation, and as Lakoff and Johnson have shown in *Metaphors We Live By*, up is a near universal signifier of good, while down is bad. The classical expression, عالي الجبين *'aaliyy al-jabiin*, forehead held high, is synonymous with noble descent and social respectability. Conversely, عفّر جبينه *'affara jabiinahu* means to humble someone, literally, to cover his forehead in dust. There are expressions meaning to bring dishonor to others, and doing so to parents had its own special term: سبّة في جبين والديه *subba fii jabiin walidayhi*, a mark of disgrace on his parents' foreheads. English provides a very contemporary, though utterly informal echo in a line from a hit Queen song, "You got mud on your face, you big disgrace!"

Looking at things from a physiological perspective, the head and forehead are well supplied with sweat glands, and as a consequence, hard work and sweaty foreheads have become closely associated. Not surprisingly, the collocation عرق الجبين *'araq al-jabiin*, the sweat of one's brow, is a popular one. In another context, Arabic uses the metaphor of a sweaty brow to indicate great social discomfort: أمر يندى له الجبين *'amrun yandaa lahu al-jabiin*, a matter for which the brow beads up with sweat, a disgraceful thing. The forehead is mentioned just once in the Qur'an, at 37:103. There, too, orientation is critical. In a sign of utter submission, once Ibrahim and his son Isma'il have accepted God's commandment that Ibrahim sacrifice him, Ibrahim has him lie down, forehead to the ground. . . . فَلَمّا أَسْلَما وَتَلَّهُ لِلْجَبِينِ.

All of those usages have a logical air to them, but in the derivations of the ج – ب – ن there is a very odd intersection of cowardice, cemeteries, and cheese. The word for coward is جَبان *jabaan* and, along with its plural جُبناء *jubanaa'*, it is ranked 4,084 in the *FDA*. The Form I verb جبُن – يجبُن *jabuna* is to be cowardly. Both الجُبن *al-jubn* and الجبانة *al-jabaana* are used as its *maSdar*, cowardice. The connection of cowardice to a cemetery, جبّانة *jabbaana*, is not so hard to grasp. To the faint of heart, a place full of corpses is very intimidating. But what can be the connection of cowards and cemeteries to cheese and of all three to the forehead? Perhaps visual and olfactory similes are responsible for such a suggestive acoustic intersection. Cheese is called الجُبن *al-jubn* or الجُبنة *al-jubna* and a cheesemaker, جبّان *jabbaan*. The Form II and Form V verbs جبّن and تجبّن both mean to make milk curdle, and also to go on to make cheese. Refrigeration lets us forget, but cheese at room temperature sweats, a visual link to a sweaty forehead. Likewise, a sweaty brow may suggest cowardice. On a multisensory front, the lumpy, wrinkled appearance of curdling milk and its sour smell may be what called to mind decomposition in a broader sense, producing the allusion to a cemetery. Curdling is an unappealing process, and when not strictly referring to cheesemaking, its associations are altogether distasteful. In English hyperbole, it collocates with blood to create the most gruesome term for horrifying: blood-curdling.

FACE
وَجْه
façade; right side of fabric, heads (coin)
جهة
side, district, administrative agency
المواجهة
confrontation
تواجه
to face each other; to meet face to face
وجهة نظر
point of view
واجه
to encounter; to stand up to, withstand, confront; to be located in front of, face something
الوجه البحري
Lower Egypt
الوجه القبلي
Upper Egypt
وجّه لِ/إلى
to steer, guide, turn someone or something toward; to address (a request) to..
اتّجه إلى/نحو
to head for, make for, turn towards
MacToot

35
Face وَجْه – وُجوه
Direction; Distinction

This word for face and its root و – ج – ه are long-lived, prolific sources of common vocabulary. Six derivatives occur seventy-eight times in the Qur'an, and وجه *wajh* and its plural وجوه *wujuuh* account for seventy-two of them. Seventeen derivatives rank in the *FDA*. Along with the face itself, five of thesc figure in the top 1,000. Seven verb forms are based on the face, five of which are in common use, and its vocabulary takes a full three pages of *Hans Wehr*. Most of its derivatives refer to physical orientation, movement in a given direction, or surfaces. Where it departs from such meanings, الوجه *al-wajh* suggests eminence, playing on the esteem traditionally associated with the face. The face can also represent the whole, an example of synecdoche. Such usage includes more than one reference to God in the Qur'an, as in 55:27: وَيَبْقَى وَجْهُ رَبِّكَ ذُو الجَلالِ وَالإِكْرام, *while your Lord's majestic and venerable face is everlasting*. In the Qur'an as well as in common parlance, لوجه الله *liwajh illaah* is a good deed, done gratis, for God's sake. The expression حفظ ماء الوجه *HafiZa maa'a al-wajh* has an echo in the English idiom 'to save face,' where ماء الوجه *maa'al-wajh* is a metaphorical equivalent of self-respect and personal honor.

The famous collocation سبب وجيه *sabab wajiih* means a valid reason, although it is more commonly—and flatly—dubbed into English as a good reason. In other contexts, the adjective means notable, worthy of regard. In the Qur'an at 3:45, Jesus is referred to as: وجيهًا في الدنيا والآخِرَة, *distinguished in this world and the next*. The فعيل pattern it is based on works as a noun, too, and وجيه *wajiih* can mean a high-ranking person, a distinguished individual. Used as a noun, وجيه takes the broken plural وُجَهاء *wujahaa'* a pattern used exclusively with human beings. From the idea of distinction and notability, it is only a short leap to الوجاهة *al-wajaaha*, repute, prestige.

In the initial position, the root letter و disappears under certain circumstances, as in جهة *jiha*, side or facet. Used in جهة رسمية *jiha rasmiyya*, it means an official agency, that is, one devoted to a particular *facet* of governmental bureaucracy. Also from Form I is وجهة *wujha* or *wijha*, direction, drift, course (of a ship), which figures in the collocation وجهة نظر *wujhat an-naZar*, a point of view. Another derivative is واجهة *waajiha*, a façade of a building, often a shop window.

Enhanced by the directional preposition إلى, Form II وَجَّه and its *maSdar* التوجيه *at-tawjiih* mean to point something at, guide something toward, or turn one's face or attention to something. Its intransitive counterpart is Form V, توجَّه إلى, to proceed in one direction or another. Form VIII is essentially synonymous with Form V, but their *maSaadir* are distinct. The Form V التوجُّه *at-tawajjuh* and its plural in *at-tawajjuhaat* refer to abstract political, religious, or other orientations. In some contexts, التوجُّه can mean favoritism or patronage. The Form VIII *maSdar* اتّجاه *ittijaah* and its plural *ittijaahaat* indicate physical directions, including north, south, east, and west. Form III واجه is unidirectional: to confront or stand up to someone or something. The interactive Form VI تواجه means to confront each other, to face off.

FACE, COUNTENANCE مُحيّا

36

Face, Countenance (1) مُحَيّا – مَحايٍ

Greetings; Life

Greetings! The part of the body sought out when offering a greeting is the face, and one of the words for it is المُحَيّا *al-muHayyaa*, literally, the greeted thing. This passive participle comes from the Form II verb حيّا to greet, a verb that can also mean to keep alive. In 58:8 of the Qur'an it is used twice: وَإِذا جَاءُوك حَيَّوك بِما لَمْ يُحَيِّك بِهِ الله, *When they come to you, they greet you with words God never used to greet you.* Logically, of course, we do not say hello to the deceased. The link between life, the origin of this word, and greeting is by no means trivial. In a near parallel in English, when asking for word from someone, we might well ask for a sign of life. Some greetings are more famous than others. In 33:44 of the Qur'an, a very particular one is mentioned: تَحِيَّتُهُم يَوْمَ يَلْقَوْنَهُ سَلامٌ, *Their greeting when they meet Him will be "Peace."*

In addition to the Form II verb حيّا discussed above, the doubly weak ح – ي – ي root produces three verb forms. Form IV is discussed in chapter 37. Form I حيي – يحيا *Hayiya* has two meanings, each with its specific *maSdar*. In a direct connection with the face, it means to be shy and takes the *maSdar* الحياء *al-Hayaa'*, shyness. This sense is the less common, but other derivatives of the root expound on it, too. There is the adjective حيي *Hayiy*, bashful, shy, modest, and the Form X verb استحيى, to be ashamed, feel embarrassed, shy, or bashful. Forms I, II, and X, with only minor sound changes, are extant in Egyptian colloquial, where we also find the charmingly named الست المستحيّة, 'the modest lady,' the Cape gooseberry fruit, a large smooth yellow-green berry completely covered in a papery veil. The same Form I verb associated with shyness has another meaning of paramount importance, to live. Its *maSdar* is الحياة *al-Hayaah*, life. The verb also refers to longevity, and can mean to live to see or witness, to experience (a life of), to live through a time. It is the basis for the traditional wish offered to monarchs at the beginning of their reigns, لِيحي الملك *liyaHya al-malik*, (long) live the king!, while patriotic Egyptians love to say تحي مصر *taHya maSr*, long live Egypt!

FACE, COUNTENANCE مُحَيّا
الحياة / مَحْيا
life
John the Baptist يَحْيى
to give new أحيا
life to;
to revive, to stage
(a performance),
to celebrate
كائن حيّ
a living thing
animal حيوان
anti-
biotic
مُضادّ حيَوِيّ
حيّة
snake, serpent, adder

37
Face, Countenance (2) مُحَيّا – مَحايٍ
Greetings; Life

Giving someone a greeting is a sign of life and vitality, and vocabulary stemming from the *maSdar* الحياة, life, is both timeless and significant. Thirteen forms of the ح – ي – ي root figure in the *FDA*, three of which number in its top 100, while fifteen forms are used 189 times in the Qur'an. Among these is the oft-quoted thirty-third verse of the chapter entitled "Maryam." Jesus, still an infant, speaks and says: وَالسَّلامُ عَلَيَّ يَوْمَ وُلِدْتُ ويَوْمَ أَموتُ وَيَوْمَ أُبْعَثُ حَيًّا, *Peace be upon me the day I was born, and the day I die, and the day I am resurrected alive.* In another Biblical tie-in, this root is the basis for the ancient name يحيى, Yahya. Names tend to be meaningful, and this one, translated literally, is He lives! Yahya has found a home in language after language, with more versions than you could shake a stick at. A few of the more common are Yohannes, Yuhanna, Hanna, Johannes, Johan, Hans, Juan, Jean, Sean, Ian, and John. According to the gospel of Matthew, Yahya was the cousin of Jesus, and he is known in English as John the Baptist.

That same word used by the Qur'anic Christ child, حَيًّا Hayyan, alive, can be used as a common noun, حيّ Hayy, a living being, an organism. Its plural, أحياء *'aHyaa'*, is the word used for a subject in many high school curricula, علم الأحياء *'ilm al-'aHyaa'*, biology. It can also mean a neighborhood or quarter, as in حيّ الجيزة, the neighborhood of Giza, one part of the larger Egyptian governorate of the same name.

Returning to the noun الحياة, life, one finds a cluster of closely related, high-frequency words. Vitality is الحيويّة *al-Hayawiyya*, and lively, vital, and vigorous are just some of the possible translations for حيويّ *Hayawiyy*. This adjective comes in handy in medical science, too, where مضادّ حيويّ *muDaadd Hayawiyy* means an antibiotic.

One curious nominal derivation from this root is حيّة *Hayya*, a serpent. The word حيوان *Hayawaan*, animal, is also a product of ح – ي – ي, and the connection between them is easily intuited. However, given the important negative associations typically made with serpents, it seems odd that it, too, should be housed here. Visually, however, it makes perfect sense. Picture a coiled snake, rearing up, head and neck erect. The snake is careful to let you see its disquieting face. Glittering eyes fix you, a forked tongue flicks back and forth. It may even issue a hiss or rattle its tail. This is a very particular تحية *taHiyya,* greeting, one to be taken most seriously.

This leaves us with the Form IV verb, أحيا. A causative pattern, أحيا means, in a literal sense, to endow with life, to bring to life, or to restore to life. It is often used Qur'anically in this last sense when speaking of how God causes the rain to fall, bringing the dry earth back to life. In a different context, it can mean to celebrate or commemorate something, especially the memory of someone who has passed away, thus keeping it alive. It can even mean to put on or stage a performance, animating it, as in أحيا المغنّي ثلاث ليال *'aHyaa l-mughanniyy thalaatha layaalin*, the singer gave three evening performances.

FACE, GUISE, LOOK
طلعة
تطلّع ب/في
to look closely at; to stare at; to gaze at
تطلّع إلى
to have an eye for something; to wait, look out for
استطلاع الرأي العام
opinion poll
طالع
to read
مطالعة
reading
اطّلع على
to study; to come to know; to become aware of; to become acquainted with
MacToot

38

Face; Guise, Look(s) (1) طَلْعة – طلعات

Rising; Visibility; Insight

Given the face's significance in interpersonal interactions, it is not surprising that Arabic coined several words for it. The metaphor at work in الطلعة *aT-Tal'a* is how careful perusal of outward appearances provides insight. English likes to say that seeing is believing. The very name of this Arabic body part seems to suggest that seeing is understanding. Although first impressions are notoriously unreliable, they are also hard to resist, and a glance at someone's face often influences our judgment, making us *feel* we understand the nature of the person we are looking at. Friend or foe? Trustworthy or treacherous? Desirable or repulsive? The significance of the face extends beyond everyday social interactions, too. Fingerprints and retinal scans are infinitely more precise, but governments and businesses have not yet chosen to dispense with the facial photograph. Outward appearance still seems to offer a more holistic suggestion of who is who. Legend and literature also combine to remind us how powerful—and dangerous—a face may be. Narcissus, of Greek myth, was so enamored of his beautiful reflection that he died gazing at it. And Christopher Marlowe's sixteenth-century description of Helen of Troy immortalized her for English speakers unfamiliar with Greek as "the face that launch'd a thousand ships."

The ط – ل – ع root is quite a large one, with six powerhouse verbs and fifteen derived nouns and adjectives. Eight different words from the root are used nineteen times in the Qur'an, and eight also figure in the *FDA*. By far the most common of these is the Form I verb طلع – يطلُع *Tala'a*, to break (of day), rise (of a star), emerge, come into view, go/come out, mount, and board. This wonderfully versatile verb ranks 306 in the *FDA*. Spoken registers use it in many of the same ways. One of Alexandria's most famous sons, the poet–composer Sayed Darwish (1892–1923) wrote: *Til'it yaa m-aHla nurha, shams ishshammuusa*, She has risen, how beautiful her light, sun, sunny sun. Orientation is a key element here: elevated position, movement, and visibility link the face and heavenly bodies.

طالع
celestial body,
star;
destiny
استطلع
to explore,
research,
inquire
طلع
to break (of day);
to rise, come into view;
to mount, board
Slope,
daybreak
مطلع
طليعة
vanguard
أطلع (على)
to come in (of a tooth);
to sprout;
to notify, tell, do
something
LOOK
FACE, GUISE
طلعة

39

Face; Guise, Look(s) (2) طَلْعة – طلعات

Rising; Visibility; Insight

The face is at the top of the body, where it is clearly visible. It attracts our gaze, as does المطلع *al-maTla'* or الطلوع *aT-Tuluu'*, rising or ascendance, of طالِع *Taali',* a celestial body. Celestial bodies may be understood to affect one's fortune, and so الطالع is also used to mean destiny. The stars and planets were traditionally viewed as presaging the onset of something. It is just a small metaphoric leap from the astronomical طالع to الطليعة *aT-Talii'a,* portents, first indications, vanguard, and even avant-garde. The *maSdar* المطلع, mentioned above, can also be used as a place noun, and meanings of this word are surprisingly varied. In modern urban construction terms, it is an up-ramp; in literature, a preface, prelude; and in poetry, a poem's opening verses.

Combining visual and literary applications, Form III gives us طالع, to read, peruse, study, as well as to give someone an insight into something. Reading as an activity is the *maSdar* المطالعة *al-muTaala'a.* The Form IV verb أطلع returns to the issue of visibility. This is a verb seven-year-olds and gardeners anxiously anticipate: to come in (of new teeth), or to sprout. As one would expect, this Form IV verb also has a transitive use. The verb–preposition idiom أطلعه عليه, means to inform someone of something, or to show someone something. Form V تطلّع إلى means to have one's eye on something, to be on the lookout for, to gaze at. Someone who does so is مُتطلّع إليه *mutaTalli' 'ilayhi* waiting, curious, eager for it. The assimilated Form VIII اطّلع على means to see something, be well informed, to have inside information. The participial phrase مُطّلِع على *muTTali' 'alaa* means acquainted with, informed about. Finally, Form X استطلع means to try to find out, to scout out, make inquiries. Its *maSdar* is one crucial tool of statisticians, استطلاع الرأي العام *istiTlaa' ar-ra'y al-'aamm*, the opinion poll. All of these derivatives are variations on a theme: using visual clues to reach a better understanding of a situation.

مئذنة
minaret
أذّن
to call to prayer
مؤذّن
muezzin
أُذُن
EAR
استأذن
to ask permission
(to seek someone's ear)
أذِن
to listen; permit
وِدن من طين وودن من عجين
'An ear of mud and an ear of dough' (Pleas falling ondeaf ears)
-Egyptian Proverb
كلّي آذانٌ صاغية
I'm all ears
آذَنَ
toforeshadow, portend, suggest
أُذَيْن القلب
auricle
-MacToot-

40
Ear أذن – أُذنان – آذان
Permission

What good does it do to ask someone's permission if they have no ear to hear your request? This is the point of the Egyptian proverb in which unlucky pleas destined for deaf ears fall on *widn min Tiin wi widn min 'agiin*, an ear of mud and an ear of dough. In fact, both standard and vernacular idioms closely link the ear with permission.

The Form I verb أذِن – يأذَن *'adhina* means to permit, along with its *maSdar* الإذن *al-'idhn*, while the Form X verb استأذن means to ask for permission. This Form X verb is an exact—though more concise—equivalent of the English expression to seek an audience. As a look at other derivatives of the Latin *audire* like audio and auditorium suggests, an audience actually means the opportunity to be heard. The pairing of the Form I and Form X verbs embodies the relationship of one who has the power to grant permission and one who can only request it. Polite usage naturally requires offering an excuse if leaving a gathering prematurely, but it also dictates acquiescence. In a dramatic example of concision, which recognizes this important little social contract, English allows an imperative: Excuse me. Arabic is also very succinct: resorting to the Form I *maSdar*, it offers the formulaic بعد إذنكم *ba'da 'idnikum* (I will leave) after (you give me) your permission.

The passive participle of Form I designates an occupation, المأذون *al-ma'dhuun*, literally the one permitted, or authorized. This is a sort of religious justice of the peace who has the authority to solemnize Islamic marriage contracts and divorces. The common noun الأذان *al-'adhaan*, is the call to prayer, a necessarily audible announcement that the permissible time for one of the five daily ritual prayers has arrived. As we have seen in the introduction, many common nouns and adjectives can be used to produce verbs, and the call to prayer الأذان is one. Form II أذّن, means to produce الأذان, that is, to give the call to prayer. The one who does so is المُؤَذِّن, commonly transliterated as the muezzin. In the olden days, a high place from which the muezzin's call could be easily heard was needed, and the instrument pattern المِئذنة *al-mi'dhana*, the minaret, was the architect's esthetic and technical solution. Someone with powerful lungs and legs was best suited to this calling. Nowadays, loudspeakers are usually affixed to all such المآذن *ma'aadhin* (plural of المِئذنة), obviating the need for a long climb and a stentorian voice.

The word أذن *'udhun*, ear, can also be used to produce one of Arabic's most endearing patterns, the diminutive. In this case, we find أُذَيْن القلب *'udhayn al-qalb*, literally 'the heart's little ear.' Its English name is essentially the same, coming straight from a Latin diminutive *auricula*. 'Auricle,' one of the chambers of the heart, was presumably named for its resemblance to a little ear. Similarly, بُطَين القلب *buTayn al-qalb*, ventricle, from *ventriculus*, means 'the heart's little belly.' Who did the naming? The Romans? Or the Arabs? Historians of science, please weigh in!

حجب
to outshine, eclipse, overshadow
حاجب
doorman, gatekeeper
to make imperceptible; حجب عن
to conceal from
to conceal oneself; to flee from sight; to veil oneself تحجّب
EYEBROW
حاجبٌ
محجوب
concealed, protected
الحجاب الحاجز
diaphragm
to veil oneself; to be covered up, hidden انحجب
Curtain, screen, veil, amulet
حجاب
to vanish, become invisible, elude perception; to cease publication احتجب
MacToot

41

Eyebrow حاجِب – حاجِبان – حَواجِب

Veiling, Protection

The 'brow' embedded in the English eyebrow suggests prominence but goes no further. Because the Arabic eyebrow, الحاجب *al-Haajib*, is built on the participial pattern فاعِل, it tells us more: someone or something is performing an action. One of the meanings of Form I حجب – يحجُب *Hajaba* is to veil, seclude, or shelter. The anatomical حاجب is thus a guardian or protector of the eye. Because the فاعل pattern is predicated on the existence of a verb, one must presume that the verb or its *maSdar* came into usage first and was the source of the body word. Before there can be a protector, the concept of protection itself must exist. As noted, the pattern فاعل can designate a person or a thing. In this case, Arabic made use of both options: in medieval texts, الحاجب referred to the guard at the castle gates. When used to indicate the latter, the broken plural الحُجّاب *al-Hujjaab* must be used instead of الحواجب *al-Hawaajib*, eyebrows.

The nefarious possibilities of being too beautiful, too desirable, too successful, and so forth were sources of age-old anxieties. The potency of an envious eye called for a variety of protections, and الحجاب *al-Hijaab*, often in the form of an amulet or talisman, served this purpose. A person wearing such a طَلْسَم *Talsam*, a word of Greek origin meaning talisman, was thereby protected, محجوب *maHjuub*. Protection from envy and ill-will could be accomplished, depending on the age and one's beliefs, with a magic formula or a Biblical or Qur'anic verse. With its reassuring connotations, محجوب has even turned into a common Arab family name. Although the high frequency word *Hijaab*—2,373 in the *FDA*—is now commonly identified with the veil women wear to protect them from the prying eyes of men, its actual meaning is thus much broader. Furthermore, it is one component of another important anatomical designation, الحجاب الحاجز *al-Hijaab al-Haajiz*, diaphragm (of course, a much later term than eyebrow). Translated literally, this all-important protective barrier between chest and abdomen would be 'the partitioning guard.'

The Form I verb حجب – يحجُب *Hajaba* has two meanings: first, to outshine, overshadow. With the addition of the preposition عن, the meaning becomes to make imperceptible, to conceal, to shelter. In both cases, reduced visibility is implied. Form II, حجّب also means to conceal or veil someone. Form V تحجّب is the reflexive of II, veiling and concealing oneself. It is also an example of a small semantic subset of Form V verbs related to clothing; تحجّب can also mean to put on a veil. See chapter 63 on اللحية for further examples. Form VII انحجب is synonymous with Form V. Most of the Form V verbs that refer to dressing have Form VIII counterparts with the same meaning. In this case though, احتجب is more likely to be a very particular metaphoric extrapolation on disappearance: to cease publication.

جفنٌ
EYELID
إنه لشديد
جَفنِ العينِ
His eyelids never tire (he can maintain an all-night vigil)
يَعْمَلونَ لَهُ ما يَشاءُ مِنْ مَحاريبَ وَتَماثيلَ وَجِفانٍ كَالجَوابِ
They made him whatever he wanted: palaces, statues, and bowls as large as water troughs
Qur'an 34:13
جفن نفسه عن
to stop oneself from
جفن السماء
Clouds
نام مِلءَ جَفْنَيْهِ
he slept soundly
جفن الطعام
to serve food in a large bowl or basin
جفّن
to produce, manufacture a large bowl or basin
أثقل الكرى أجفانه
he fell asleep (sleep weighed his eyelids down)
large wooden or copper bowl
جَفْن السيف
scabbard of a sword
جَفْنة
جفّن له
to serve someone food in a Jafna
MacToot

42

Eyelid جَفْن – جَفْنان – جُفون / أَجْفان

Shielding; Generosity

It is not surprising that the eyelid, الجفن *al-jafn*, that built-in shield for generating a bit of darkness, should be most commonly used in expressions directly connected to sleep. The proverbial إنه لشديدُ جفنِ العين *innahu lashadiid jafn al-'ayn*, he has a powerful eyelid, describes someone who can resist sleep and stay awake through the night. Few are able to do so, however, and أثقل الكرى أجفانه *'athqala al-karaa 'ajfaanahu* describes someone whose drooping eyelids signal a surrender to sleep. One may say of a person who sleeps very soundly, ينام مِلْءَ جَفْنَيْه *yanaamu mil'a jafnayhi*, the gist of which is that one's very eyelids get their fill of sleep. Colloquial English offers a different body analogy: to pound one's ear.

Al-jafn has two homonyms, as well. Both, like their phonetic twin, shield something of great value. First, from the practical world of valuable gear comes جفن السيف *jafn as-sayf*, the scabbard, which sheathes a warrior's precious sword. In a poetic meditation on nature, we find the Bedouin trope جفن الماء *jafn al-maa'*. This is a metaphor for السحاب, clouds, which hold within themselves life-sustaining rain.

The most important derivative of the eyelid is الجفنة *al-jafna*, a classical word for a very large bowl or basin. Presumably it is the saucer-like shape that links these utensils to anatomy. The plural is جفان *jifaan*, a word that figures just once in the Qur'an, at 34:13: يَعْمَلُونَ لَهُ مَا يَشَاءُ مِنْ مَحَارِيبَ وَتَمَاثِيلَ وَجِفَانٍ كَالْجَوَابِ, *They made him whatever he wanted—palaces, statues, and bowls as large as water troughs.* Such basins could also be used for kneading dough. Another meaning of جفنة was a small water well. Once again, the shape of the well's mouth might suggest a large bowl. Its function as a container for water links it to the basin as well.

English serving platters are rarely so generous, making the expression 'to dish out food' a rather pallid equivalent of the Form I جفن الطعام *jafana aT-Ta'aam*. When used for serving, such a bowl was said to hold enough to feed ten men. By extension, someone who would treat his guests to such impressive feasting was to be admired, and the word جفنة *jafna* could also designate a generous, hospitable host. The Form II verb جفّن is denominative, to produce or manufacture a large bowl. It can also mean to serve someone food in a جفنة. A quite different sense is produced by adding the preposition عن to the Form I verb. This preposition typically designates movement away from, and جفن عن means to avoid, shield, or screen oneself from something, a functional analogy to the role the eyelid plays in protecting the eye. Thus, جفن نفسه عن كل مكروه *jafana nafsahu 'an kulli makruuh* means 'He avoided all reprehensible things.' Unlike the English 'to shut one's eyes to something' or 'to turn a blind eye to it,' the Arabic expression does not imply ignoring bad things that happen, but rather declining to participate in them.

طائر أهدب
bird with long feathers
هُدْب
EYELASH
long-lashed
هَدِب/أَهْدَب
هَدَب
drooping branches
لحية هدباء
long, flowing beard
أهداب
eyelashes, cilia
هدب
to milk a cow with the fingertips
هدّب
to pick fruit, to decorate with a fringe
MacToot

43
Eyelash هُدْب – أَهْداب
Fringe

The ancient Arabs contemplated the graceful eyelashes and named them الهدب *al-hudb*, the fringes, a word which emphasizes their feathery, drooping beauty as well as their peripherality. It is interesting to note that *both* هدب (the collective term) and أهداب *'ahdab* (the broken plural) are translated in the plural in English. To speak of just one eyelash, ة must be added to the collective هُدب form, as in هدبة سوداء طويلة *hudba sawdaa' Tawiila*, a long black eyelash. Collective designations are often linked to things typically found in multiples or large numbers. Examples abound in the natural world (البقر cattle; الشجر trees; السحاب clouds; الموج waves) but are not confined to it (الطوب bricks, الورق paper). The contrasting plural forms tend to emphasize abundance or variety.

These eyelashes even provided cell biology with a bit of poetry. The microscopic fringes on a cell, whose *lashing* movements help it locomote, are also called الأهداب, cilia. In fact, this is a fairly old import. Dutch tradesman and scientist Antonie van Leeuwenhoek (1632–1723), known as the father of microbiology, was the first to observe *and* document cilia, not to mention bacteria and spermatozoa. In the late seventeenth century, microscopy was in its infancy, and van Leeuwenhoek, a tradesman, sent accounts of his amazing observations to many 'proper' scientists. He is also the one who baptized the anatomical cell, basing its name on the resemblance, in his judgment, to a monk's quarters!

In the case of الأهداب, it is hard to say whether the *source* word for the ه – د – ب root vocabulary is eyelashes or leaves. Verbally, هدبت العين *hadibat al-'ayn* means to be long-lashed, but in terms of trees, هدبت الشجرة *hadibat ash-shajara* means to have low-hanging branches. Just one word, هدبة *hadaba,* succinctly describes a drooping branch. Narrow, drooping leaves like those of a cypress are collectively termed هدب *hadab*. The flora and fauna of the natural world were also sources of poetic inspiration. Whether the Bedouin decided that eyelashes were like slender drooping leaves, or vice versa, is arguable. Either way, this root has a number of figurative uses like تمسّك / تعلّق بأهداب الأمر, to hold firmly to a course of action. In this analogy, an abstract matter is portrayed as tangible and subject to control, if one can just get a good grip on some accessible feature of it, الأهداب.

The أفعل adjective pattern with this root creates أهدب. A long-lashed person is أهدب العينين *'ahdab al-'aynayn*. Other facial hair, and things like it, can be described using this same descriptor. A flowing beard is لحية هدباء *liHya hadbaa'*. The animal world is fair game, too. A horse with a long, flowing forelock is called فرس هَدِب *faras hadib*. Since birds have feathers rather than hair, a well-endowed bird, so to speak, can be called طائر أهدب *Taa'ir 'ahdab*. Even more metaphorically, a long, drooping ear, like that of a rabbit, is أذن هدباء *'udhun hadbaa'*.

The Form I verb هدب – يهدَب *hadiba* means to milk a cow with the ends of the fingers. Form I and the Form II هدّب can both mean to pick fruit from a tree where it dangles from the end of the branches. Form II هدّب can also be used in the realm of embellishment: *haddaba* thus means to decorate a garment with a fringe, or to add a decorative fringed edge or border to something.

رمش
EYE-LASHES
يا رمش العين اللي جرحني
- محرم فؤاد
Oh eyelashes that have wounded me
-Muharram Fouad 1934-2002
أرمش
long-lashed
رمشت
ترمش العين
to blink, wink
رمشت العين
to have a nervous tic; to flutter (of the eyelid)
رمّش
to pick something up by the tips of the fingers
MacToot

44

Eyelash رِمْش – رُموش

Blink; Graze

The most common derivative of the ر – م – ش root is الرمـش *ar-rimsh*, a modern term for the eyelashes, themselves, and the one that the spoken register prefers. They are closely associated with blinking, and yet the connection is more esthetic than functional. These fluttering eyelashes bewitch and enthrall, and they are dangerous.

Many great voices have sung to the eyes, but few have gone on to address the seductive lash. One of the pillars of the golden age of Egyptian cinema and song, singer Muharram Fouad, crooned: رمـش عينـه اللـي جرحنـي, Oh, (my love's) eyelash that has wounded me. Strangely, unlike هـدب *hudb*, رمـش is *not* a collective; it is just one lash. To indicate many, use its plural, رمـوش *rumuush*.

The object of a long-lashed gaze, the song suggests, will be struck and smitten by its beauty, as if those very lashes were projectiles. Dangerous though they may be, eyelashes seem to be universally admired, and using the أفعـل pattern in combination with this root, Arabic can describe a person or an animal endowed with this beguiling feature: أَرْمَـش / رَمشـاء / رُمـش *'armash / ramshaa' / rumsh* (in this order: masculine, feminine, plural).

There are other expressions, though they are much less common, based on the significant relative location of the eyelashes, the edge. The Form I verb رَمَـش – يرمُـش *ramasha* can mean to touch or pick something up by the tips of the fingers. In this analogy, the fingertips are to the hands as the eyelashes are to the eyelids. This is similar to the Form I and Form II verbs of the ه – د – ب root mentioned in the previous chapter. An expression from the pastoral world plays on this simile of the lashes as extremities: رمشـت الماشـية, the livestock grazed very lightly. As in English, grazing suggests a light touch.

More commonly, however, الرمـش is directly associated with the eye. The Form I verbal expression رمشـت العيـن *ramashat al-'ayn* means to blink or wink, with the *maSdar*, الرمـش *ar-ramsh*, blinking. From the *maSdar* comes the countable instance noun, رمشـة *ramsha*, a blink. In addition to referring to individual blinks, this word figures in expressions of dramatic rapidity, just as in English. For example, one might say أسـرع مـن رمشـة العيـن *'asra ' min ramshat al-'ayn*, quicker than the blink of an eye, in the twinkling of an eye. A small modification of the vowel produces رمِشـت العيـن *ramishat*, indicating an abnormal condition. It may mean to have conjunctivitis, an infection in which secretions of the eye make it red and puffy, and cause the eyelashes to become matted. Given the discomfort, such a condition makes its sufferer prone to blinking. Less dramatically, this phrase also describes a nervous tic or tremor of the eye, due to which it involuntarily flutters.

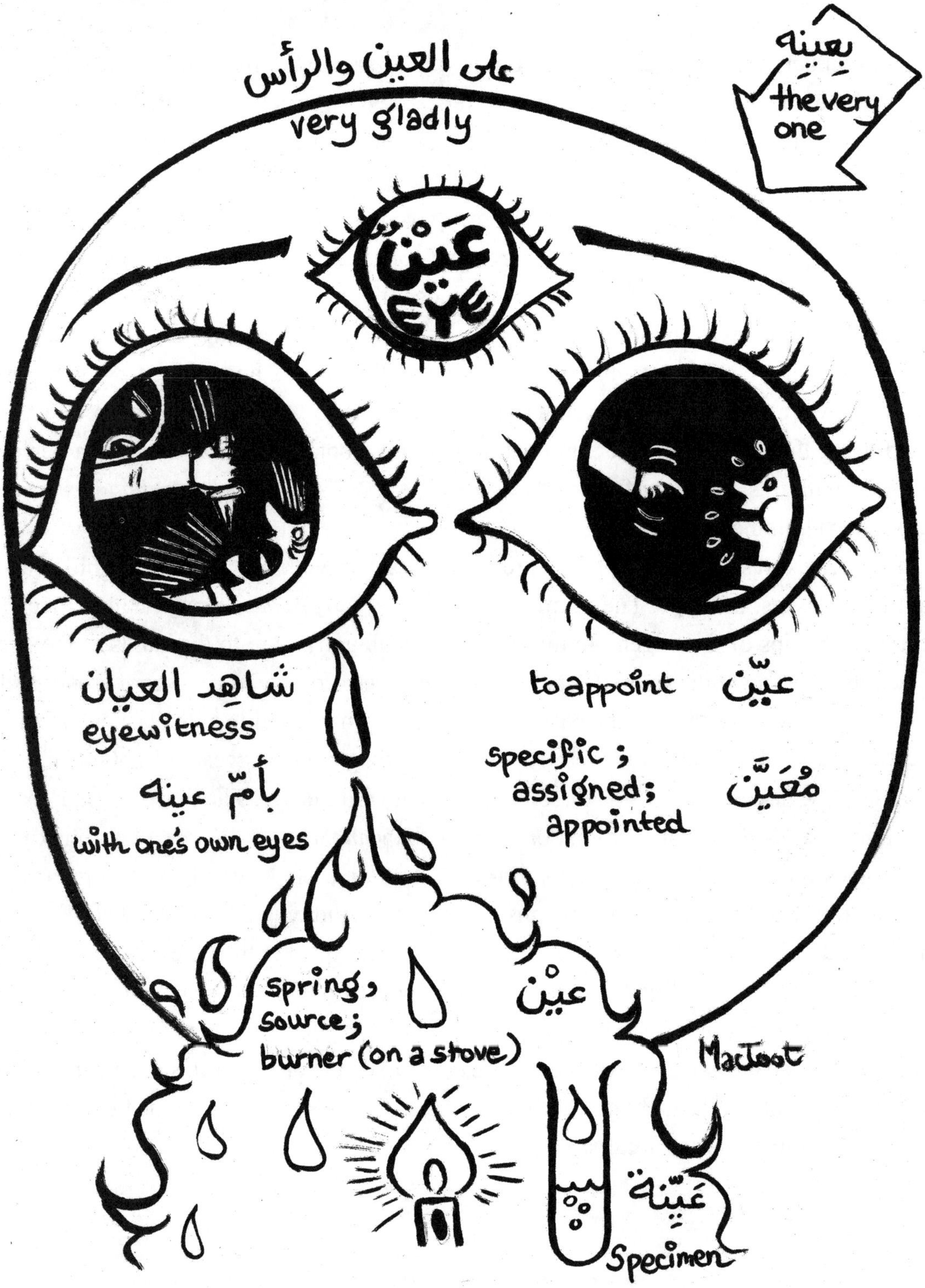

على العين والرأس
very gladly
بعِينه
the very one
عيْن
EYE
شاهِد العيان
eyewitness
بأمّ عينه
with one's own eyes
عيّن
to appoint
مُعَيَّن
specific; assigned; appointed
عيْن
spring, source; burner (on a stove)
MacToot
عَيِّنة
Specimen

45
Eye عَيْن – عَيْنان – عُيون / أَعْيان
Outlet; Scrutiny; Witnessing

Logically, of course, the eye العين *al-'ayn* is what we see with, and sometimes what we see is what we want. When our eye alights on something, we mark it, or using an English body metaphor, we earmark it. This is the idea behind the Form II verb عيّن, to specifically designate, assign, or appoint, and its *maSdar* التعيين *at-ta'yiin*. In English, *eyeing* someone for a position is just a first step in the decision process. In Arabic, it is actually the result of the scrutiny, the appointment, itself. The passive participle of this verb means specifically designated: شيء معيَّن *shay' mu'ayyan* is therefore something which has been singled out, a specific or particular thing.

The anatomical eye is the source of two additional verb forms. Like it, they are based on the ع – ي – ن root. Form III عاين means to inspect something, or to see it with one's own eyes. Nominally, using the form's available *maSdar* patterns, it is possible to specify which is intended: المعاينة *al-mu'aayana*, inspection or supervision, or العِيان *al-'iyaan*, witnessing. The latter is echoed in the English eyewitness, شاهد العيان *shaahid al-'iyaan*. Form V تعيّن is the reflexive equivalent of II, to be earmarked, appointed, assigned. The addition of the preposition على signals the logical consequence of formally being chosen for something. It indicates obligation and duty: تعيّن عليه أن يساعدهم *ta'ayyana 'alayhi 'an yusaa'idahum*, he had to assist them. From there, it can acquire a more general sense of necessity: تعيّن عليه أن يرتاح *ta'ayyana 'alayhi 'an yartaaH*, he had to rest.

The physical eye is only one of the meanings of العين. It has many other figurative senses. All of them share the idea of being an outlet for something. In the English saying, the eyes are the windows of the soul. The implication is that one can see *into* another's very soul through the eyes. In Arabic, however, that directional implication is reversed. It is not that we see in, but rather that something emanates from العين. In its use as the word for a spring, water gushes forth. As a burner on a stove, flame is emitted. In commercial parlance, العين is an outlet where business is transacted, from which profit, it might be hoped, will issue. Another metaphoric category of العين is based on the organ's beauty. In this sense, it refers to the prime of something, as in عين الشباب *ayn ash-shabaab*, the flower of youth. Furthermore, it can be used to convey the idea of the central locus of something, as in عين العقل *'ayn al-'aql*, the epitome of reason. This idea of the eye as essence allows it to take a possessive suffix and be used in apposition, the way 'self' is in English. For example, جاء الرئيس بعينه *jaa'a ar-ra'iis bi-'aynihi*, the president himself came. Its alternative plural أعيان *'a'yaan* means people of distinction, eminent men, a term which combines the idea of being seen and being chosen. In selecting a translation for 'senate,' some Arab countries preferred the Greek (and English) style مجلس الشيوخ *majlis ash-shuyuukh*, council of elders, but others gravitated to the alternative مجلس الأعيان, council of the distinguished.

The anatomical importance of العين, its many secondary meanings, and its seemingly endless metaphoric dimensions, make the eye, after القلب *al-qalb*, the heart, the most frequently used body part in the *FDA*, ranking 130.

مقلة
eye
مقل
to feed a baby camel milk from one's palms ; to drizzle water down a baby camel's throat if it is not strong enough to drink on its own
مقل- يمقّل
to give someone a look
MacToot
مقل
to dive (for pearls)
مقل
فيه
to dive into
مقل
the sandy bottom of a well
مقل
to measure water rations with a pebble's worth of water

46
Eye مُقْلة – مُقْلتان – مُقَل
Pearl in Water

Whereas much of the quite common vocabulary derived from العين means to scrutinize and witness, المقلة *al-muqla* has its own, mostly quite specialized, associations. Some of them are functional and others are based on resemblance.

The eye's raison d'être is vision, and in fact Form I مقل – يمقُل *maqala* means to give someone or something a look, to regard. However, the م – ق – ل root also has a close connection to water and diving. First, المَقْل *al-maql* means diving in the ocean, and especially diving for pearls. These precious, lustrous spheres have obvious parallels with the eye. In addition, the eye, like the ocean, is a source of salty water. Second, this same noun also refers to the sandy, pebbly bottom of a well. Pearls were to be found in oysters, and oysters had to be retrieved from the sandy ocean floor. Not only is the bottom of the well reminiscent of the ocean floor; the rounded shape of a well's shaft may also evoke the eye. Whether in pearl diving or fetching water from the well, a plunge—of the diver or the bucket—was the only way to obtain what was desired.

In addition to the sense of looking at, the Form I verb مقل - يمقُل *maqala* has two very specialized meanings, each of which gives us a fascinating glimpse of Bedouin problem-solving. In the first instance, مقل describes a very specific veterinary practice. Baby camels in distress from an inability to nurse properly and at risk of dehydration from the heat could in the short term be hand-fed by their owners. Two methods are specified: allowing the animal to drink from one's palms, or should it be unable to do so, moving its tongue to the side, bypassing the uvula, and gently trickling water down its throat. This latter tactic is even preserved in a line of poetry: إذا استحرَّ فامْقلوه مَقْلاً . . . في الحَلْقِ واللَّهاةِ صُبّوا الرِّسْلا *'idhaa astaHarra famquluuhu maqlan . . . fi-l-Halqi wa-l-lahaati Subbuu ar-risla,* If it gets heatstroke, give it the 'maql' treatment . . . into its throat and (past) the uvula, pour slowly.[13]

In the second instance, مقل describes another technique for apportioning water that is in very short supply. In this case, the drinkers are human. Small pebbles (حصى *HaSaa)* would be thrown into a drinking vessel, and water poured to barely cover them. Rationing with 'the apportioning pebbles,' حصى القسم *HaSaa al-qasam*, would be repeated to guarantee a fair allotment to each drinker.

In all contexts, the م – ق – ل root is rare, and in modern usage, المقلة, the eye, is the only familiar word. Largely confined to poetry, this body part is closely associated with romance. In "Hadhihi laylati" (this is my night), a masterpiece of a song written by the Lebanese poet George Jerdaq and full of references to the body, Umm Kulthum famously sings والحبّ في مقلتينا *wa-l-Hubb fii muqlataynaa*, And love was in our eyes.

حدق/أحدق
to surround, encircle
خَطَرٌ مُحدِقٌ
imminent danger
حديقة الحيوان zoo
garden حديقة
حدّق
أحدق في /إلى/ب
to look, glance, gaze
حدّق/أحدق النظر في
to fix the gaze on
حدقة
MacToot

47

Pupil حَدَقة ـ حَدَقتان ـ حَدَقات / حَدَق / حِداق / أَحْداق

Encircle

Surrounded by the colorful, circular iris, the perfect, dark circle of the pupil الحدقة *al-Hadaqa* is an opening into the eye. The shape of the pupil, itself, ringed by the iris, suggests encircling or being encircled, and this metaphor animates the whole ح – د – ق root family. The most common noun from this root, ranking 1,624 in the *FDA*, is حديقة *Hadiiqa,* a garden. Especially in classical parlance, it refers to a garden *surrounded* by a wall rather than an open one (روضة *rawDa*). Besides the fact that a walled garden suggests a small contained space, the metaphoric link of the pupil to a garden is clear: in desert life, a garden would be hard to tear one's eyes away from. In modern usage, the walled versus unwalled distinction has been lost. Consequently, حديقة is used to refer to any garden, including حديقة الحيوان *Hadiiqat al-Hayawaan*, the zoo, literally, the animal garden. Gardens of all varieties held a fascination for desert dwellers, and in fact, Paradise الجنّة *al-janna* is typically described in the Qur'an as gardens, حدائق *Hadaa'iq*, with rivers, as in 78:32. This plural is the only derivative of the root to figure in the Qur'an. The common word for garden in spoken Egyptian Arabic, جِنَينة *gineena*, is actually the diminutive form of paradise.

As a plural, أحداق *'aHdaaq* can mean pupils or glances, and the three verb forms derived from the ح – د – ق root all mean to glance, look, or stare at. Form I حدق - يحدِق *Hadaqa* is transitive, and the eye is often specifically mentioned. One might say, for example, حدقها بعينه *Hadaqahaa bi 'aynihi*, he looked/glanced at her. Forms II حدّق and IV أحدق may use any of three prepositions for their objects بها / فيها / إليها. By adding النظر as a direct object, the sense is to fix one's gaze on someone or something, as in أحدق النظر بها *'aHdaqa an-naZar bihaa*, he stared at her/it. The English word pupil comes from the Latin *pupa*, doll or girl, a playful term derived to describe the tiny mirrored image one sees reflected in another person's eyes. Arabic, however, did not take this playful metaphoric path. Instead, the active participle from the Form IV أحدق verb contemplates the potential perils of encirclement. A danger ready to pounce on one from all sides is خطر مُحدِق *khaTar muHdiq*. It has the unfortunate victim in its sights, and is poised to close in and encompass him.

قرنيّة
CORNEA
وحيد القَرْن
rhinoceros
قرن
to couple, yoke together; to hitch together
قِرن
(matched) opponent in battle; equal, peer
أقرَن
horned
قَرْن
animal's horn, insect tentacle, feelers; century
مَقرون
having eyebrows that meet
MacToot

48

Cornea (1) قَرْنيّة – قَرْنيّتانِ – فَرْنيّات

Horns; Yoking; Marriage

Anatomical terminology of the eye is remarkably similar in Latin, Greek, and Arabic. In addition to discoveries in fields as diverse as astronomy, navigation, and mathematics, these ancient civilizations shared medical lore, a fact confirmed by the similarity of terms like cornea, auricle, ventricle, and others. The Greek word *keras* means horn, a root that English used to coin *keratin*, a fibrous protein that forms the chemical basis of horny epidermal tissue like hair and nails, while keratosis is an abnormal overgrowth of such tissues that may produce corns. In short, corn and horn are cognates. In Latin, the word for an animal's horn is *cornu*, from which comes the easily recognizable *cornea.* The Arabic word for horn is قرن *qarn*, and its *nisba* adjective, turned into a noun by the definite article, is القرنية *al-qarniyya*, the cornea.

Animals' horns are the inspiration for a large family of words, and Arabic exploited analogies based on them in ingenious ways. The magnificent oryx is just one of the native horned species ancient Arabs had occasion to observe. To describe such an eye-catching feature, they chose the أفعل pattern, producing أقرن *'aqran,* and its feminine form قرناء *qarnaa'*, horned. It was the *paired* nature of horns and their resemblance to each other that Arabic used as a metaphor in ق – ر – ن vocabulary. Athough not primarily an agricultural people, the Bedouin were great traders and travelers, and had undoubtedly seen buffalo yoked together to plough. The Form I verb to couple, yoke, or hitch together is قرن – يقرَن *qarana.* Using this as a point of departure, they coined the term مِقرن *miqran* for the wooden yoke so visually reminiscent of the horns of a buffalo that could be used to yoke a pair of them. Consequently, a rhinoceros, وحيد القرن *wahiid al-qarn*, was a truly amazing creature, given its iconoclastic single frontal horn. While the Greek name that English adopted means 'nose horn,' the Arabic means 'single of horn.'

قرنية
CORNEA
قارن بين (وبين)
to compare, draw a parallel between two things
مُقارَنة
comparison
قارن إلى/بـ...
to link something to
to associate something with
قِران
marriage
قرين
associated; associate, comrade, spouse
قِران
close connection; marriage
MacToot
اقترن بِـ...
to be joined, connected, linked, married, to get 'hitched'
قارن
to unite forces; to be simultaneous, go hand in hand

49
Cornea (2) قَرْنيّة – قَرْنيّتانِ – قَرْنيّات
Horns; Yoking;Marriage

The word قَـرن *qarn*, horn, has an exact homonym, and it is also a very old word. Used in the Qur'an, it refers to generations from bygone eras. Commentators differed greatly in saying how long such generations lived. Consensus gradually settled on one hundred years, a century. The semantic scope of القـرن and specifically the link between horn and century is impossible to pin down with confidence, but perhaps it had to do with the one hundred years as the *shared* lifespan of a generation of people. Primarily because of its meaning as century, this word is the most common of the ق – ر – ن root in modern usage, ranking 883 in the *FDA*. As we have seen, one of the meanings of the Form I verb قـرن – يقـرَن *qarana* is to hitch together, and this verb also produced a playful extrapolation on the idea of horned animals. Its passive participle is مقـرون *maqruun*, and describes someone whose eyebrows meet above the nose.

A minimal vowel change to the word for century produces قرن *qirn*, an equal, a peer, or an opponent in battle, but one who is a match. Although زوج is more common, another word for a spouse is قريـن *qariin*. The marriage contract is عقد القران *'aqd al-qiraan*, and to be joined in marriage can be expressed by the Form VIII verb, اقتـرن, and its *maSdar* الاقتـران *al-iqtiraan*. It is fascinating to note that the image of a yoke inspired the quite formal words قران ,قريـن, and اقتـران, while in English it gave rise to the very slang and not entirely enthusiastic expression for getting married, 'to get hitched.'

The Form II verb مُقَرَّنِين refers to a physical binding or shackling together, and its passive participle is used this way in 14:49 of the Qur'an: وَتَـرَى الْمُجْرِمِيـنَ يَوْمَئـذٍ مُقَرَّنِيـنَ فـي الأَصْفـادِ, *you will see the sinners on that Day, bound in fetters*. Form IV أقرن can have this same meaning, and its active participle is so used in 43:13. In fact, eight derivatives of this root are used forty times in the Qur'anic text. But Form IV also means to link or combine two things. For example, one may say أقـرن بيـن الحـجّ والعمـرة *'aqrana bayna l-Hajj wa-l-'umra*, he combined the major and minor pilgrimages.

The Form III verb قارن is commonly used with بين, which may be repeated, meaning to compare (between) two things, as in قـارن بيـن الظبـي وبيـن الغـزال *qaarana bayna aZ-Zabiyy wa-l-ghazaal*, he compared the antelope and the gazelle. Once again, the fact that an animal's horns tend to resemble each other is what prompted this semantic outgrowth. The *maSdar* is المقارنـة *al-muqaarana*, comparing or comparison, and it ranks 1,401 in the *FDA*. In modern academia the passive participle of this verb figures in the name of one of the branches of study available to university students, الأدب المقارَن *al-'adab al-muqaaran*, comparative literature.

DIMPLE غمّازة
غمز ب/على ...
to slander, calumnate
تغامز
to signal to one another; to wink at one another
غمزة ج غمزات
sign, signal, wink; hint;
غمز ب ...
to wink at
غمز
to make a sign, signal; to wink at
غمز ب ...
to feel, touch, palpate someone with something
غميزة = مَغمَز ج مغامز
failing, shortcoming, character blemish, weak spot which invites innuendo
مَغْمَز
weak point; failing, shortcoming
اغتمز
to detract from; to belittle, disparage; to find someone's weak point

50
Dimple غمّازة – غمّازات
Signal; Innuendo

The dimple, الغمّازة *al-ghammaaza*, associated with the cuteness of childhood and the allure of femininity, is deemed an attractive facial feature in many societies. The result of recessive genes, it is also a relative rarity, giving it added cachet. English tends to associate dimples with the cheek and chin, but other bodily locations with a little extra fat will do. English dimples aren't necessarily human or even animate: golf balls, for example, have them, too. In Arabic, the charming dimple is intimately linked to innuendo. Closely associated with the eye, the غ – م – ز root is all about winking, nodding, and making surreptitious critical signals. Arabic dimples are therefore strictly animate.

Form I غمز – يغمِز *ghamaza,* and its *maSdar* الغمز *al-ghamz*, are ancient and have a variety of meanings. One of them is to touch, and the noun غمّاز *ghammaaz* came to indicate something frequently pressed, including the finger pad or key on many musical instruments. The verb also means to nudge, beckon, signal, and wink. Exploiting this image, the Arabs dubbed the eye-catching float on a fishing line, which seems to wink as it bobs on the surface of the water, غمّاز *ghammaaz*. In a particularly creative neologism, they used the same term to name the blinker or flasher on an automobile.

When the Form I verb is used with the preposition على, an important shift in meaning results. The ancient Arabs had a great ear for rhyme, and sonorous overlaps suggestively link certain roots. Of relevance to the discussion of *ghamaza* is a different rhyming duo in the Qur'an, at 104:1, which shares those last two consonants. Castigating those it describes as *humaza lumaza*, the verse says: وَيْلٌ لِكُلِّ هُمَزَةٍ لُمَزَةٍ, *Woe to every backbiting slanderer!* The shared rhyme suggests that those who engage in winking and nodding in reference to a third person are mocking a defect in their target. In the root in question, the place pattern identifies it, too: مغمز *maghmaz*, a weak spot, a shortcoming or flaw of character that could expose one to ridicule. Hence, like these two roots with which it rhymes, غمز على can mean to slander.

The dimple itself does not appear in the Qur'an, but the root's checkered aura is represented once again in the Form VI verb تغامز. This form spells out the shared nature of this social action. In 83:30, the subdued but unsettling gestures designed to undermine confidence are referenced again: وَإِذَا مَرُّوا بِهِمْ يَتَغَامَزُونَ, *And when they pass by them they nudge one another*. Gibran Khalil Gibran (1883–1931) provides a modern echo: وأخذوا يَتَغَامَزُونَ وَيَضْحَكُونَ وَيُشِيرُونَ نَحْوِي مُسْتَهْزِئِين, They began winking at each other and laughing and pointing at me mockingly.[14] The Form VIII verb اغتمز, to detract from or to disparage, rounds out this verbal gallery of derision. Together, these usages allow us to see how gestural innuendo can constitute unnerving social criticism. Humans are conditioned to read a lot into facial gestures, and what links the charming and not-so-common dimple to these other not-so-innocent signals seems to be the fact that it appears and disappears on the face, just like a wink and a nod.

أَنْف
NOSE
مذكور آنِفاً
abovementioned
النَّفْسَ بِالنَّفْسِ وَالعَيْنَ بِالعَيْنِ وَالأَنْفَ بِالأَنْفِ
a life for a life, an eye for an eye, and a nose for a nose
Qur'an 5:45
قَصَبة الأنف
الجُيوب الأنفيّة
sinuses
رَغمَ أنفِه
in spite of him
كسر أنفه
to humiliate someone
استأنف
to recommence, to resume
قدّم استئنافاً
to appeal (a verdict)
MacToot

51
Nose أَنْف ــ أُنوف
Pride, Haughtiness

The nose is a prominent feature of many a Middle Eastern profile. Observing the rugged topography of the area, as they had ample opportunity to do, the likeness of the spur of a mountain to the nose must have prompted the Arabs to give it the very same name, الأنـف *al-'anf.* Simple directionality is another meaningful aspect of vocabulary derived from the nose. In a text, therefore, the phrase مذكـور آنِفًا *madh-kuur 'aanifan* is the equivalent of 'see above.' Proximity to the nose also played a role in the creation of vocabulary: the *nisba* adjective is used to describe the troublesome cavities behind the nose which may subject their owners to seasonal misery, الجيـوب الأنفيّـة *al-juyuub al-'anfiyya*, the sinus cavities, literally, the nasal pockets. Such miseries make speech distinctly nasal, and it is no accident that in many languages, the word for the organ itself has onomatopoeic overtones. The Arabic nose, *al-'anf*, suggests just this sort of nasal twang.

Of course, it is possible for one's nose to be physically broken, انكسـر أنفُـه *inkasara 'anfuhu*, and for someone to break it, كسـر أنفَـه *kasara 'anfahu.* But this last phrase has a metaphorical meaning as well. If one insists on rubbing someone's nose in his defeat, so to speak, that same phrase كسـر أنفـه means to utterly humiliate. Proper orientation, as we have seen elsewhere, is up.

English sometimes associates the nose with haughtiness. Snooty people are 'stuck up'; they may even 'thumb their noses' at others. Similarly, the Arabs' meditations on the nose were not confined to its physical properties or the organs adjacent to it. A sharp, disdainful nod upward in many Arab societies signals rejection, and at some point, the word أنـف also came to mean pride. Thus, doing something against another's will came to be phrased رغم أنفه *raghma 'anfihi*, literally, despite his nose. In Egyptian vernacular the simile carries over into eating habits. A finicky eater, someone exceedingly difficult to please, is said to be إنِـف *'inif*, ready to turn his nose up at the first opportunity.

The association of the nose with rejection carried over into the verbal domain, too. The Form I verb أنـف ــ يأنَـف *'anifa* means to reject something. One could disdainfully refuse to *do* something with the addition of مـن أنْ and a following verb. In English judicial parlance, if one decides to challenge a legal ruling, one appeals, asking, even pleading, for a different decision. In Arabic's corresponding اسـتأنف, asking is implied by the three-letter prefix that marks every Form X. What the haughty nose root adds to the picture is the intent to reject that judgment, a clearly more opinionated, prideful stance. An appeals court, where one might send one's lawyer to contest a decision, is محكمة الاستئناف *maHkamat al-isti'naaf.* In non-judicial contexts, this same verb اسـتأنف means to resume, to recommence after a pause, as one must do in the appeals process.

مِنْخارٌ
NOSTRIL
نَخَرَ
to snore
Snorting, Snoring نَخْر
Snoring, Snorting, snore, grunt نَخير
to be worm-eaten, decayed, full of holes نَخِرَ
أَئِذا كُنّا عِظامًا نَخِرَةً
When we have become crumbling bones? Qur'an 79:11
نَخْر rottenness, decay
MacToot

52
Nostril مِنْخار – مِنْخاران – مَناخير
Decay

Nostril is a pleasant enough sounding word in English, although its pre-twelfth-century origin is actually the very inelegant 'nose hole.' This image also comes into play in the case of the Arabic word for nostril, but the word choice is not just a visual metaphor. The ingenious منخار *minkhaar* operates on several levels simultaneously.

First, as an acquaintance with patterns teaches us, the instrument pattern مِفعال is created from فعل or a close associate, and not vice-versa. Therefore, we must look to ن – خ – ر and its closest derivatives to understand how the nose or nostril could be understood as an instrument. The answer is a simple one. The Form I verb نخـر – ينخُـر / ينخِـر *nakhara* means to snore and to snort; its *maSdar* النخيـر *an-nakhiir* is snoring, snorting, and grunting. Consider the phonetics of *nakhara* and *nakhiir*. Both are classic examples of onomatopoeia. Having arrived at a word that cleverly mimicked the distasteful sounds of snoring, all that remained was to label the nostril its instrument. In fact, Egyptian speakers use the plural مناخيـر *manakhiir* for all ordinary references to the nose, rather than the formal أنـف *'anf.*

The phonetics of the verb نخَر suggest how *sonorously* disturbing the Arabs found snoring. With the addition of a simple preposition, something graphically lurid: نخـر فـي *nakhara fii* means to burrow or bore into something, and is especially said of a worm. An alternate voweling, نخِر – ينخَر *nakhira* yields an intransitive counterpart, to be worm-eaten and decomposing, in a state of putrefaction, an English verb which conveys a vivid sense of revulsion. Old English unsqueamishly labeled the nostrils nose holes, but they must have been *visually* disconcerting to the Arabs, too, vaguely suggestive of worm-eaten offal. The adjective decayed, worm-eaten is نَخِـر *nakhir*, a word used once in the Qur'an at 79:11, in a passage describing the fearful strangeness of Judgment Day. Awakened from the dead by a blast of the trumpet, people wonder aloud at the fact that they have risen when in such a state of decay: أئِـذَا كُنَّـا عِظَامًـا نَخِـرَةً, *when we have become crumbling bones*?

MUSTACHE شارِب
شرّب = أشرب
to give a drink to,
to make drink
beverages مشروبات
شارب
have a drink with
شرِب
to drink
شَراب
a drink
MacToot

53

Mustache (1) شارِب – شارِبان – شَوارِب
Drink

Embodiment is not merely a question of specific body parts; body *processes* are also an integral part of the field. This chapter looks at the process of drinking, while the following one focusses on nominal derivatives of drinking, including the mustache. The primordially important verb شَرِب – يشرَب *shariba*, to drink, is the source of a large body of vocabulary that has been a constant over the centuries. The verb and seven of its derivatives occur in thirty-nine places in the Qur'an. Of them, this Form I verb is the most commonly used. This is also true in modern usage, although three of the root's other derivatives figure in the *FDA* as well.

Let us consider the four (principal) verbal derivatives of this root. Form II شرّب is to give someone something to drink, or even to force someone to drink. Form III شارب signifies to drink with someone, and one must not use the preposition مع with this verb, as the sense of 'with' is built right in. Form V تشرّب adds intensity to the Form I verb: to soak up, absorb, be filled or imbued with. It may be literal or figurative; a towel can soak up a spilled liquid, and a person can soak up an atmosphere. Interestingly, Form IV أشرب may be synonymous either with the causative Form II, to make someone drink, or the intensive sense of Form V, to be imbued with. In the story of the Israelites and the golden calf in 2:93 of the Qur'an, the Form IV verb is used in the passive voice with the causative meaning. وأُشْرِبوا في قُلوبِهِمُ العِجْلَ, *And they were made to imbibe (the love of) the calf (deep) into their hearts*. A fifth verb, technically considered to be from a separate quadriliteral root, ش – ر – أ - ب, is the Form IV اِشْرَأَبَّ, *ishra'abba*. It means to stretch or crane the neck in order to see something, to raise the head conceitedly. The semantics of this verb, focusing as it does on a movement of the neck, suggest the possibility of an underlying connection to drinking. Form IV quadriliteral verbs are exceedingly rare in Arabic; the very pattern makes one want to crane one's neck for a good close look.

شارِبٌ
MUSTACHE
يَخْرُجُ مِنْ بطونِها شَرابٌ مُخْتَلِفٌ أَلْوانُها
from (the bees') bellies comes a drink of diverse hues
Qur'an 16:69
شَرْبة
sip, swallow; potion; laxative
شرّب ب...
تشرّب ب...
to saturate something with
تشرّب
to soak up, absorb; to be permeated, infused with
MacToot

54
Mustache (2) شارِب – شارِبان – شَوارِب
Drink

Among the important nominal derivatives of شرب is its active participle, الشارب *ash-shaarib*, the mustache. As the word suggests, an imperfectly trimmed mustache tends to drink along with its owner. Its name, 'the drinker,' is a gentle jab at the owner of those sometimes sodden whiskers. Just as it may designate the mustache, this same word refers to the person who drinks as well. The casual imbiber has two intensive counterparts, شِرّيب *shirriib*, and شَرّاب *sharraab*; both are drunks. Note the role of the *shadda* in each of these words. It is this phonetic feature that gives the words their added intensity. In the proper sense of drinker, as opposed to mustache, the noun شارِب, also has a passive counterpart, مَشروب *mashruub*, (something) drunk. Used in the plural form, it is the common word for beverages, المشروبات.

There are plenty of other nominal derivatives of شرب, too. One even made its way into English some four centuries ago, via Persian and Turkish. This is sherbet, from the Arabic شربات, *sharbaat*, originally a cool, sweet fruit-based drink. At modern Egyptian weddings, a drink of the same name, though now sadly artificial, is *de rigeur*. The singular of this word, شَرْبة *sharba*, a drink, sip, or swallow, is distinctly unfestive, a potion or a laxative! The word used to mean honey in the Qur'an is شَراب, *sharaab*, still a common word today for any drink. A derivative of the place noun also played a role with this root. In the days before refrigeration, Egyptians stored drinking water in clay pots or jugs which they called قلل *'ulal*. These jugs promoted condensation and a slight natural cooling of the contents. To enhance this cooling property, people of means whose houses had such a feature placed القلل in the houses' most well-aired spot, المشربية *al-mashrabiyya*. This was a projecting bay window of sorts, enclosed not by walls but by ornamental wooden latticework that conveniently provided shade, a relatively cool place to sit, screened from view, and cooling breezes. Clever, rudimentary refrigeration is no longer sufficient for most modern tastes, and nowadays, as a consequence, المشربية has lost its functional architectural role, and designates just the beautifully ornamental latticework itself.

شَفَوِيّ/شَفَهِيّ/شفاهِيّ
oral
امتحانات شفهيّة
oral exams
الحروف الشفهيّة
the labials (B, F, M, W)
أشفى على
to be very close to,
to be on the verge of
شَفاً
edge, rim,
border, brink,
verge
على شفا ...
on the verge of...
مُشْفٍ على الموت
on the brink of death
شفة
شِفاه
شَفَوات
شَفائف
lips
the upper lip
الشفة العُليا
LIP
الشفة السُفلى
the lower lip
MacToot

55
Lip شِفة ـ شِفتان ـ شِفاه
Brink

The lips are the gateway to the mouth, and vocabulary derived from the lip makes use of both elements of this linkage. Considering the lips and the critical role they play in speech, the Arabs coined the phrase بنت شفة *bint shifa*. Translated literally, this charming collocation says 'daughter of a lip.' Its meaning, quite simply, is a word. The Form III verbal derivative of a lip also takes the mouth as inspiration: شافه *shaafaha* means to speak to someone face to face. This meaning is utterly devoid of the connotations of the English admonition against cheekiness: Don't give me any lip!

In Form IV, أشفى على, Arabic creates a metaphor of the lip as a gateway. This verb is derived from a related common noun شفًا *shafan* rim, edge, verge. The شفة / شفًا duo have an obvious semantic connection. In English, the figurative use of lip is confined to physical resemblance, as when we say the lip of a container, meaning its lip-like edge. However, in Arabic, الشفا has *negative* metaphoric associations. For example, one cannot say that someone is on the brink of a discovery using أشفى على. The kind of brink inspired by the lip is a perilous one, as in in أشفى على الهلاك, to be on the brink of destruction. A fall of one sort or another is anticipated, the imminence of which is suggested by the active participle in the expression مشفٍ على الموت *mushfin 'alaa al-mawt*, (teetering) on the brink of death.

The lip and its derivatives come from a rather schizophrenic root. The *taa marbuuta* is never a root letter, so in its singular form, شفة is missing its third root letter. To deduce what the missing letter is, an examination of related vocabulary ought to steer one in the right direction, but here, it leaves the searcher in a quandary. Lip has several plurals, the most common of which is شفاه, suggesting that the third root letter is 'ه,' a hypothesis backed up by the *nisba* adjective شفهيّ, *shafahiyy*, labial, oral, and the Form III verb شافه. However, there is another plural, too, شفوات *shafawaat*, which suggests that the third root letter is a 'و.' This is backed up by the *nisba* adjective شفويّ *shafawiyy* and the Form IV verb أشفى. That said, if these two roots were originally distinct, over time they have infiltrated each other's territory, and can now be more practically considered together. To be thorough, one must add that there is a third plural for lips شفائف *shafaa'if* (and in Egyptian parlance, شفايف *shafaayif*), thus suggesting a 'ف' as the hidden third root. However, most vocabulary derived from the شفف root has to do with transparency and translucency, and so this last hypothesis must be discarded.

فوّهة
mouth, opening, Vent; muzzle
MOUTH
فو - فم
أفاويه
aromatics spices
How well you have spoken!
literally, May your mouth not be closed! لا فضّ فوكَ
فاه = تفوّه
to pronounce, utter, voice, say
مفوّه
eloquent
لم يتفوّه بكلمة
He didn't utter a word
MacToot

56

Mouth (فَم – أَفْواه (فُو / فَا / فِي – أَفْواه

In! And Out!

The mouth in all its guises is a strange and fascinating body word. Using it metaphorically to describe things in nature, sometimes in terms of appearance, but more often in terms of function, the Arabs also elaborated on it etymologically.

First of all, the mouth is quite special in terms of its spelling. It has two basic forms, فـو *fuu* and فـم *fam*. The latter has taken over in modern usage for the organ itself, but the very old *fuu*, quite particular in and of itself, is the basis for all the derivatives. The first thing to notice about the word فـو is that it is declinable, varying with its function in the sentence. The nominative or subject case is فـو, and there are two others فـا : *faa* and فـي *fii*. This last one is an exact homonym of the preposition فـي, meaning in, and as Mohsen Esseesy shows in his work on prepositions, it is most probably derived from this very body part.[15] The mouth, after all, is a container of sorts, and it practically begs for things to be put into it. In(to) the mouth, فـي الفـي *fi-l-fii*, is a primordial functional association.

The Arabs were great travelers, whether by land or sea, and much travel was in fact done by night. Reliable navigation was essential, and over time, they learned how useful careful observation of the stars could be. Mapping the nighttime skies in great detail, they gave constellations many a colorful name. Western languages have preserved a rough facsimile of some of these Arabic originals, but their speakers can only appreciate these names phonetically. Their poetic content is sadly lost. Such is the case with Fomalhaut, which comes from فَـم الحـوت *fam al-Huut*, the whale's mouth. Inspired pictorial descriptions like this had pedagogic value, too. As is the case with the names of major constellations that many of us still learn as children—Orion's Belt, the Big Dipper—once the image association is made, it lasts. The Arabs found mouths not only in the sky but on earth as well. They decided, as did English speakers, that the opening of a volcano resembled a mouth, and dubbed it فوّهـة *fuwwaha*.

Words issue from the mouth, and the Arabs chose it as a functional basis for the Form I verb فـاه – يفـوه *faaha* and Form V تفـوّه, to say something, to utter a word. In doing so, they regularized its weak shape, augmenting the two-letter original with a final ه. An eloquent speaker is the Form II participle مُفـوّه *mufawwih*. However, it is not only words that issue from the mouth, but also odors. In a charming extrapolation on that image of wafting scents, Arabic offers the word أفاويـه *'afawiih*, aromatics, spices.

احتنك
to devour;
to eradicate;
to have complete control of, to lead around by the nose/mouth (as with a bridle)
PALATE
حنكيّ palatal
لَأَحْتَنِكَنَّ ذُرِّيَّتَهُ إِلَّا قَلِيلًا
Indeed I would bridle his descendants, all but a few Qur'an 17:62
سدّ الحنك
Sadd il Hanak dessert
حِناك
rope used to bridle a mount
حنك = حنّك = أحنك
to render experienced through trials;
to polish and sophisticate, to make wordly-wise
مُحنّك
worldly wise; experienced and sophisticated, shrewdly capable
حنيك
glutton; voracious
MacToot

57
Palate, Roof of the Mouth حَنَك – أَحْناك
Halter

The palate, both hard and soft, is الحنك *al-Hanak*. Letters pronounced in its immediate vicinity (ج/ش/ي) are called حروف حنكية *Huruuf Hanakiyya*, palatals. Less technically, الحنك is the roof of the mouth. Classically, it is used with humans and animals. In some *spoken* registers, it refers primarily to an animal's mouth. As with snout and muzzle—conveyed by خطم *khaTm* in Arabic—using it for people can be demeaning. One of the meanings of a classical term, حنيك *Haniik*, is voracious and gluttonous, linking it with a popular Egyptian confection, سدّ الحنك *sadd il-Hanak*. Both insinuate a reproachable connection between the palate and overindulgence. The latter is indisputably a palate pleaser, but also the final act in a meal, a trap shutter, so to speak, given its elevated sugar content.

Four verb forms are based on the ح – ن – ك root; three of them are largely synonymous. These are Form I حنك – يحنُك *Hanaka*, Form II حنّك and Form IV أحنك, to sophisticate and polish through extensive trial and experience. One might say أحنكه الدهر, *'aHnakahu ad-dahr*, time made him worldly-wise. Adjectivally, someone sophisticated and capable, might be described as محنَّك *muHannak*. Vocabulary derived from these forms exploits the sense of the nouns الحنك / الحنكة *al-Hink*, *al-Hinka.* Also pronounced *al-Hunk*, *al-Hunka*, these are the confluence of the wisdom and insight gained from worldly experience. But what links this to the mouth and palate? If one were a bon vivant, it would be tempting to tie the analogy to the sophisticated *tastes* someone with extensive experiences out in the world might be expected to acquire. However, something quite different is operative here. The ح – ن – ك root has links to the world of domesticated animals and to bridling and haltering. To understand the metaphor, a look at some old vocabulary from the world of animal husbandry is useful.

As embodiment theory demonstrates in case after case, ideation proceeds from the concrete to the abstract. One such word from the classical register is الحناك *al-Hinaak*, the rope used to bridle a mount. It is this noun that is elaborated on by the Form VIII verb احتنك. This very old verb means to have complete control of, to lead around by the mouth (or nose), as with a bridle or halter. In 17:62 of the Qur'an, it is used with an 'energetic' suffix, adding further to its already graphic power. In this verse, Satan makes a boast to God of how thoroughly he could assert his will over most human beings (Adam's offspring): لَأَحْتَنِكَنَّ ذُرِّيَّتَهُ إلّا قليلاً, *Indeed I would bridle his descendants, all but a few.*

That image is undeniably a negative one, but one must bear in mind that the Arabs were great riders and trained their mounts extensively, especially their horses. The Bedouin, expert breeders, did not geld horses and considered the males too difficult to train. Instead, they chose the mare, الفرس *al-faras*, as a war horse. Therefore *faras*, rather than *HiSaan*, a male horse, is the basis of the word فارس *faaris*, horseman or knight, and الفروسية *al-furuusiyya,* chivalry. Experienced battle horses had a rough life, but were highly prized. It seems that an analogy can be made between them and the capable people to whom time and experience has taught hard lessons, and whose resulting wisdom makes them similarly masterful. This explains the other sense of the gluttonous حنيك, mentioned above; in the context of worldly wisdom, it designates an experienced elder.

لسان
TONGUE
لسِن
to be eloquent
لسان القفل
bolt, deadbolt
ألسنة النار
tongues of fire
لسان العرب
The Tongue of the Arabs
definitive 13th century dictionary
لسّن
to sharpen something
MacToot
تلاسن
to give each other a tongue lashing
ملسون
liar
deceitful ذو لسانين

58
Tongue لِسان - أَلْسِنة
Speech

In culture after culture, Arabic included, the tongue is used as an allusion to language as a whole, and to the character of individuals' speech as well. It follows that لسان *lisaan* has a very high ranking—1,026, to be exact—in the *FDA*. The tongue's metaphoric reach is epitomized in the name of classical Arabic's most authoritative dictionary, written in the thirteenth century: *Lisaan al-'arab*, the tongue of the Arabs. The tongue and the spoken word are intimately linked because the organ is essential to the clarity of speech. One who has difficulty enunciating due to some physical impairment is said to be ثقيل اللسان *thaqiil al-lisaan*, heavy of tongue. In 28:34 of the Qur'an, Moses describes his brother as أفصح . . . لسانًا *afSaH . . . lisaanan*, more eloquent, an example of the grammatical category of *at-tamyiiz*, specification. Here, the tongue, standing in for speech, is specified. The fact that the tongue and its plural ألسنة *'alsina* appear twenty-five times in the Qur'an suggests just how important eloquence was in classical Arab culture. To be eloquent even has its own verb, the Form I لسِن– يلسَن *lasina*. From this comes the *maSdar* لَسَن *lasan*, eloquence, and the adjective لَسِن *lasin*, eloquent. Very interestingly, لسان also has an elative (comparative) form. When أفعل takes a body part as its root, it most commonly depicts a defect. In the case of the tongue, however, this is not so: أَلْسَن *'alsan* means more/the most eloquent.

The tongue can also be used for devious purposes, and ملسون *malsuun*, the passive participle of the Form I verb, means to be untruthful, said especially of one who is all talk and no action. Expressions signaling a departure from standard anatomy often suggest something undesirable or even reprehensible. One should, of course, have just one tongue. Having two is a metaphor for duplicity and double-dealing: ذو لسانين *dhuu lisaanayn*, 'two-tongued,' meaning deceitful. In parallel fashion, English offers 'to speak with a forked tongue.' Back in the verbal domain, Form VI تلاسن is the explicitly mutual 'to give each other a tongue-lashing.'

This vocabulary describes functional aspects of the tongue, speaking and deceiving, but physical *appearance* is also the basis for some vocabulary based on it. In the domestic sphere, one such shape metaphor is لسان القفل *lisaan al-qifl*, the bolt that slides into a lock. Along with the body, fire was another important ancient preoccupation. English tends simply to call them flames, but Arabic focuses on the shape, and says ألسنة نار *'alsinat naar*, tongues of fire. Arabic also has a transitive verb based on the shape of the tongue. Form II لسّن *lassana* means to sharpen something, making it long, tapered, and pointed, as a carved piece of wood or a hammered metal point. However, the addition of the preposition على allows for a return to the speech domain. English is also wary of someone with a sharp tongue, but the expression is stronger in Arabic: لسّن على جاره *lassana 'alaa jaarihi*, he spoke ill of his neighbor, he tarnished his neighbor's name.

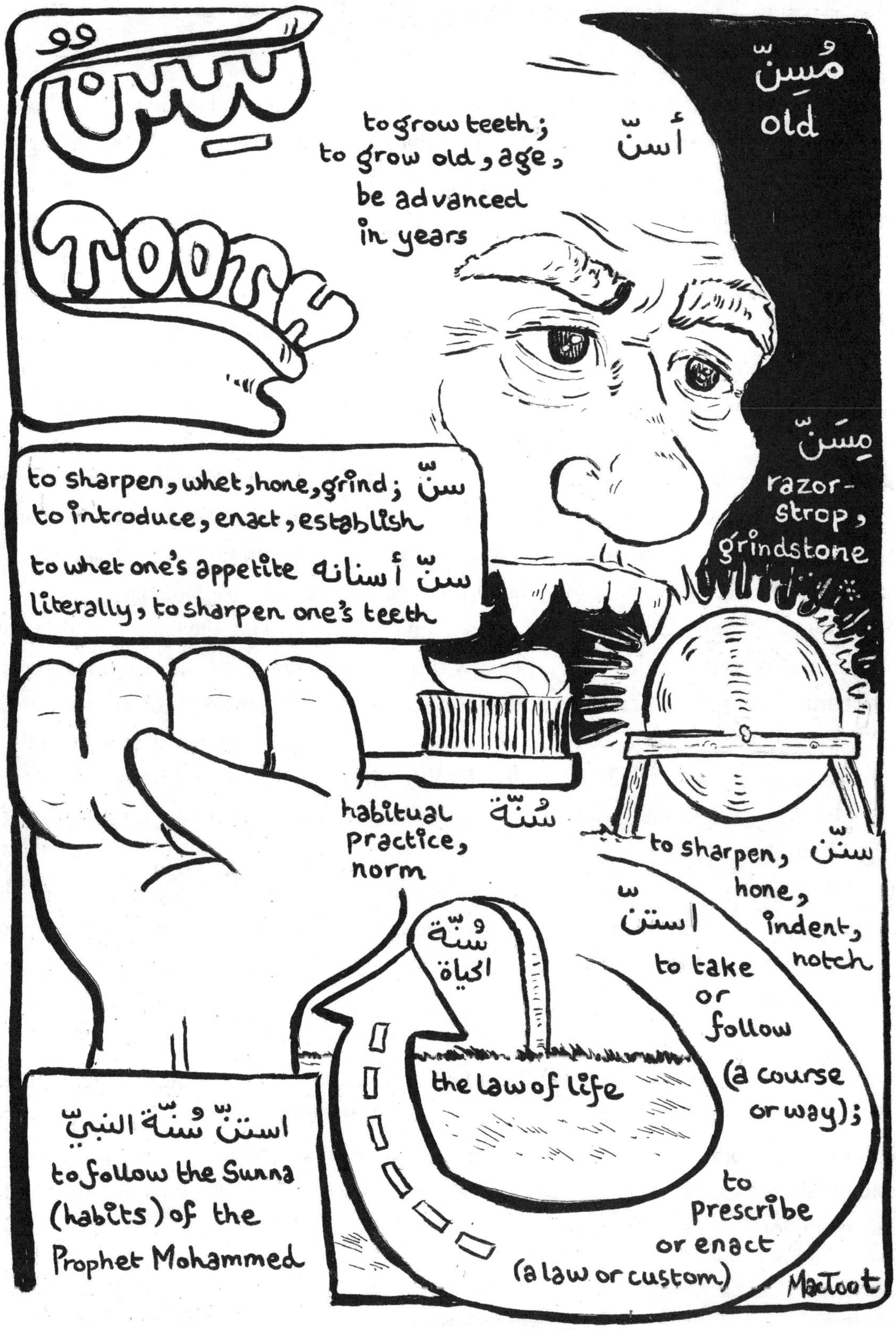
سِنّ
TOOTH
مُسِنّ
old
أسنّ
to grow teeth; to grow old, age, be advanced in years
سنّ to sharpen, whet, hone, grind; to introduce, enact, establish
سنّ أسنانه to whet one's appetite
literally, to sharpen one's teeth
مِسَنّ
razor-strop, grindstone
سُنّة
habitual practice, norm
سنّ
to sharpen, hone, indent, notch
استنّ
to take or follow (a course or way);
to prescribe or enact (a law or custom)
سُنّة الحياة
the law of life
استنّ سُنّة النبيّ
to follow the Sunna (habits) of the Prophet Mohammed
MacToot

59
Tooth سِنّ – أَسْنان
Sharpness; Age; Law

With its sharp serrations, the initial سـ of the word tooth, سِنّ *sinn*, visually suggests teeth. Even the name of the letter, *siin,* echoes the word for tooth, *sinn*. This link between the anatomical tooth and the letter 's' or 'sh' can be found in other old Semitic languages like Aramaic and Hebrew, suggesting that this letter began as a stylized pictograph of a tooth.

In the literal realm, السِنّ, as one might expect, is all about sharpness. It can refer to a variety of pointy things, like the nib of a pen, the tooth of a comb, or the tip of a nail. It also figures in an expression for the tusk of an elephant. Ivory, العاج *al-'aaj*, is loosely referred to as سِنّ الفيل *sinn al-fiil*, the elephant's tooth. The literal sense of the Form I verb سَنّ – يسُنّ *sanna* is to hone something like a knife. From this starting point, Arabic offers the figurative سَنّ أسنانه *sanna 'asnaanahu*, he sharpened his teeth, in anticipation of a hearty meal. English also links sharpening to hunger in the collocation 'to whet the appetite.' In both languages, the expression is figurative, describing the eager, perhaps greedy anticipation of a profitable or satisfying encounter, and not just a good meal. Form II سنّن has a number of meanings, including to sharpen. This can be done on a مِسَنّ *misann*, a grindstone, easily identifiable as an instrument with its signature *mi-* prefix.

Teething is the harbinger of growth in a baby, and to teethe is another of this form's meanings. The teeth grow for a while as one ages; their eventual deterioration is a typical marker of old age. Form II also means to estimate age based on the appearance of the teeth, a broadly cross-cultural concept. The English proverb 'don't look a gift horse in the mouth' is based on how much one can tell about a horse's age from its teeth. Having received a horse as a gift, it would be exceedingly bad form to inspect its teeth in an effort to determine its market value. In Arabic, Form IV أسنّ means to grow teeth, and hence to be advanced in years. An old horse, therefore, could be called حصان مسنّ *HiSaan musinn*, using that verb's active participle.

In human anatomy, the teeth are likewise associated with strength and vigor. This fact is borne out by a critical derivation of the س – ن – ن root in the cultural realm. The noun سُنّة *sunna* refers to a widely accepted norm, a habitual practice. It is famous in the collocation سُنّة الحياة *sunnat al-Hayaat*, loosely, the law of life, the way things are. This noun is at the root of an important juridical term. In addition to its literal sense of sharpening something, Form I سَنّ can mean to introduce or enact a law. In English, one may call regulations 'toothless' when they cannot be enforced. Arabic's word for toothless, أدرد *'adrad*, is from a completely different root.

Using the س – ن – ن root to depict weakness would be counterintuitive. Instead, the verb سَنّ embodies a veiled warning: سنّوا قانونا يحظر الازدراء بالأديان *sannuu qanuunan yaHZur al-izdiraa' bi-l-'adyaan*, they enacted a law forbidding disparagement of religion(s). This is a directive with teeth! Form VIII استنّ has this same legalistic meaning, and shows the fundamental connection between law and accepted good practice. One of the primary doctrinal divisions of Islam is, of course, السُّنّة *al-sunna*, the Sunna, commonly contrasted with الشّيعة *ash-shii'a*. This designation developed from the desire of early Muslims to emulate the typical practices of the Prophet, سُنّة الرسول *sunnat ar-rasuul*. A follower of this doctrine is therefore described as سُنّيّ *sunniyy*, a Sunni.

حَلْقٌ
THROAT
حلّق ... to hover ... fly over, to make round, ring shaped ... to encircle
على surround
تحلّق
to form a circle, gather in a circle, sit in a circle
حلّاق
barber
حلق
to shave
حليق
clean-shaven
صابون الحلاقة
shaving cream
إذا بلغت الحُلْقومَ
when it reaches his throat
Qur'an 56:83
حَلَق
Earrings
حلقيّ
pharyngeal, guttural
حَلقة
link; study circle
MacTout

60
Throat; Larynx حَلْق – حُلوق / أَحْلاق (حُلْقوم – حَلاقيم)
Circle

Among Arabic's rich vocabulary for the throat area are الحلق *al-Halq* and الزور *az-zawr* (see the next chapter). The more common of the two is الحلق. It has three verbal derivations and quite a few nominal offspring. Anything related to the throat, especially phonetic sounds called pharyngeal or guttural, can be described by the *nisba* adjective, حلقيّ *Halqiyy*. Arabic also has a word specifically for the larynx, الحنجرة *al-Hanjara*, commonly used when referring to a physician's specialty, along with the ear and nose, الأنف والأذن والحنجرة *al-'anf wa-l-'udhun wa-l-Hanjara*. In Arabic, the pharynx is called البلعوم *al-bal'uum*, a word derived from the verb بلع *bala'a*, to swallow, helpfully identifying it as the tube leading to the stomach. Consequently, speaking of a sore throat will entail reference to either الحلق or الزور or الحنجرة, but *not* to البلعوم. The ح – ل – ق root also has a rather rare relative, الحُلقوم *al-Hulquum*, throat, gullet, windpipe, a word found in 56:83 of the Qur'an: إذَا بَلَغَت الْحُلْقُومَ, *when it (the soul of someone dying) reaches the throat.*

To better understand الحلق, imagine the tonsure-style haircut typical of medieval monks. The perfect circle of the shaved scalp with its fringe of hair mimics the circular shape of the throat, viewed from the inside. To shave, whether head or face, is expressed by the Form I verb حلق – يحلِق *Halaqa*. The professional who performs the operation of shaving, الحِلاقة *al-Hilaaqa*, is a barber, حَلاّق *Hallaaq*. This is the pattern فعّال, one of Arabic's workhorse patterns for occupations. Shaving 'cream' in Arabic is 'soap,' صابون الحلاقة *Sabuun al-Hilaaqa*, and the adjective حليق *Haliiq*, clean-shaven, follows the hyper-common adjective pattern فعيل.

Jewelry makes good use of this root, not for rings, but rather for another body ornament, a pair of earrings, حَلَق *Halaq*. Earrings come in many shapes, but as their English name also implies, the traditional one is circular. Multiple pairs of earrings are the quite broken plural حُلقان *Hulqaan*. One of a single pair, however, can *only* be expressed by the *iDaafa* phrase فردة حلق *fardat Halaq*. The addition of a *taa marbuuta* creates another circular item, حَلَقة *Halaqa*, a link in a chain. By metaphorical extension, the physical link in a chain or a necklace became the traditional word for a circle of students gathered before a teacher or a circle of devotees in a Sufi dhikr ceremony. In modern academia, حلقة can mean a research circle. The chain metaphor has also extended to the world of broadcasting, where it means one episode in a radio or television serial. Given the power of modern mass media, حلقة is extraordinarily common, ranking 1,213 in the *FDA*, even more common than the word for air الهواء *al-hawaa'*.

In the verbal domain, Form II حلّق means to hover, an intensive take on the idea of a circle. Careful observation of hawks and other birds circling round and round high overhead must have prompted this. The expression من حالِق *min Haaliq*, from above, suggests the same. To form a circle, the reflexive of Form II, is Form V تحلّق.

THROAT
زَوْر
UPPER CHEST
أزْوَر slanting, crooked, oblique; cross-eyed
زار to visit, call on; to afflict
زوّر to forge, falsify, counterfeit
زُور lie, falsehood; force
تزاور to exchange visits
التزوير في أوراق رسمية forging official documents
شهادة زُور false testimony
بالزُّور by force, forcibly
ازْوَرّ عن to turn aside from; to be averse to
ازْوَرّ به عن ... to alienate someone from someone else
ازْوِرار aversion

61
Throat; Upper Chest زور – أَزْوار
Slanted

Sources describe الـزور *az-zawr* anatomically as the meeting point of the bones of the chest. Viewed in profile, the upper part of a person's chest where it meets the throat is slanted, oblique. This visual take on the region is the key to the root's metaphoric coherence. In normal usage, though, الـزور is a simple reference to the throat, viewed from the inside, like الحلـق *al-Halq* (see previous chapter).

Metaphorically speaking, though, oblique is not straight, and not straight as an orientation suggests shady business. A minimal internal vowel change yields الـزور *az-zuur*, falsehood. This word is the crucial half of the judicial collocation شهادة زور *shahaadat zuur*, perjury. The same word can mean force, in a negative sense, as in to be compelled to do something بالـزور *biz-zuur*, by force. Introducing two short internal vowels yields a new word, زَوَر *zawar*. When describing the gaze, زَوَر means a squint. Returning to the gaze, زَوَر can be modified to fit the أفعل elative pattern. Like أعـور *'a'war*, one-eyed, أزْوَر *'azwar* is a bodily defect or anomaly, meaning slightly cross-eyed, as if peering down one's nose, trying to see one's own upper chest. In other contexts, زَوَر means a slant, or crookedness, and as in English, crookedness in interpersonal dealings is malicious. In some instances, it may be translated as perfidy.

The Form I verb زار – يـزور *zaara* and its exceedingly common *maSdar* الزيـارة, which ranks 490 in the *FDA*, mean to visit. Visiting can be a back and forth social interchange, so specified in Form VI تـزاور. We may also explicitly long for someone's visit, the Form X اسـتزار, and yet visiting seems like a very strange departure from the core meaning of the root. However, if something *unfortunate* should metaphorically visit us, the verb loses that harmless quality and becomes to afflict, with all its ominous associations.

A few weak roots like ز – و – ر have unusual voweling, and زوِر - يَزْوَر *zawira – yazwar*, to slant or become crooked, is one of them. This verb is used of deformities of the chest, when one side becomes higher than the other. Egyptian colloquial gives another sense to its equivalent زِوِر - يِزْوَر *ziwir – yizwar* to choke on food, the result of an improperly functioning throat. At best, eating alone is viewed as regrettable, at worst as stingy and anti-social. The Egyptian proverb says اللـي يـاكل لوحـده يـزور *illi yaakul liwaHdu yizwar*, he who eats alone chokes. Form II takes the noun الـزور, falsehood, and turns it into a verb, زوّر, to falsify, to forge, whether a signature or money. Forgery is the *maSdar* التزويـر *at-tazwiir*; a forger is مُزوِّر *muzawwir*. With a simple vowel change from *kasra* to *fatHa*, that active participle, like all its derived counterparts, becomes passive, مـزوَّر *muzawwar*, forged.

This root also has a Form IX, the least common of the ten principal forms of a root. This is ازورّ, to turn aside from. Deviation from normal orientation is the semantic core of this verb. Typically used with the preposition عـن, which enhances the sense of negativity, the phrase can mean to dissociate oneself from, or be averse to someone or something. With a second prepositional object, ازورّ به عن *izwarra bihi 'an*, the sense becomes causative, to make someone averse to or alienate someone from someone else.

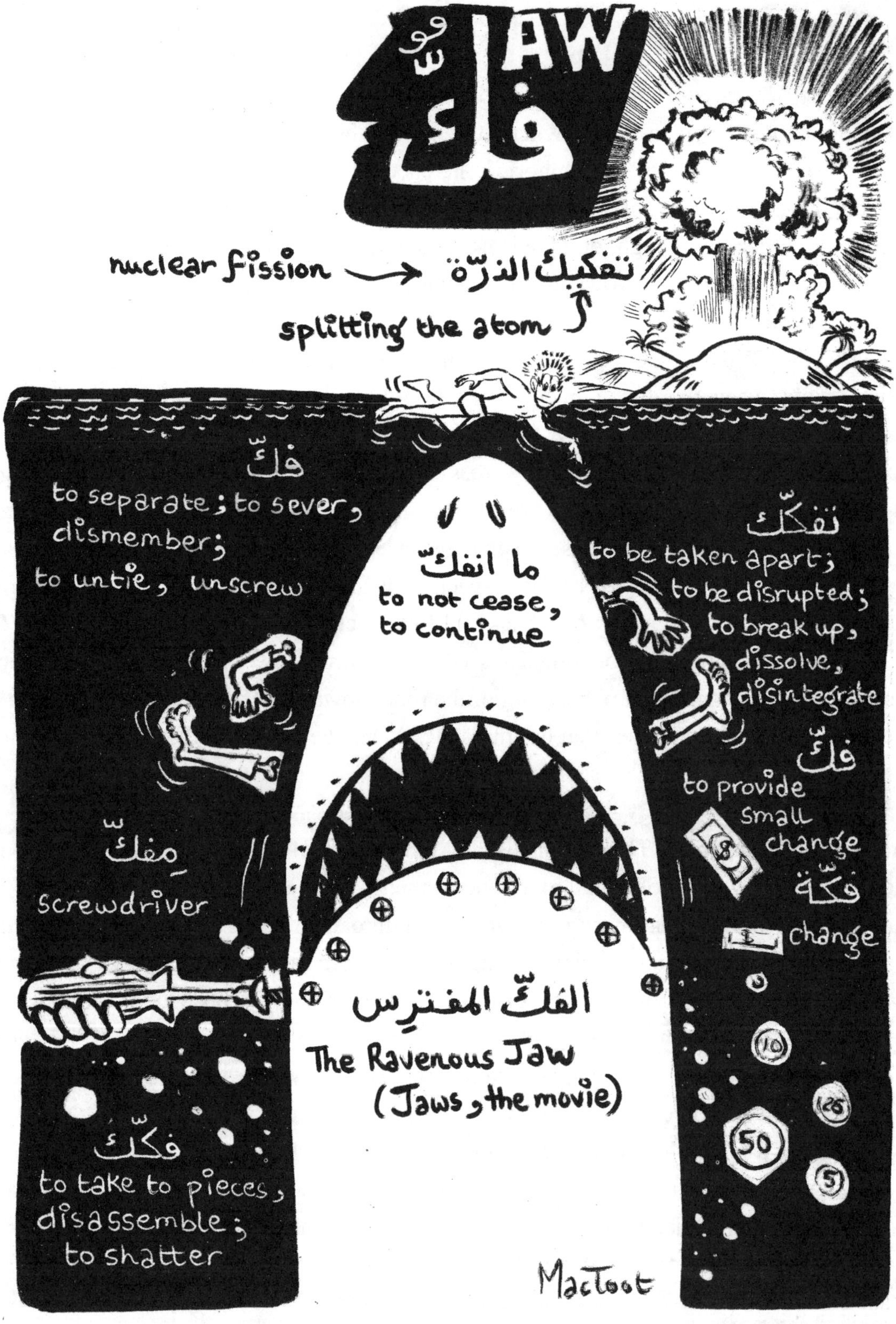
JAW
فكّ
nuclear fission → تفكيك الذرّة
splitting the atom
فكّ
to separate; to sever, dismember; to untie, unscrew
ما انفكّ
to not cease, to continue
تفكّك
to be taken apart; to be disrupted; to break up, dissolve, disintegrate
فكّ
to provide small change
فكّة
change
مِفكّ
screwdriver
الفكّ المفترِس
The Ravenous Jaw (Jaws, the movie)
فكّك
to take to pieces, disassemble; to shatter
MacToot

62
Jaw فَكّ – فُكوك
Dismemberment

Relative to its weight, the jaw muscle is the strongest muscle in the human body, and is capable of exerting about 90 kilos of pressure on the molars! By 1748, English speakers were already using the verb "to jaw" as a succinct metaphor for long-winded or abusive talk. The Arabs, however, focused on the power of الفكّ *al-fakk* and the damage it allows the teeth to inflict, creating a family of vocabulary that elucidates the many ways in which dismemberment can occur.

The noun most closely resembling the word for jaw itself is فكّة *fakka*, change, whether coins or bills, for a larger sum of money. As a verb, Form I فكّ – يفُكّ *fakka* can thus mean to provide change, breaking a larger sum into smaller component parts. In a broader sense, it means to take something apart, disassemble or undo it. One might, for example, take a gadget apart or undo the buttons of a shirt. A common tool used to accomplish physical disassembly is مِفكّ *mifakk*, a screwdriver, of the instrument pattern مِفعل. Driving a screw into something suggests assemblage, even coupling, but the gist of the Arabic word, because it is based on the jaw, is just the opposite. The Form I verb also has the more abstract, metaphoric sense of to relieve. This meaning has amazingly broad applications, from—in the informal register—relieving the pressure of a full bladder, to nullifying the effects of a magic spell.

Like Form I, the Form II verb فكّك is transitive, and conveys an intensive permutation of Form I: to shatter, to take to pieces. This verb's *maSdar* is used in the term تفكيك الذرّة *tafkiik adh-dharra*, splitting the atom, or nuclear fission. Its Form V counterpart تفكّك is intransitive and reflexive, to disintegrate, dissolve, come apart. This disintegration can be a physical or a figurative process, as in تفكّك الأسرة *tafakkuk al-'usra*, the fragmentation of the family. Although that is a well-known collocation, the only two items from the ف – ك – ك root to figure in the *FDA* are the Form I and II *maSaadir*, فكّ *fakk* and تفكيك *tafkiik*, untying, and splitting / taking apart, respectively.

Form VII انفكّ is compliant with Form I, to be loosened, unfastened, detached. By compliant, grammarians mean that since Form I *fakka* means to disassemble or undo something, the subject of Form VII complies with that action, becoming loosened or detached. With the addition of the preposition من *min*, from, the Form VII verb can mean to be or become separate, from, to disengage oneself from. Form VII has another important phrasal use, too. The classical duo ما انفكّ *maa infakka* means not to cease, to continue. It is one of the 'sisters of كان,' a group of verbs with specific grammatical effects on other elements of the sentence. The key to this change in meaning is the initial negative ما, an element found in some of the other sisters of كان, like ما زال *ma zaala*. Here, it specifies that there is no separation from whatever situation or action is being designated.

Finally, completing the gallery of verbs derived from this root is Form VIII افتكّ, which has both concrete and figurative applications. Like Form I, it can mean to take something apart, but it also means to free (a prisoner), or to redeem (a pledge, from a pawnbroker), further exploiting the underlying idea of disentangling things.

BEARD
لحا = لحى
to insult, abuse, revile
أطلق لحيته to grow one's beard
التحى to grow a beard
ألحى long-bearded
JAWBONE(S)
لَحْي (لَحْيان)
تلاحى
to call each other names, heap abuse on each other
لا تأخُذْ بِلِحْيَتي
Do not insult me
Lit. Do not grab my beard
Qur'an 20:94
MacToot

63
Jawbone لَحْي – لَحيان – لُحي
Beard لِحْية – لِحًى / لُحًى
Insult

Both the jaw and the beard have verbal incarnations in English, and though the second is quite uncommon, each has negative associations. To jaw, as mentioned in the previous chapter, is to engage in long-winded and perhaps abusive talk, while to beard someone is to confront or oppose him with effrontery. In Arabic, these two weak roots ل – ح – و / ل – ح – ي, produce three verbs. Two of them, Form I and Form VI, like their English counterparts, suggest a link between verbal invective and a jaw thrust forward in an aggressive posture. Although لَحْي *laHy*, jaw, is not a common word, logic and morphology both suggest that it is the source of لحية *liHy*a, beard. Logically, beards are specific to jaws, and while jaws are universal, beards are not. Morphology backs this assumption up, because لحي is the shorter of the two, and thus the more likely source.

Beards are among the most visible tokens of masculinity, and in many cultures they have been a fashion concomitant of manliness and maturity. In the famous classical expression that appears in the Qur'an at 20:94, لا تأخذ بلحيتي, *Do not insult me (by grabbing my beard),* a tug on the beard is identified as a grievous affront to one's dignity. Arabic has other verbs meaning to insult that are not based on the body, including أهان *'ahaana* and سبّ *sabba*. This Form I verb, however, has two distinct spellings, لحا – يلحو and لحى – يلحى. The past tense verbs are pronounced identically *(laHaa)*, but their present tenses diverge (*yalHuu* versus *yalHaa*). In the nominal domain, the word for insult and invective is لَحْو *laHw*. Putting the possibilities of mutuality to excellent use, the Form VI verb تلاحى succinctly expresses an action that requires five or six words in English: to call each other names, to heap abuse on one another.

The other derivatives of jaw and beard have to do with appearance. Form VIII التحى is to grow a beard. It is interesting to note that one very small but particular semantic domain of Form VIII is donning clothes. Examples include to get dressed (رِداء) ارتدى, to put on a turban (عِمّة) اعتمّ, put on a belt (حِزام) احتزم, and to put on shoes (نَعل) انتعل. This suggests that beards were seen as another element of manly attire. The active participle of التحى is ملتح /الملتحي *multaHi*, the very common descriptor 'bearded.' The less common elative adjective ألحى *'alHaa* means having a long beard.

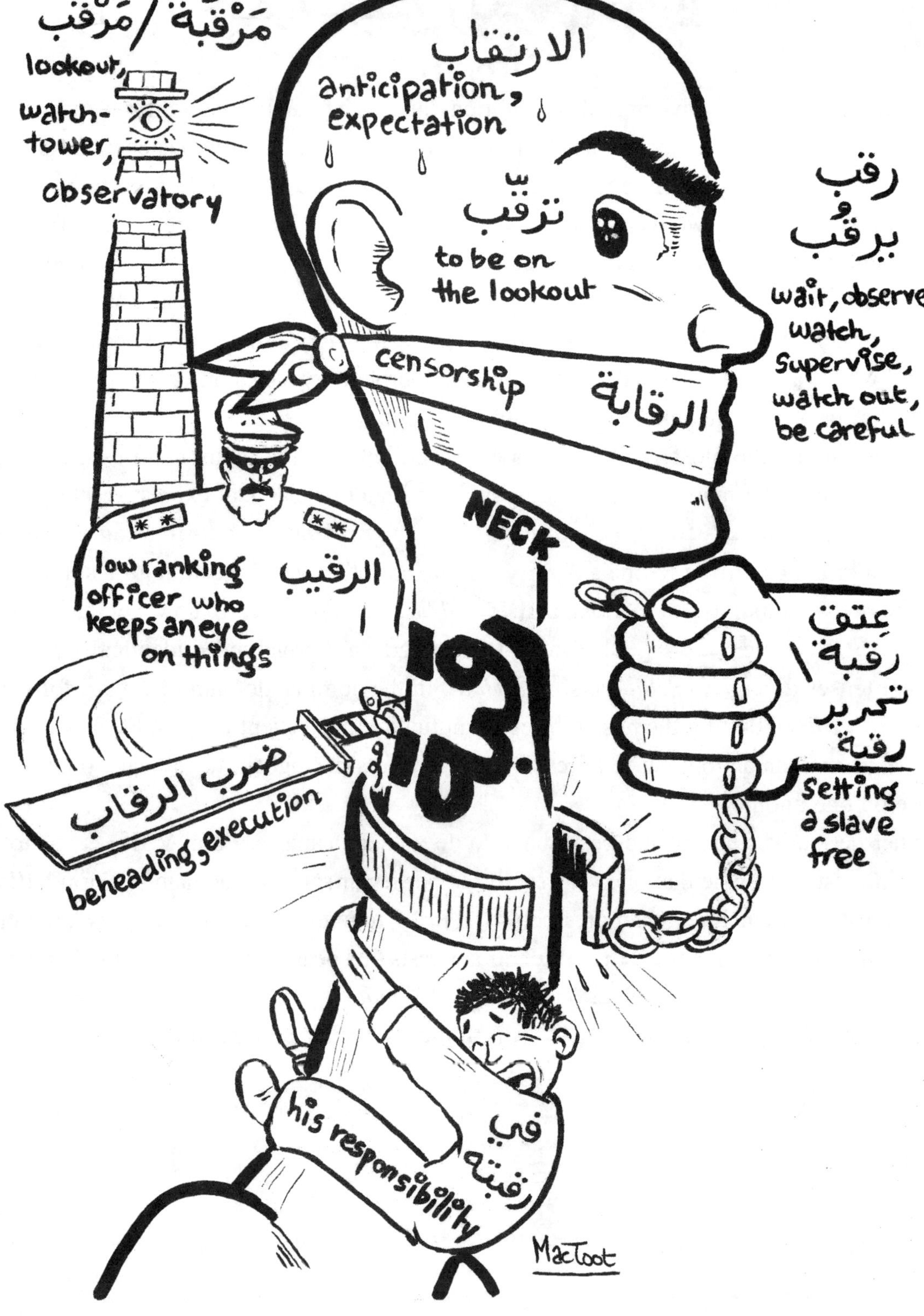
مَرْقَبة / مَرْقَب
lookout, watch-tower, observatory
الارتقاب
anticipation, expectation
ترقّب
to be on the lookout
رقب و يرقب
wait, observe, watch, supervise, watch out, be careful
censorship
الرقابة
NECK
رقبة
الرقيب
low ranking officer who keeps an eye on things
عتق رقبة / تحرير رقبة
setting a slave free
ضرب الرقاب
beheading, execution
في رقبته
his responsibility
MacToot

64
Neck رَقَبة – رِقاب
Watchful Waiting

In its incarnation as الرقبة *ar-raqaba*, the neck is the limb that allows for careful tracking of the environs. Meticulous watching necessarily entails waiting, and derivatives of الرقبة often suggest both. As a consequence, much of this vocabulary has connections to the security and surveillance domains. The Form I verb رقب – يرقب *raqaba* means to wait, as well as to observe or supervise. It may also mean to watch out, be careful. From it comes الرقابة *ar-raqaaba*, censorship. The noun الرقبة and six of its derivatives figure in the *FDA*. Of them all, censorship is the most common! Military terminology includes الرقيب *ar-raqiib*, a low-ranking officer whose original job description must have included keeping a close eye on things. The word رقيب is also Qur'anic. In that context, it is not a military designation, but rather a close observer, a keeper. The ر – ق – ب root also generates two place patterns on the same theme, مَرْقَب *marqab* and مَرْقَبة *marqaba*, lookout, watchtower.

Both Form I رقب and Form III راقب mean to watch or observe, but Form III suggests a personal object: to keep a watchful eye on someone. Introducing Allah as the object produces the collocation راقب الله فيه *raaqaba Allaaha fiihi*, to do right by someone for fear of God. This moral injunction is a reminder that one's selfish inclinations may have a negative impact on others. God—a synecdoche for God's laws, here—should therefore be kept carefully in mind for guidance. Unlike the 'Golden Rule,' with its implicit expectations of reciprocity, this admonition urges one to be scrupulous, never losing sight of an ultimate reckoning.

Form V ترقّب and Form VIII ارتقب are quite similar. Form V often suggests added attention or effort to the sense of a Form I verb, and it may thus be translated 'to be on the lookout.' Like Form VIII, it can also mean to expect, anticipate, eagerly await. It follows that the *maSaadir* of الترقُّب *at-taraqqub* and الارتقاب *al-irtiqaab* are largely synonymous: anticipation, expectation.

This neck also has several nominal metaphoric uses. One is the issue of responsibility. Something worn around the neck or tied to it is impossible to ignore. Hence, في رقبته *fii raqabatihi*, common in written and spoken registers, means to be one's responsibility. In classical usage, the word رقبة may be a legal reference to a person, and especially to a slave, and it is used in this way the Qur'an (for example, 58:3). The expression 'a hundred head of cattle' reduces cattle to their heads. Monetary value is all that is at stake. Similarly, calling people 'necks' is dehumanizing and degrading, identifying them as possessions, no more than assets. The term for setting a slave free was تحرير رقبة *taHriir raqaba* or عِتق رقبة *'itq raqaba*, freeing a neck, perhaps a literal reference to removing the physical chain. But an enemy of the state could also be referred to as رقبة, with its plural رقاب *riqaab*. In medieval times, when the weapon of choice was the sword, a term for execution, which might well entail beheading, was ضرب الرقاب *Darb ar-riqaab*, literally striking the necks. Off with their heads!

griffin العنقاء
اعتنق
to embrace a doctrine
عنّق
to nab someone physically
NECK
تعانق
to embrace each other
to embrace عانق
عنق الرحم
cervix
MacToot

65

Neck عُنُق – أَعْناق

Embrace

A nimble neck is important for ease of surveillance, but necks can also be metaphors for affectionate proximity. When this is the case, derivatives of العنق *al-'unuq* come into play. This version of the neck has produced four verbal derivatives, as well as some famous collocations. In the Qur'an, however, العنق is markedly less common than الرقبة *ar-raqaba*. None of its verbal derivatives appear therein, and as a noun, the singular is used just twice, and the plural, seven times. By contrast, الرقبة and its derivatives turn up twenty-four times. In modern usage, though, العنق is slightly more frequent than الرقبة, with *FDA* rankings of 3,122 and 3,859 respectively.

As is typically the case in Form III verbs, عانق refers to action on a recipient: to hug someone. The English verb 'to neck' refers to a sexually charged embrace, but in Arabic, the image is simply one of an affectionate clinch. Explicit affectionate reciprocity is conveyed by the Form VI تعانق. Form VIII transfers this embrace to the abstract domain; اعتنق is the enthusiastic embrace of a doctrine, or even conversion to a religion. Affection, however, is not associated with the Form II verb عنّق at all. Instead, this verb paints a picture of a very particular use to which the neck may be put. To convey nabbing someone, English uses a clothing reference: 'to collar.' Instead, Arabic suggests the best way to apprehend a miscreant is with a firm grip on the bare neck.

In nominal uses, two famous expressions come to mind. One is the technical medical term, عنق الرحم *'unuq ar-raHim*, 'the neck of the uterus,' the cervix. The other is the literal and figurative عنق الزجاجة, the neck of a bottle and a bottleneck. The latter sense plays on the shape of a bottle's neck to convey a similarly long, narrow, and difficult-to-navigate passage.

Much less common is the word for the griffin, العنقاء *al-'anqaa'*, a mythological creature, part bird, part lion, that figures in the art of many old cultures. A bronze griffin head dating from the seventh century BC is part of Greece's Olympia museum collection, and even older images of this hybrid creature appear in neighboring cultures' art, from Susa in Iran, to pharaonic Egypt, to Knossos in Crete. The statue of a griffin probably made in eleventh-century Andalusian Spain was later nabbed in a raid. It ended up decorating the tower of the Pisa Cathedral for some six hundred years, until removed in the mid-nineteenth century. In choosing a good name for the griffin, the Arabs took its signature sinuous neck as inspiration.

THROAT / NECK
خُناق / مُخَنَّق
اختنق
to die of strangulation, choke to death; to be tight, constricted (of the throat); to be suppressed
مختنق بِ
crammed, chock full of
مخنوق
strangled, stifled
خُناق
suffocation; angina
خِناق
strangling cord
خنق
to choke someone; to strangle someone; to cut, check, suppress
انخنق
to be strangled
خانق
to quarrel with someone, to have a fight with someone
تخانق
to quarrel, be at each others' throats
الخانوق
quinsy, diphtheria
MacToot

66

Throat, (Lower front of the) Neck

خِناق / مَخنَق – مَخانِق

Strangling, Suffocating

As we have seen, Arabic has a well-elaborated vocabulary for the throat and neck, and the best way to appreciate its subtleties is to follow the metaphoric associations of the derivatives of each element. The throat's circular shape is imaginatively exploited in variations on الحلق *al-Halq*, while the sloping orientation of الـزور *az-zawr* suggests the slippery slope of dishonesty. The خ – ن – ق root has much in common with النحـر *an-naHr* (see next chapter), and it shares a tactical take on this part of the body. While النحـر has applications to both people and animals, الخنـاق *al-khinaaq* focuses on humans. In addition to being a name for the throat and lower neck, seen from the front, الخنـاق is a murder weapon, a cord devised specifically for strangling! As a comparative look reveals, the Arabs portrayed المخنـق *al-makhnaq* as the ideal locus for stifling the breath, and المنحـر *al-manHar* as that for slitting the throat.

Feelings of suffocation can't be ignored, and painful medical emergencies that involve them rely on this root. Angina, marked by a suffocating pain, is called الخنـاق *al-khunaaq* or الخَنـوق *al-khanuuq*, and diphtheria, an inflammatory disease named for the leathery membrane that often forms in the throat, as well as quinsy, a bacterial disease producing an abscess on the tonsils, can be called الخنـاق *al-khunaaq* or, with its two long vowels, the even more dramatic الخانـوق *al-khaanuuq*.

Five verbs are based on this root. Form I خنـق – يخنُـق *khanaqa* means to choke or strangle someone. By figurative extension, it means to cut, check, or suppress something, as if choking it off. The passive participle مخنـوق *makhnuuq* means literally unable to breathe, or figuratively, to feel stifled, very distressed. In the expression مـات مخنوقـا *maata makhnuuqan*, murderous intent is not the necessary cause of death by suffocation; one may also accidentally die from asphyxiation. To squabble with is conveyed by the Form III verb خانـق, to engage someone in a خِناقـة *khinaaqa*, a quarrel. If the quarrel is expressly mutual, Form VI تخانـق is used. Form VII انخنـق is the pseudo-passive, to be strangled. Finally, Form VIII اختنق is to die by strangulation, to choke to death. In this case, no foul play is implied; the focus is rather on the manner of death. As is the case in the Form I verb, the figurative sense of being suppressed may also apply here. The active participle مختنِـق *mukhtaniq* may mean choking, or chock full of, crammed with, so full that there seems to be no air left.

انتحر to commit suicide
الانتحار suicide
نحر
to slaughter (an animal by slitting the throat)
نَحْرٌ
مَنْحَرٌ
THROAT
NECK
UPPER CHEST
نِحر / نحرير
Skillful
تناحر
to slaughter each other, to hack each other to pieces
MacToot

67

نَحْر / مَنْحَر – نُحور / مَناحِر

Throat, (Lower front of the) Neck

Slaughter

The ن – ح – ر root, like its semantic cousin خ – ن – ق, offers a very particular meditation on the strategic importance of the *outer* throat and the neck, as seen from the *fore*. The anatomical النحر *an-naHr* and المنحر *al-manHar* are the core of a small family of words with technical religious meanings and combative associations. The key to understanding them is the Form I transitive verb, نحر - ينحَر *naHara*, to properly butcher an animal, and its *maSdar*, النحر *an-naHr*. Doctrinally speaking, this can only be properly done by cutting an animal's throat, hence the neck's synonym المنحر *al-manHar*, an explicit noun of place. By morphologically linking slaughter to the throat and neck, the Arabs cleverly identified this area of the body as a site of particular physical vulnerability. Observant Muslims everywhere who have the financial means to do so commemorate the Prophet Abraham's slaughter of a ram or a sheep instead of his son by sacrificing an animal on the tenth day of the month of Dhu l-Hijja. This is the culminating element of Hajj, the pilgrimage to Mecca, and the day is called يوم النحر, *yawm an-naHr*. Although the nouns النحر and المنحر are not used in the Qur'an, the imperative does occur once, in 108:2.

The ن – ح – ر and خ – ن – ق roots have brutal overtones, but in fact English and French (no doubt among many other languages) also link the throat to physical attack. To *throttle* someone means to choke, or to kill by choking, and is derived directly from the Middle English word for throat. French comes even closer to the Arabic by linking the throat 'la gorge,' directly to the verb 'égorger,' to slit the throat. 'To be at each other's throats' is another English metaphor for being involved in aggressive conflict. This expression has a near equivalent in Arabic's Form VI تناحر. Conceding that slaughter is not always confined to the world of the butcher, this one word embodies the mutuality of a ferocious conflict, akin to the violent English expression to hack each other to pieces. The pivotal importance of the throat and its vulnerability in physical combat is what animates the Arabic—and French—verbs, unlike the more general English phrase. Form VIII انتحر completes the verbal derivatives of this version of the throat. Generally speaking, Form VIII can be difficult to pin down semantically, but occasionally, as is the case here, it offers a reflexive take on Form I. Rather than slit the throat of an animal, the perpetrator—at least metaphorically—slits his own, committing suicide by any means. In a comment on contemporary trends, the only word from the ن – ح – ر root to figure in the *FDA* is انتحر, where it ranks a distressingly high 3,865.

In modern urban life, at least in the developed world, slaughterhouses are at a careful physical and psychic remove from the consumer. Slaughtering is not only distasteful, but without industrial backup, slaughtering a sizeable animal is also no easy feat and requires considerable expertise. Two adjectives meaning skillful are thus directly linked to the practice. By analogy, anyone proficient in accomplishing a challenging task may be described as نِحر *niHr*, or its very unusual intensive form نِحرير *niHriir*, skilled and adept.

كتف
SHOULDER
أكتف
broad shouldered
تكتّف = استكتف
to fold one's arms across the chest
تكاتف
to join forces, act in solidarity
to stand shoulder to shoulder
كتاف
shackles, handcuffs
كتف / كتّف
to straitjacket, bind the hands
tie up
يَعلمُ مِن أين تُؤكل الكتف
He knows how to make his way in life;
He always knows just what to do
MacToot

68
Shoulder كَتِف – كَتِفان – أَكْتاف
Solidarity, Immobility

The noun كتف *katif* is the most common word for the anatomical shoulder, ranking 3,278 in the *FDA*. Arabic's two other nouns for the shoulder are less common: عاتق *'aatiq* ranks 4,897, and منكب *mankib* does not figure in the top 5,000. This shoulder, الكتف, is the basis for five verbs and a small family of other vocabulary. Neither it nor any of its derivatives is mentioned in the Qur'an.

Rather than considering the shoulder in terms of the weight it can bear, as English tends to do, the ك – ت – ف root elaborates on the shoulder region's capacity for solidarity, stability, and immobility. The intransitive Form V تكتّف and Form X استكتف both indicate the familiar gesture of folding one's arms across one's chest. Form I كتف – يكتِف *katafa* and Form II كتّف, however, are both transitive, and denominative, as well. The noun كتاف *kitaaf* is one of Arabic's word for shackles or handcuffs, and Form I is thus to shackle someone, forcing him to adopt a posture that immobilizes the shoulders. Form II is transitive and causative, and depicts the act of tying or pinning someone's arms behind the back. It can also mean to straitjacket someone. In contrast, Form VI, تكاتف offers a very positive depiction of this part of the anatomy. From the literal act of standing shoulder to shoulder with others, it depicts the metaphoric act of standing in solidarity, from that same image of closing ranks. This root has one more positive take on the shoulders, the أفعل adjective أكتف *'aktaf*, broad-shouldered. Here, the description is not of a defect but rather of something unusual and noteworthy in the body.

The shoulder also occurs in two proverbial usages that need unpacking. We find ما هكذا تؤكل الكتف *maa haakadhaa tu'kal al-katif*, literally, that is not how the shoulder is eaten, and يعلم من أين تؤكل الكتف *ya'lamu min 'ayna tu'kal al-katif*, he knows where (to start) eating the shoulder from. Both expressions use the passive voice تؤكل, to be eaten, and employ a concrete activity from daily life as a metaphor for a broad range of challenging situations. The shoulder, like most body parts that comes in pairs, is feminine, and so the verb is conjugated with an initial تـ. The image depicts eating the meat from a shoulder cut of lamb, presumably a challenging process that requires some experience and a degree of dexterity. Being stymied by the process, as in the first expression, suggests a lack of ability at rising to other more serious challenges. Knowing how to proceed, on the other hand, suggests an ability to deal with other tricky tasks.

مَنْكِبٌ SHOULDER
نكبت الريح
the wind shifted
Ill-fated, منكوب stricken
catastrophe, نكبة disaster
to make unhappy, distress نكب
تنكّب على to lean on
to swerve, veer off نكب عن
to deviate from, swerve تنكّب عن
نكّب to divert, deflect
تنكّب to shoulder something (a bow, etc), to avoid, shun, give someone the cold shoulder
MacToot

69
Shoulder, (Upper) Flank مَنكِب – مَنْكِبان – مَناكِب
Shift, Turn away

The shoulders are a prominent feature of the body, and Arabic chose to endow the shoulder region with more than one word. In this case, المنكب *al-mankib* is somewhat more specific than its English counterpart. Though often translated simply as shoulder, it is said to be located just below العاتق and therefore may include the upper flank and upper lateral back. Arabic offers the collocation عريض المنكبين *'ariiD al-mankabayni*, to be broad-shouldered or have a broad upper back, as a mark of attractive strength. In addition to its anatomical sense, المنكب can also be used topographically to mean upland or highland. It is easy to imagine a resemblance between sloping ground and a shoulder or upper flank. In 67:15 of the Qur'an, the plural of the word is used to describe the earth, in a verse that suggests appealing breadth and height:هُوَ الّذي جَعَلَ لَكُمُ الأَرْضَ ذَلولا فَامْشوا فِي مَناكِبِه, *It is He who has made the earth navigable for you, so travel its regions.*

Human anatomy makes shouldering a physical burden a familiar sight; from there, shouldering a responsibility is a short metaphoric step. Arabic uses this root, in the Form V verb تنكّب to convey this. That said, the choice of the ن – ك – ب root to express the shoulder in the first place seems very odd, because the *primary* semantic associations of Form I نكب - ينكُب *nakaba* are distress and affliction. Originally, النكبة *an-nakba* could designate any catastrophe or disaster, but since the mid-twentieth century, it has become synonymous with the creation of the state of Israel and the consequent displacement of tens of thousands of Palestinians. The passive participle منكوب *mankuub* depicts someone or something disaster-stricken, as in الرحلة المنكوبة *ar-riHla al-mankuuba*, the ill-fated journey and المنكوبون *al-mankuubuun*, the unfortunate victims.

However, the Form I verb can also refer to the wind: نكبت الريح *nakabat ar-riiH* means the wind shifted, and the implication is one of distressing consequences. This is a deviation from normal that spells trouble. Verse 23:74 of the Qur'an illustrates how the preposition عن enhances the lateral implications inherent in the ن – ك – ب root: وَإِنَّ الّذِينَ لا يُؤْمِنونَ بِالآخِرَةِ عَنِ الصِّراطِ لَناكِبونَ, *And those who do not believe in the Hereafter will certainly veer off the Path.* Form II, نكّب, is a causative verb meaning to deflect something, or divert it from its (proper) trajectory. The Form V verb discussed above, but with the preposition عن, also takes this tack. Its meanings include to swerve, to steer clear of, and to shun. This dismissive physical turning away from someone is reminiscent of English's 'to give someone the cold shoulder.' The underlying metaphor in English is a censorious lack of body heat. Such a cold English shoulder also involves a visible spurning to show disapproval and social rejection. The sense of veering, shifting, and swerving may also explain why 'shoulder' found a home with the نكب root. What كتف lacks is any connection to mobility, a void which منكب nicely fills.

عاتِق
SHOULDER
عِتْق
age, vintage;
emancipation
أخذ على عاتقه
to shoulder
عِتْق
emancipation
to be emancipated عتق
to free, set free, emancipate أعتق
to free, rid oneself of انعتق من
عَتيق
old, antiquated, mellowed, aged (wine)
MacToot

70
Shoulder عاتِق – عاتِقان – عَواتِق / عُتَّق
Ancient; Emancipation

In Arabic's trio of words for the shoulder, العاتق *al-'aatiq*, technically speaking, is said to be located above المنكب *al-mankib* and below the neck. Somewhat less common than الكتف *al-katif*, Arabic's workhorse for the shoulder, العاتق nevertheless figures in the *FDA*, ranking 4,897. There is another derivative of the ع – ت – ق root that outdoes it in terms of frequency; the adjective عتيق *'atiiq,* ancient ranks 3,724 in the *FDA*. This is, in fact, an ancient word, used twice in the Qur'an to describe the Kaaba, in 22:29 and 22:33. That expression has more than one interpretation, but it is most commonly translated 'the ancient house,' as the Kaaba was already a very old structure. In modern usage, the only common meaning of the adjective عتيق is ancient or aged. It is used to describe quite a variety of things, including customs, historical sites, and, in the culinary domain, wine and cheese. Used transitively, with these latter as objects, Form II عتّق means to age.

A more transparent semantic connection can be made between العاتق and the physical properties of the shoulder region. One such property is the capacity to support weight. Perhaps the most famous expression involving this word for the shoulder is أخذها على عاتقه *'akhadhahaa 'alaa 'aatiqihi*, to shoulder (a responsibility). It is also possible to place responsibility for something on someone else's shoulder, ألقاها على عاتقه *'alqaahaa 'alaa 'aatiqihi.*

The other important sense of the ع – ت – ق root is emancipation. Form I عتق – يعتق *'ataqa* means to become emancipated, to leave a state of bondage. Its *maSdar* appears in the phrase عتق رقبة *'itq raqaba*, emancipating a slave. A literal translation is 'freeing a neck.' One can imagine two links to the shoulder. First, there is the question of appearance. As in English, bondage refers directly to the captive's being bound. When the hands are no longer bound, the shoulders naturally expand. The other connection is to age: many slaves, if ever set free at all, were emancipated after long years of service, during which time they had aged. To emancipate is conveyed by the Form IV verb أعتق and its *maSdar* الإعتاق *al-'i'taaq*. Finally, with the addition of a preposition, Form VII انعتق من means to free oneself of something. This connection between the shoulder and emancipation is the source of the other possible sense of البيت العتيق *al-bayt al-'atiiq* in reference to the Kaaba in the Qur'anic verses mentioned above. This would render it *the freed house*, probably in reference to a famous historical attack on the Kaaba by the Abbyssians, with an army of elephants, described in Sura 105.

ذريع
rapid, torrential, sweeping
Power, ability, capability
الذرع
ذرع
to measure, take the measure of; to cover (a distance), traverse (an area)
to use as a pretext, excuse
تذرّع بذريعة
فشل ذريع
an abject failure
cubit ذراع
ذَرْع
measurement in cubits
ذريعة
means, pretext, excuse
ARM, FOREARM ذِراع
to put in a good word for someone ... ذرع لـ
- MacToot -

71
Forearm ذِراع – ذِراعان – أَذْرُع
Power

In addition to its literal, functional sense, الذراع *adh-dhiraa'*, the arm, is a symbol of power. It is also a convenient instrument with which to measure length. The Qur'an makes use of all three meanings. People are not alone in having ذراعان *dhiraa'aani*, two arms. In Arabic, animals have them as well. In 18:18 of the Qur'an, there is a description of the 'people of the cave' who lay down to sleep with their dog posted as guard at the cave's entrance, and woke only to find that they had slept for many long years: وَكَلْبُهُم باسِطٌ ذِراعَيْهِ بالوَصِيدِ, *with their dog stretching out its forelegs at the entrance.*

In 29:33 comes the famous phrase ضاقَ بِهِمْ ذَرْعًا *Daaqa bihim dhar'an*, one that has a range of possible translations. The literal meaning of the initial verb is to become narrow; that narrowness is then specified as being in terms of the arm, and by extension, in terms of power and ability. Arabic portrays narrowness in a very negative light, one suggesting distress. As a whole, the expression can mean he was hard put to deal with them, he was discomfited by them.

The ancient cubit, a word derived from the Latin word for the *elbow*, designates the approximate length of the arm from the elbow to the tip of the middle finger. Likewise, this Arabic word for the physical forearm also signifies that rough measure of length. Ancient Egyptian illustrations show that, long before the Romans, they made calculations using the length of the elbow to the fingertip in their impressive feats of engineering. Over the centuries, this understanding must have been shared with peoples far and wide. In one verse of the Qur'an, 69:32, we find the word for cubit as well as another of the root's derivatives, ذَرْع *dhar'*, the act of measuring something in cubits: ثُمَّ فِي سِلْسِلَةٍ ذَرْعُها سَبْعُونَ ذِراعًا فاسْلُكُوهُ, *then, in a chain seventy cubits long, tie him up.*

The Form I verb ذرع – يذرَع *dhara'a* can mean to measure something, such as a piece of fabric, or to cover or traverse a distance on foot, as in ذَرَعَ المسافر الصحراء *dhara'a al-musaafir aS-SaHraa'a*, the traveler crossed the desert. In either case, the length of the forearm is the key to the idea. Adding the preposition لِـ *li* to this verb creates the idiom ذرع له *dhara'a lahu*, to put in a good word for someone, to act on someone's behalf. Here, the idea of intercession suggests using one's power for someone else, and perhaps, shielding another from trouble. This is spelled out more clearly with the noun ذريعة *dharii'a*. The arms make useful shields, and a cringing gesture made with them to shield oneself from something is the image behind this noun, which has literal and figurative meanings. These include means, medium, expedient, pretext, excuse. This noun is at the root of the Form V verb تذرّع بـ, to use as a means (to an end); to use as a pretext, to make excuses for oneself.

سَعدان ape
سَعِد و سُعِد to be happy
السعيد
the happy one, the lucky one
ساعد هو FOREARM
السعدانة areola
ساعد to help
المساعدة help
MacToot

72

Forearm (1) ساعِد – ساعِدان – سَواعِد

Fortunate Assistance

In English, when needing assistance, we may say, "Would you mind giving me a hand?" A considerate listener may then offer 'to lend a helping hand.' Some types of assistance, however, require more muscle, and when Arabic speakers offer to help, ساعَدَ *saa'ada*, they are generously offering not just a hand, but the whole forearm, الساعِد *as-saa'id*. What luck, السعد *as-sa'd*, for the happy one, السعيد *as-sa'iid*, who needs help, المساعدة *al-musaa'ada*!

The starting point for this semantic cluster is undoubtedly السعد, good fortune. With luck on one's side, of course, happiness may not be far behind. The Form I passive voice سُعِدَ *su'ida* means to be the recipient of good fortune, to be blessed. Furthermore, the concepts of good fortune and help are very closely linked in this root. For example, the first element of the man's name سعد الدين, *sa'd*, should be understood as assistance or support. The whole name, Sa'd ad-Diin—one of the many compound male names formed with the word الدين *al-diin*, religion, grammatically a *muDaaf ilayhi*—means the support of religion, that is, one who acts in its support. In fact, four other common given names discussed below are also based on س – ع – د an excellent measure of how very positive its connotations are.

Form I سعِد – يسعَد *sa'ida* means to be happy or lucky. Its very common *maSdar* is السعادة *as-sa'aada*, happiness. This association of happiness and luck is not entirely foreign to English, either, as evidenced in the expression 'happy-go-lucky.' English, however, does not link being carefree and light-hearted with any expectations of help. The س – ع – د root is also the source of two rather unexpected nouns, one from the animal kingdom, سَعْدان *sa'daan*, ape, and the second yet another body part, السعدانة *as-sa'daana*, the areola, the pigmented skin surrounding the nipple. What connection might they have to the root? The choice of this root to designate an ape is surely a reference to its powerful arms. Furthermore, among Arabic's many names for a monkey is ميمون *maymuun*, which also means fortunate or blessed, and it may be that some kinds of monkeys and apes were, at least at some point, considered happy-go-lucky or fortunate. As for the areola, its association with happiness is hardly surprising, nor are the erotic connotations of its counterpart, الحلمة *al-Halama*, nipple.

The close resemblance of ساعِدة *saa'ida*, a tributary, to الساعِد *as-saa'id*, the forearm, suggests a strong semantic link between the two. This link is not one of function, but rather of appearance. Considered along with its twig-like fingers, the forearm quite resembles a branch, and ساعدة may thus be understood as a *branch* of a river. A more common word for tributary is رافد *raafid*, derived from a verb that also means to help or support. The word رافد (*FDA* 4,071) undoubtedly owes its high frequency to the fact that it became the epithet, in its dual form, for the Tigris and the Euphrates: together, these two iconic rivers are famous far and wide as الرافدان, *ar-raafidaan*.

Note that the plural of both forearm ساعِد and tributary ساعدة is سَواعِد *sawaa'id*. The فواعل pattern is the expected plural for words of the pattern فاعل (and some instances of فاعلة) that have *inanimate* referents. Hence, the plural of the noun رافد is روافد *rawaafid*.

ساعِدٌ
FOREARM
أسعد
to make someone happy; to help somebody
ساعِدة
tributary
branch of a river
مُساعِد
aide, assistant
مُسعَد
fortunate
مَسعود
happiness
السعادة
سَعد
good luck
the Kingdom of Saudi Arabia
السعوديّة
سعادتكم
Your Grace
MacToot

73

Forearm (2) ساعِد – ساعِدان – سَواعِد

Fortunate Assistance

The causative Form IV, أسعد is to make someone happy or to help someone. However, the idea of fortune is also embedded there, and the verb's passive participle مُسْعَد *mus'ad*, a proper name, is typically translated as fortunate. The more or less synonymous مسعود *mas'uud*, another proper name, is a Form I passive participle. In both cases, the passivity is not to be overlooked. The idea of divine agency behind this good fortune is palpable. There is, however, another common word for happy, سعيد *sa'iid*, also a popular given name, and it does not have that same ring to it. Applying the comparative pattern أفعل to the adjective سعيد yields أسْعَد *'as'ad,* happier (again, a popular name) and it is particularly redolent of maternal optimism. Form III, ساعد, to help, is the root's most frequently used verb (*FDA* 1056). Its *maSdar*, المساعدة *al-musaa'ada* is even more common (*FDA* 692).

There remains a key word to address, the one which ranks highest, for this root, in the *FDA*. Politics is a powerful generator of vocabulary, and we find it hard at work here in the *nisba* adjective السعوديّة *as-su'uudiyya*, the common abbreviated version of its longer official name, المملكة العربية السعودية *al-mamlaka al-'arabiyya as-su'uudiyya,* the Kingdom of Saudi Arabia The reference is to سعود *su'uud*, progenitor of the family that has ruled the modern kingdom since its rather recent inception in 1932. This royal family is sometimes referred to as آل سعود *'aal su'uud*, the House of Saud. As in western designations like the House of Windsor, it is not the domicile that is so described, but the family. Arabic has many words for family, clan, and kin, of which آل is one.

In addition to the country's religious primacy, major financial clout helps make this particular word, سعود, a winner in the frequency domain, at an eye-popping 479. The next most frequent word from this root is السعادة *as-sa'aada*, happiness (*FDA* 753), the Form I *maSdar* discussed in the previous chapter. This word, too, owes its ranking to power and politics, because in addition to its literal meaning, it also functions as an honorific. Used with a possessive ending, it is like 'Your Honor,' 'Your Worship,' and 'Your Grace,' used deferentially when addressing a person of elevated rank. This and other examples of discourse etiquette are alive and well in written and spoken Arabic.

كَوَّعَهُ بالسيف
to cut someone down with a sword
elbow joint of a pipe, drain pipe
كوع الماسورة
كوّع
to curl up and take a nap
كوع
ELBOW
كوع
bend, angle
لا يعرف الكوع من البوع
He doesn't know his elbow from the metatarsal bone in his foot
Mactoot

74
Elbow كُوع – أَكْواع – كِيعان
Bend

The ع – و – ك root designates the anatomical elbow, الكوع *al-kuu'* as well as things that resemble it in shape. Common uses of this sort include the elbow joint of a drain pipe or the angle of a smoking pipe that leads to its bowl. In the spoken Egyptian register, it may also refer to a bend in the road.

Speaking proverbially of stupidity and incompetence, one may say لا يعرف الكوع من البوع *laa ya'rif al-kuu' min al-buu'*, he doesn't know his elbow from his metatarsal. American English preferred a different and considerably coarser body metaphor: he doesn't know his ass from a hole in the ground. In another famous phrase from the spoken Egyptian register, سقيته المرّ من كيعانه *sa'eetu-l-murr min ki'aanu*, I gave him something bitter to drink from his elbows. This depicts particularly malevolent intent by coupling a bitter drink with an anatomically agonizing position. The idea, of course, is to give someone a very hard time.

Unlike أكتف *'aktaf*, broad-shouldered, which describes an unusually positive physical feature, the adjective أكوع *'akwa'* depicts someone with strangely outsize elbows. There is also a Form I verb, كوِع – يكوع *kawi'a – yakwa'*, with two meanings. It may be the verbal equivalent of أكوع, having massive elbows, or it may describe a particular gesture: to bring the hands together, thus lifting and bending the elbows, and making them prominent.

The Form II verb كوّع has had a long and varied semantic life. It can be found in an ultra-classical expression. A swashbuckling warrior might cut someone down كوّعه بالسيف, *kawwa'ahu bi-s-sayf*, literally, striking him with the sword until he bent double. This old verb, however, is still alive and well in modern Egyptian speech. Transitively, كوّع means to bend something—a pipe cleaner, for instance—into the shape of an elbow. Intransitively, it means to curl up and take a nap, or to fail in an exam. This last sense even manages to suggest that same doubling over caused by a mortal blow of the sword.

ELBOW
مِرْفَق
Kindness الرفق
to be kind, رفق ب /على friendly, gentle to
ترفّق مع؟ ب
to display kindness toward someone in something
رفيق السوء
bad fellow, friend of the wrong sort
to utilize something ارتفق
أرفق
to be useful to someone
رافق
to be a companion, comrade; to accompany, escort
رفيق / رفيقة العمر/الحياة
husband/wife
lit. life's companion
أرفق
to be useful to someone; to attach, enclose, append
to travel together ترافق
EGYPTAIR
MacToot

75

Elbow مِرفَق / مَرفِق – مَرافِق

Attachment; Camaraderie

Body language has a lot to say a lot about the nature of relationships. Comrades, الرفاق *ar-rifaaq*, are often pictured walking arm-in-arm. A gesture of fellowship common to many societies is that of close companions out for a stroll, arms linked and bent at the elbow. This physical attachment speaks volumes about the rapport of those involved. Attachment, both physical and emotional, is thus the mystery behind this name for the elbow, المرفق. Interestingly, the Arabs gave this same consonantal shape two distinct vowelings. One may pronounce it *mirfaq*, the instrument of camaraderie and attachment, or *marfiq*, their place.

There are, of course, many kinds of comrades and companions, and the assumption is that they ought to be of the most desirable sort. This makes Rafiiq and Rafiiqa popular given names. A spouse may be optimistically called رفيق العمر *rafiiq al-'umr* or رفيق الحياة *rafiiq al-Hayaat*, life's companion. The appropriate gender, of course, designates the spouse. Another famous collocation is رفيق الدرب *rafiiq ad-darb*, fellow wayfarer, that friend or colleague right at your elbow on a literal or figurative journey or mission. Many companions are, in fact, of the desirable sort, but there may also be رفيق السوء *rafiiq as-suu'*, a morally objectionable fellow, association with whom leads one into trouble.

Both companions and elbows are good things to lean on. Comfort is highly desirable, and when opportunity allows, societies have demonstrated a penchant for more, and more elaborate, tools of comfort on which to lean. Taking inspiration from those functional, convenient elbows, المرافق *al-maraafiq*, the Arabs went on to call the convenient accoutrements of technical and social progress by the very same name. Like the elbow, itself, this is a term that covers a host of utilitarian devices or installations. For instance, المرافق العامّة *al-marafiq al-'aamma* are public utilities.

In the verbal domain, the Form VIII verb ارتفق is also a functional designation, to lean on one's elbows. With the addition of the preposition بِـ - *bi* it means to utilize something, or to profit from doing so. One may also be useful to someone else. This is Form IV أرفق. With the preposition بِـ, this same verb means to attach or enclose something. Its passive participle is used in the collocation مرفق به *murfaq bihi* and مُرْفَق طيّه *murfaq Tayyahu*, enclosed, included.

The Form I verb رفق – يرفَق بـ/ على *rafiqa bi / 'alaa*, to be kind, friendly, or gentle to someone is the source word for most of the rest of these derivatives. The Form III verb, رافق *raafaqa*, is, as usual, transitive and implies someone else's involvement; this is to escort or accompany someone, to act as someone's companion. One who does so can be dubbed مُرافق *muraafiq*. Finally, Form V ترفّق معه بـ *taraffaqa ma'ahu bi* means to display kindness toward someone in an undertaking or encounter, or to proceed gently with someone in something. This suggests an attitude or comportment quite similar to Form I, if somewhat more deliberate.

آه من قيدِكَ
أدمى مِعْصَمي
Aah, your hand! It has bloodied my wrist
الأطلال
العصمة في يدها
She retained her independence (and right to initiate divorce) at marriage
عاصمة capital
مِعصَم
WRIST
معصوم
inviolable, sacrosanct; sinless
MacToot
عصم
to hold back, restrain; to safeguard
العصمة
bond; protection; modesty; virtuousness impeccability
عاصِم protector
عِصاميّ
distinguished (on one's own merits)
اعتصام
demonstration, sit-in
اعتصم
to seek refuge; to go on a religious retreat; to picket, demonstrate, to cling to, adhere, to maintain
عُصمة
neckband or collar
عِصام
strap, thong
اعتصم = استعصم
to cling to; to resist temptation
اعتصم بالصمت
to maintain silence

76

Wrist مِعْصَم – مَعاصِم

Restrain; Cling to

The wrist is one element in a constellation of vocabulary derived from the Form I verb عصم – يعصِم *'aSama* whose principal meaning is to restrain or hold back. Built on an instrument pattern, المعصم *al-mi'Sam* shows its functional link to restraint. Another common noun in this semantic family is عِصام *'iSaam*, a thong or strap. The choice of عُصمة *'uSma* for neckband or collar is also a visual link between ع – ص – م and cords tied around limbs. In "al-Atlal" (the ruins), Umm Kulthum sings: آه من قيدِك أدمى مِعْصَمي, Aah, your bond! It has bloodied my wrist. The Form I verb, however, has another crucial meaning: to protect and safeguard. Qur'anically, it is used in 33:17 to ask a rhetorical question with more than a little menace: مَن ذا الَّذي يَعصِمُكُم مِن اللهِ, *Who is it that might protect you from God?*

From the combined senses of restraint and protection, the culturally loaded noun العصمة *al-'iSma* draws its complex nuances. Meaning hindrance, preservation, or protection, this noun has a special affinity with marriage and is used in the collocation عصمة النكاح *'iSmat an-nikaaH*, the bond of marriage. Combining the associations of marriage and restraint, العصمة also came to mean chastity and purity. With its trademark Ottoman spelling, عصمت, Ismet, is a popular name, used both for men and women. Two other popular men's names typically transliterated without their long vowels or any indication of their initial consonant are عِصام, Isam, thong or strap, and عاصِم, Asim, protector or guardian. The popularity of these names says volumes about gender and social attitudes. Noteworthy adjectives are عصامي *'iSaamiyy*, distinguished, self-made (rather than having come to prominence through family or other connections, عظامي *'iZaamiyy*) and the elative pattern, أعصَم *'a'Sam*, white-footed, and by extension, excellent, precious.

Men had—and have—considerable authority over women, and one way of describing a woman under a man's authority is with the phrase في عصمته *fii 'iSmatihi*, (she is) in his custody, meaning she is married to him. A woman may, however, retain her independence at marriage by specifically asking that this question of custody be 'in her hand.' This would give her the prerogative to initiate a divorce, should she wish to do so. However, social disparagement of the request for العصمة في يدها *al-'iSma fii yadihaa* continues to make it difficult for a woman to do so.

Two more verbs are derived from this root. Form VIII اعتصم has the sense of to seek refuge, or to adhere to something (like silence, or calm). Along with the high frequency word عاصمة *'aaSima*, capital of a country, the only derivative of ع – ص – م that appears in the *FDA* is الاعتصام *al-i'tiSaam*. In addition to the sense of adhering to something, this *maSdar* has acquired religious and political dimensions. Religiously, it is a prayer retreat practiced during Ramadan, when men may go to a mosque for days or weeks at a stretch in an expression of deep spiritual devotion. In the modern political sphere, it is a sit-in or demonstration. In both cases, practitioners stick to a practice as if they were bound to it. Form X استعصم is sometimes synonymous with VIII, but more commonly it means to resist (a temptation). What is sought is العصمة, the restraint of virtue, or the virtue of restraint! This verb is used in 12:32 of the Qur'an to describe Joseph, who resists the attempted seduction of his owner's wife: وَلَقَد راوَدْتُهُ عَن نَفْسِهِ فَاسْتَعْصَمَ, *and I tried to seduce him but he showed restraint.*

HAND, FORELEG, HANDLE
يدٌ
helping hand
يد العون
بَين يَدَيهِ
before him,
in front of him
وَيَدٍ تَمْتَدُّ نَحْوي
كَيَدٍ من خلال المَوْج
مُدَّتْ لغَريق
And a hand reaching out to me like a hand amidst the waves, extended to one drowning
Ibrahim Nagi
as sung by Umm Kulthum
له يَدٌ في
to have a hand in
رَحْب اليدين
generous, capacious of hand
يدان
forelegs of felines, dogs, rabbits and primates
MacToot

77

Hand; Foreleg; Handle (1) يَد – يدان – أيدٍ / أيادٍ

Power; Giving

Classical grammarians identify the root of يـد *yad* as ي – د – ي, backing up their judgment, in part, on its plural form أيـدٍ *'aydin* and the plural of that plural, أيـادٍ *'ayaadin*, both of which point to a finally weak root. Badawi and Hinds in *A Dictionary of Egyptian Arabic* consider the Egyptianized form of the word hand, إيـد, and link it to the Form II verb أيّـد, to support, a verb common in the spoken register and the news media, and used in Qur'anic Arabic as well. This choice is intriguing because it allows for the expansion of the semantic domain of such a crucial part of the body—and the psyche—to include two important verbs with strong associations to the hand. It is the proposal adopted here.

In hand and handle, English etymologically highlights the functional connections between the anatomical hand and the hilt of a tool. Manufactured handles, the very word suggests, share much with the human counterpart for which they are named, and yet still need to be differentiated from it. Handle also morphs into a verb in English, and designates taking something into one's hand and manipulating it, as in 'handle with care!' More abstractly, handling means coming to *grips* with a situation, *dexterous* problem-solving, so to speak. The adjective handy and its use in the expression 'to come in handy' and 'handyman' offer more evidence that functional utility is a prime English association with the hand. By contrast, Arabic uses one and the same noun for hand and handle, and it does *not* use يـد verbally for the functions of picking up, holding, or manipulating.

That said, Arabic has many, many different metaphoric associations with اليـد. Two classical expressions very similar in meaning are رحـب اليديـن *raHb al-yadayni* and سـبط اليديـن *sabT al-yadayni*. Translated literally, they are capacious of hand and loose of hand; because the hands are instruments of giving, the real meaning of both is simply generous. An expression which illustrates the importance of generosity in Arab society is اليـد العليا *al-yad al-'ulyaa*, the upper hand. Unlike the English phrase 'having the upper hand,' it designates the person who bestows gifts liberally. Someone whose limited means put him strictly on the receiving end of such generosity is اليـد السـفلى *al-yad as-suflaa*.

HAND
FORELEG
HANDLE
اليد
power, authority, influence
اليد العاملة
man power
أيّد
to support, strengthen, corroborate
تأيّد
to be supported
مؤيّد
Supporter
التأييد
Support, backing, confirmation, endorsement
MacToot

78
Hand; Foreleg; Handle (2) يَد – يدان – أيدٍ / أيادٍ
Power; Giving

Lending a hand means providing practical assistance in English, and يد العون *yad al-'awn* is that helping hand in Arabic. When she sang Ibrahim Nagi's classic poem "al-Atlal" (the ruins), Umm Kulthum gave voice to the powerful seduction of love, embodied in a hand: وَيدٍ تَمْتَدُّ نَحْوي كَيَدٍ مِن خِلالِ المَوْجِ مُدَّتْ لِغَريق, And a hand, reaching out toward me like a hand amidst the waves, extended to one drowning.

The hand's functions are not limited to giving and helping. Physical orientation is the key to understanding the idiom بين يديه, *bayna yadayhi*, before him. Instead of the preposition 'between,' which the Arabic expression uses, English chooses 'before.' This is not a temporal expression. Instead, it pinpoints position, as when one stands 'before a judge.' Another metaphor that correlates with the hand is involvement: له يد فيه *lahu yad fiihi* means to have a hand in something. Like the arm, الذراع *adh-dhiraa'*, the hand is also a symbol of power. The phrase اليد العاملة *al-yad al-'aamila*, labor or manpower, is a nominal example.

Verbally, Form II أيَّد, means to support, strengthen, corroborate. The *maSdar* التأييد *at-ta'yiid* is support, backing, or confirmation. This is the most frequent of the root's derivatives, ranking 3,244 in the *FDA*. From this Form II verb comes مؤيِّد *mu'ayyid*, supporter. Form V تأيَّد offers a reflexive or passive counterpart to these meanings, to be supported. Oddly, this is a verb whose *maSdar* is rarely used.

Common usage in English tends to restrict the term 'hand' to humans and primates; most clawed animals that walk on all four are said to have paws; those with horns on their feet have hooves. The Arabic يد, however, designates just the hand, or the hand and the arm up to المنكب *al-mankib*, the shoulder. Furthermore, يدان *yadaani* commonly refers to a range of animals' forelegs, with the general exception of beasts of burden. For example, small animals like dogs, rabbits, mice, and rats have them. Primates and felines of all sizes have them, as do some other large animals. Perhaps a rather restrictive conception of dexterity had something to do with English's comparatively narrow, anthropomorphic view of the hand.

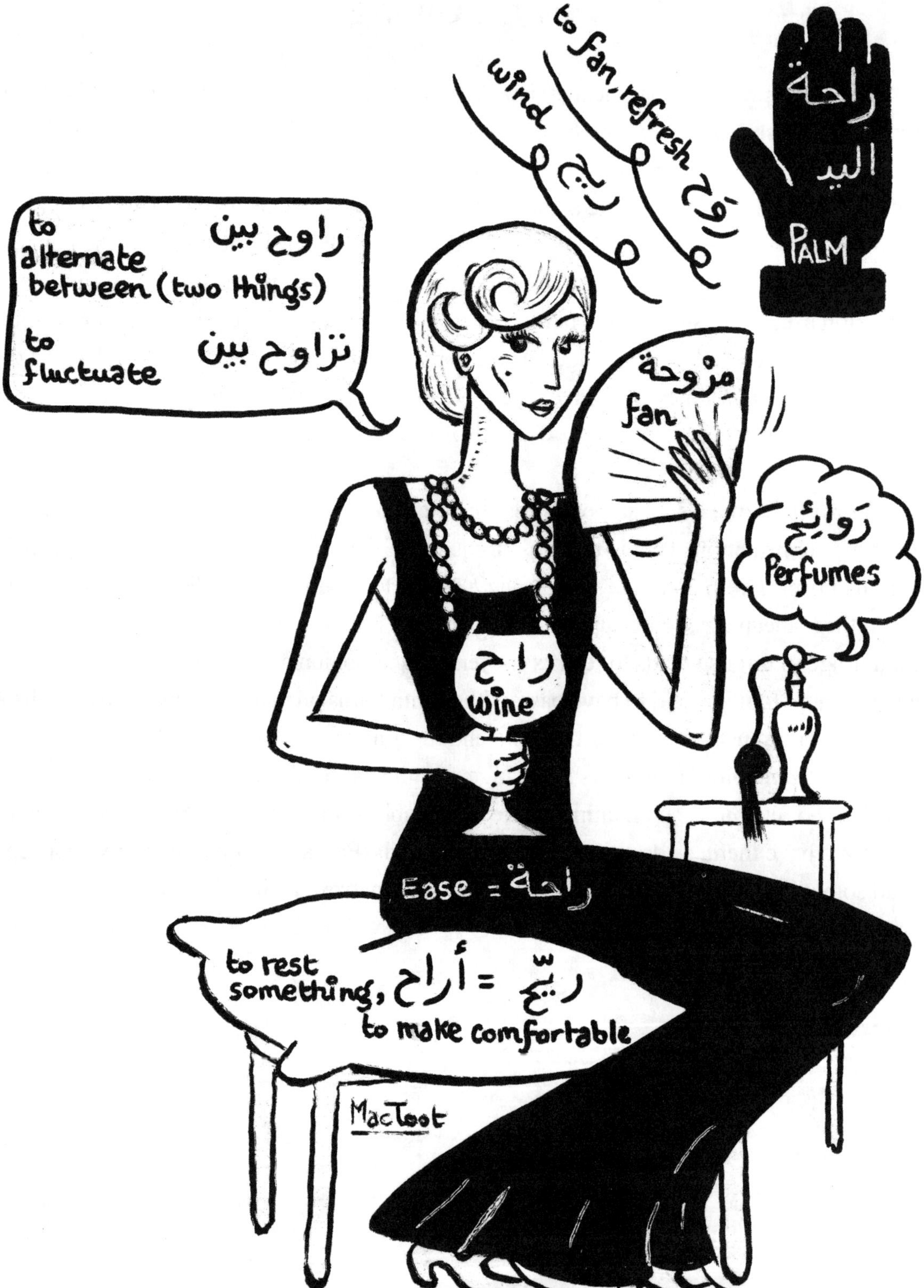

راحة اليد
PALM
to fan, refresh روّح
wind ريح
to alternate between (two things) راوح بين
to fluctuate تراوح بين
مروحة fan
روائح Perfumes
راح wine
Ease = راحة
to rest something, to make comfortable أراح = ريّح
MacToot

79

Palm راحة – راحتان – راحات / راح

Comfort; Volatility

This chapter returns to the ر – و – ح and ر – ي – ح roots examined in the chapter on الـروح *ar-ruuH*, the soul, to consider their links to the palm. Try to imagine a scorching day in the ancient Arabian Peninsula. Longing for a cool breeze, desert dwellers would have endless opportunities to contemplate the comfort that fanning could provide. The palm is the primordial fan, and in fact the *palm* and *comfort* are one and the same word, الراحـة *ar-raaHa*. Before long, an actual fan مِرْوَحـة *mirwaHa*—an instrument pattern—would have been devised. What a blessing, in the absence of wind, الريـح *ar-riiH*. For on-the-spot relief, though, the oscillations of the palm would suffice. The palm has other morphological relatives, too. A minimal spelling change, from راحة into راح *raaH* transforms that comforting palm into classical Arabic wine! In a post-classical poem of the موشّحـات *muwashshaHaat* genre comes the sensual line: وشربتُ الراحَ مـن راحتـه, And I drank (the) wine from the palm of his hand.[16]

This verse confirms that abstention was not always the rule, especially in cosmopolitan Andalusia! It is interesting to note that English can do something similar with a minimal spelling change. One little letter transforms airy spirit into liquid, alcoholic spirits.

As discussed in the chapter on الـروح, some classical verbs of motion like راح – يـروح *raaHa* were associated with movement and time. What more comfortable time to set out on a journey in a desert environment than in the evening? Another possible connection to comfort and time can be seen in the Ramadan evening prayers, التراويح *at-taraawiiH*. After a long day of fasting, the evening is surely a comfort, as well as a time to consider matters of the spirit.

Changing the medial root letter to ي in the Form II verb creates ريّـح. This verb and its Form IV synonym, أراح mean to set at ease, to comfort, simple causative elaborations on the noun الراحـة *ar-raaHa*, comfort.

The essential experiential link between movement of the palm and comfort sets the stage for a variety of important vocabulary, and in fact two verbs derived from it also refer to movement. Form III راوح means to alternate between two things. Form VI, تـراوح, its reciprocal counterpart, means to fluctuate, moving back and forth. Both of these are based on an image: the sinuous undulations of one's palm, or a fan, as it rises and falls between two points. They are therefore both used with the adverb بيـنَ *bayna*, between.

Form VIII ارتـاح returns to the underlying idea of comfort, and means to find relief for oneself. One may specify relief from what with the addition of the preposition من *min*, from. Form VIII and Form X, اسـتراح, are similar in meaning. It is a reflexive counterpart of Form IV, أراح and means to seek rest and find it, to take a break. Adding the preposition إلى *ila*, to, instead of من, conveys being pleased or happily comfortable with something or someone.

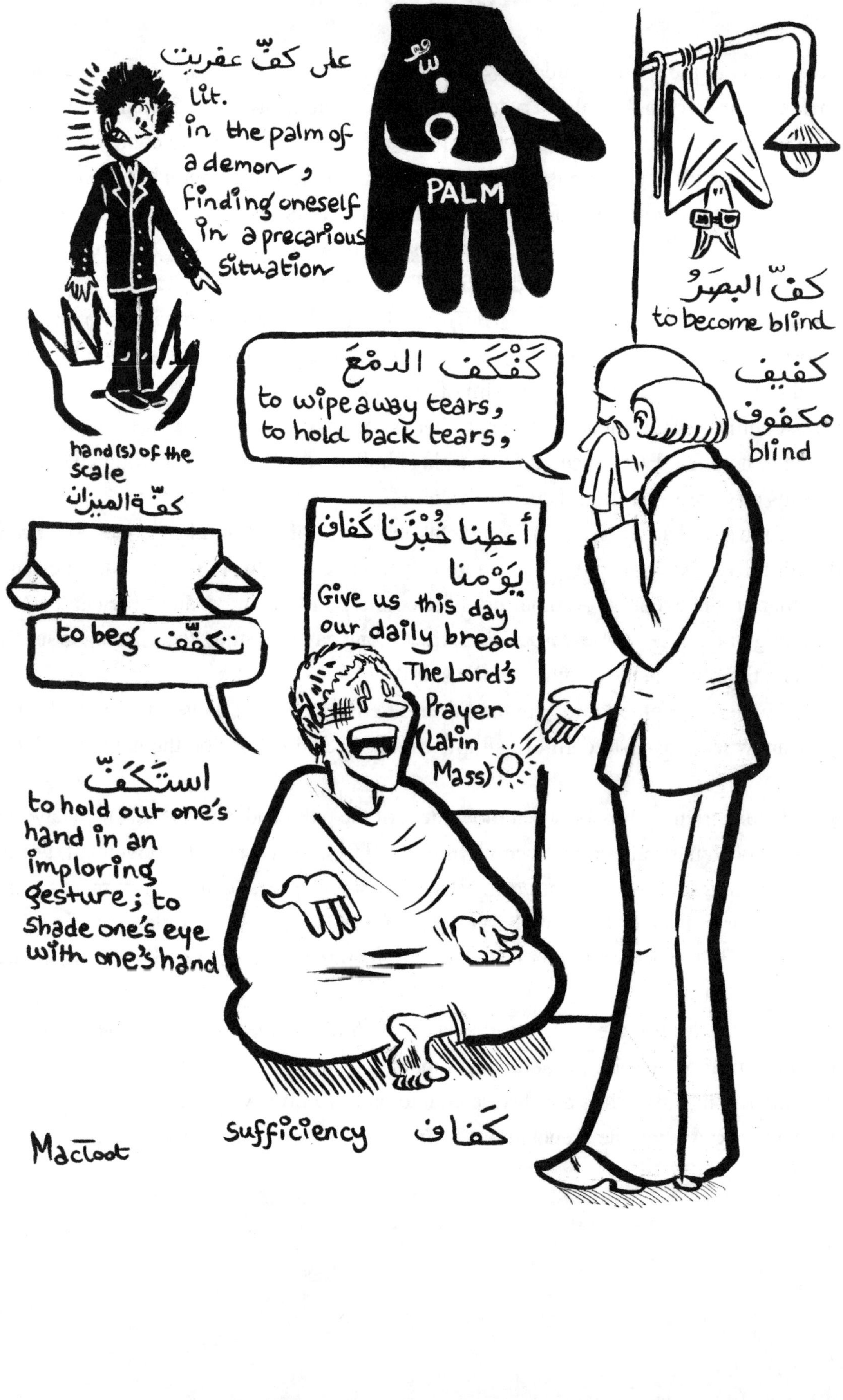
على كفّ عفريت
lit.
in the palm of a demon, finding oneself in a precarious situation
كف
PALM
كفّ البصرُ
to become blind
كفيف
مكفوف
blind
كَفْكَفَ الدمْعَ
to wipe away tears, to hold back tears,
hand(s) of the scale
كفّة الميزان
to beg تكفّف
أعطِنا خُبْزَنا كَفاف يَوْمنا
Give us this day our daily bread
The Lord's Prayer (Latin Mass)
استكفّ
to hold out one's hand in an imploring gesture; to shade one's eye with one's hand
sufficiency كَفاف
Mactoot

80

Palm كفّ ـ كَفّان ـ كُفوف / أَكُفّ

Stopping; Hemming in

Unlike الراحة *ar-raaHa*, this second word for the palm, الكفّ *al-kaff*, has no homonym; it is unambiguous. A palmful of food is just enough to get by on, a sufficiency, كفاف *kafaaf*. A phrase in the Lord's Prayer—أَعْطِنا خُبْزَنا كَفافَ يَومِنا *'a'Tinaa khubzanaa kafaafa yawminaa*—asks God to give us our bread, enough for a day's sustenance. The palm also figures in a famous metaphor for solicitous care. Being catered to hand and foot is being treated على كفوف الراحة *'alaa kufuuf ar-raaHa*, on the palms of comfort, or, as English body language prefers, in the lap of luxury. Actually, though, most associations with الكفّ have little to do with ease and opulence. They may even be alarming, as in على كف عفريت *'alaa kaff 'ifriit*, literally in the palm of a demon, used to convey finding oneself in a most precarious situation.

Resemblance to a palm is the basis for one common derivative: كِفّة الميزان *kiffat al-miizaan*, the 'palm' of a scale. The scale's opposing palms rise and fall depending on which is heavier. From this image comes the collocation الكفّة الراجحة *al-kiffa ar-raajiHa*, the preponderant option, the most likely case. The physical actions conveyed by Form V تكفّف and Form X استكفّ are broadly cross-cultural. To extend an openhanded, outstretched palm is one of the gestures associated with begging. If one is destitute, stretching out the hand to ask for something may put a stop to that hunger and need. Since asking for something related to Form I is a typical semantic association with Form X, استكفّ also conveys asking for that same كفاف, what suffices to keep hunger at bay, mentioned in the Lord's Prayer.

Arabic has two adjectives from this root meaning blind, كفيف *kafiif* and مكفوف *makfuuf*. The intransitive Form I verbal phrase كفّ البصر *kaffa al-baSar*, means to become blind. When transitive, Form I كفّ – يكُفّ *kaffa* means to prevent something, to stop it. This sense is also at work in the verb كَفْكَف *kafkafa*, an unusual doubling of the root, with a link to another gesture made with the palm. It is famous in the phrase كفكف دموعه *kafkafa dumuu'ahu*, he held back his tears.

In the Form I verb, the preposition عن *'an* accentuates this sense of impeding. One may say كفّه عن الكلام *kaffahu 'an il-kalaam*, he stopped him from speaking. The Form I verb is used eight times in the Qur'an, including in 5:11: فَكَفَّ أَيْدِيَهُم عَنْكُم, *He stayed their hands from you.* Form VII انكفّ is largely synonymous with كفّ عن. The Form I and Form II verbs كفّ and كفّف can both mean to hem a garment, a denominative formation from كُفّة and كِفاف, a seam, hem, or border of a garment. Curbing is the key here, too. The hem is the end of the garment; hemming what one wears limits or restricts its length. Tellingly, English uses the phrase 'to be hemmed in' to express a stifling sense of restriction.

The most common word of all from this root (693 in the *FDA*) is كافّة *kaaffa*, altogether. One might speculate that its connection to the palm is in the sense that when the palm closes on something it acts as a sort of container. What it holds thus becomes a contained whole.

الاعتقال
arrest, detention
مُعتقَل
detainee; detention camp, prison
العِقال
Sturdy Cord
المَعقِل
Stronghold, fort, Sanctuary
KNUCKLE JOINT
عُقلة
MacToot

81
Knuckle; Joint عُقَل – عُقْلة
Physical Restraint

The word عقلة *'uqla* has two basic meanings. It can designate a joint in the body, especially the knuckle, or an articulation in a plant's stem, a knob or a node, such as one might find in sugarcane or bamboo. It seems reasonable to assume that human anatomy was the source of the name for these knobby protuberances of the botanical world. However, there is another possibility. As we know, the camel herd was a precious asset in Bedouin society, and it had to be well managed. But camels have a mind of their own, so to speak, and occasionally stray. To keep losses to a minimum, the Bedouin needed to limit the roaming power of potentially restless animals. Necessity is the mother of invention, and the answer came in the form of a very sturdy cord, العِقال *al-'iqaal*, one woven, irony of ironies, from camel hair. Typically, one of the camel's front legs would be bent at the articulation, العقلة, and tied with العِقال. Camels thus hobbled could move about and graze, but not run far. In naming the cord, the joint was the key point of reference, and the association of joint with restraint was made. Although uncertain, it is not inconceivable that the camel's knuckle inspired the designation of the joint in humans.

The *act* of hobbling needed a name, too; and the Form I verb عقل – يعقِل *'aqala* expressed it. Applied to people, it could mean to detain, confine, or arrest. By metaphoric extension, the physical hobbling then became a term for *financial* hobbling. In the Bedouin justice system, a payment could be made to indemnify a family for the injury or death of one of its members. This practice, made to prevent long and debilitating blood feuds, has a very old name in English, 'wergild' (literally, man payment), a system codified in Germanic law and practiced far and wide in medieval Europe. Obligation to pay a substantial sum of money to avoid a cycle of dangerous reprisals acted as an impediment to reckless assault. The place pattern made use of this root, as well. The place where people could be detained was called المَعْقِل *al-ma'qil* and came to mean a stronghold, a fort, and even a sanctuary.

That sturdy cord described above, العقال, was a multipurpose invention. It acquired a sartorial function as well, tying the traditional head garment known as الكوفية *al-kuufiyya* in place, and it is still in use today. It has a close morphological relative, العقل, the mind, discussed in chapter 29. This is the rational mind, the mind which restrains impulsive actions.

It follows that the cord was essentially seen as a restraint, hobbling wayward camels and firmly securing crucial headgear.

Echoing Form I in the sense of detaining and arresting is Form VIII اعتقل (*FDA* 2,202). Sadly, after العقل, the two most common of the other eight derivatives of ع – ق – ل that figure in the *FDA* are both related to arresting: the *maSdar* الاعتقال *al-i'tiqaal*, detention, ranks 1,782, and its passive participle, مُعتقَل *mu'taqal*, both a detainee and a detention camp, is close behind, at 1,858.

إصبع
أصبوع
DIGIT, FINGER, TOE
عضّ أصابعه ندماً
he bit his fingers in remorse
صبع على/ب ...
to point at derisively
أشارت اصابع الاتّهام إليه
the fingers of accusation pointed to him
صبعه
to injure someone else's finger
صبع فرخة
to insert a finger into a chicken's cloaca/vent to see if it is about to lay
ما صبع في الطعام
he didn't touch the food
MacToot

82

Digit: Finger, Toe إصْبَع / أُصْبوع – أصابع

Point

The fingers الأصابع *al-'aSaabi'*, are sensitive and versatile. Crucial in our exploration of the immediate environment, they send detailed mountains of data to the brain. Before table manners are instilled in us—and even after—we delight in 'finger food,' which allows us the pleasures of earliest childhood when tactile feedback was a necessary part of eating. From time immemorial and all around the world, fingers have also been adorned. English and Arabic agree on the uniqueness and importance of the fingers, and honor each with a name. Strangely, the Arabs had trouble agreeing on a single spelling and pronunciation for the finger. There are two spellings. The less common is أصبوع *'uSbuu'*. The shorter أصبع is the more common, and it has a variety of vowelings too, including, but not limited to *'iSba'* and *'uSbu'*. One thing English and Arabic seem to disagree on is exactly what الأصابع encompass, a problem solved by more exactly translating the word as digits. The Arabic word refers equally to fingers *and* toes. However, both languages use the expression 'ten fingers' while neither ever specifically calls the thumb الإبهام *al-'ibhaam*, a finger.

The finger is used nominally in a couple of notable collocations that describe physical gestures, including أشارت أصابع الاتّهام إليه *'ashaarat 'aSaabi' al-ittihaam 'ilayhi*, the fingers of accusation pointed to him. The English equivalent is verbal: to finger someone for something, especially a crime. Arabic also has the classical عضّ أصابعه ندمًا *'aDDa 'aSaabi'ahu nadaman*, to bite one's fingers in remorse.

Arabic fingers have a verbal life, as well. Form I صبع – يصبَع *Saba'a* with the preposition على *'alaa* or بـ *bi* is an example of a verb directly linked to a gesture: to point at, especially derisively. With the preposition في *fii* it means to put one's finger into something, from which comes the figurative expression ما صبع في الطعام *maa Saba'a fi-T-Ta'aam*, he didn't touch the food, he ate nothing. Without any preposition, this verb has some quirkier classical meanings. The first is combat-related. Descriptions of mortal wounds are more common, but the Arabs decided that the danger of having fingers that don't function properly also merited its own designation: صبعه *Saba'ahu*, to injure someone else's finger. Second, describing what can only be termed a very hands-on animal husbandry technique, is the expression صبع فرخة *Saba'a farkhatan*, to 'finger a hen,' that is, to insert a finger into its vent or cloaca to determine if it is about to lay!

إبهام
THUMB
BIG TOE
مُبْهَم
Obscure, dark, Cryptic
∞
عدد مُبْهَم
abstract number
بَهيمة ج بهائم
animal, quadruped, pl. large domesticated animals
بهيميّة
bestiality, brutishness
بَهيم ج بُهُم
jet black
العصب المُبْهَم
the vagus nerve
بهيميّ
bestial, brutish
أبهم
to make obscure, dubious, unintelligible
MacToot

83

Thumb / Big Toe إبْهام – إبْهامان – أباهيم / إبْهامات

Behemoth; Dim-witted; Obscure

Animals come in all sizes, but بهيمة *bahiima* refers specifically to a sizeable one, such as a cow, a water buffalo, or an ox. What connection large animals have to the thumb is at first quite obscure, مُبهم *mubham*. That vein of obscurity leads to an unusual color reference: بهيم *bahiim* means black, as in ليل بهيم *layl bahiim*, pitch-black night. When applied to animals, بهيم can also mean all of one color, with no distinguishing marking. Of a voice, it means of one unvarying pitch, without any quaver. In any case, بهيم is not common; مبهم, on the other hand, is a familiar word. In addition to its commonplace sense of obscure, this adjective has technical applications, including عدد مبهم *'adad mubham*, an abstract number, and in medicine, العصب المبهم *al-'aSab al-mubham*, the vagus nerve. Which language or culture named this nerve first is a matter of some vagueness and obscurity to those outside the history of science!

In any case, to grasp the origin of the word for thumb and big toe, one must consider domesticated animals, and the question of size. The word بهيمة is a very old one, occurring three times in the Qur'an. In fact, English has a direct cognate through its Hebrew and Aramaic origins. In the Bible story of Job (40:15–24), behemoth refers to a mighty animal. Modern English usage gives the word some leeway, and it now refers to anything monstrously large or powerful. It seems reasonable to speculate that the thumb and big toe were named for their impressively large size and strength in the hand and foot. The metaphoric sense of obscure, and thick, in the slangy sense of someone slow to understand, seems to have come from a condescending view of animal intelligence. Anthropocentrically speaking, beasts are obtuse. In modern times, we (or perhaps those of us who do not work with them on a daily commercial basis) have much affection for barnyard animals, but the designation بهيمة carries none of those tender feelings. In fact, بهايم *bahaayim* (for the formal بهائم *bahaa'im*) is a very demeaning insult in today's Egypt, characterizing people as dim-witted brutes. Taking بهيمة for inspiration, the Form V and Form X verbs, تبهّم and استبهم both mean to be obscure, ambiguous, unintelligible. The same is true of the causative Form IV أبهم, the source of the adjective مبهم, a deliberate attempt to make something obscure.

سبّابة
INDEX FINGER
تسبّب في
to be instrumental in
سبّب
to be caused, be the consequence of
سَبّة
period of time
سَبّة الآلام
Passion Week
بسبب
because of
تسبّب في
to be to blame for
أسباب الراحة
comfortable accommodations
سَبَب ج أسباب
tent rope (classical); reason, cause
سبّب
to cause, provoke, bring about
تسبّب عن
to be caused by, be the result of

84
Index Finger (1) سَبّابة – سَبّابات
Cause; Insult

The Arabic index finger, السبّابة *as-sabbaaba*, is a digit with clout. As the English word suggests, the index finger makes a practical pointer, indicating whatever it is we choose to single out. Arabic takes this a big step further. It endows السبّابة with the power to blame as it identifies the reason or cause السبب *as-sabab*, of an event, establishing responsibility and/or guilt. The plural الأسباب *al-'asbaab* has some particular idiomatic uses in addition to its ordinary meanings of reasons and causes. In legal terms, أسباب الحكم *'asbaab al-Hukm* is the text of a judicial opinion, which documents the grounds for the decision. On the other hand, أسباب الراحة *'asbaab ar-raaHa* is conveniences, comfortable accommodations, luxurious means. These expressions can be seen as outgrowths of another older and more concrete meaning of الأسباب, the ropes used in pitching and securing a Bedouin tent. Keeping the tent upright literally hung on these crucial ropes. By extension, the judge's verdict hinges on certain elements of the case, and the designation of comfortable accommodations depends on certain crucial accoutrements.

Adding the preposition بـِ to our source word creates the conjunction بسبب *bisabab*, because of. As in English, this is not the equivalent of because; instead, it is always followed by a noun or pronoun. One may say, for example, كلها بسببك *kulluhaa bisababika*, it's all because of you! This is basic, vital vocabulary: cause and because of, together, rank 117 in the *FDA*. Just a tiny derivational step away, we find the altogether sophisticated السببيّة *as-sababiyya*, causality.

Also derived directly from that little سبب are Form II سبّب, and Form V تسبّب. These two verb forms are semantically similar, but Form II must have a direct object, as in سبّب البرق حريقا هائلا *sabbaba al-barq Hariiqan haa'ilan*, the lightning caused a huge fire. Form V, on the other hand, always takes a prepositional object. With في *fii*, the sense is to be instrumental in, to be to blame for; with عن *'an*, it means to be caused by, or to be the result of, the consequence of, as in تسبّب انهيار البورصة عن مكائد التاجر *tasabbaba inhiyaar al-burSa 'an makaa'id at-taajir*, the stock market crash was due to the trader's skullduggery.

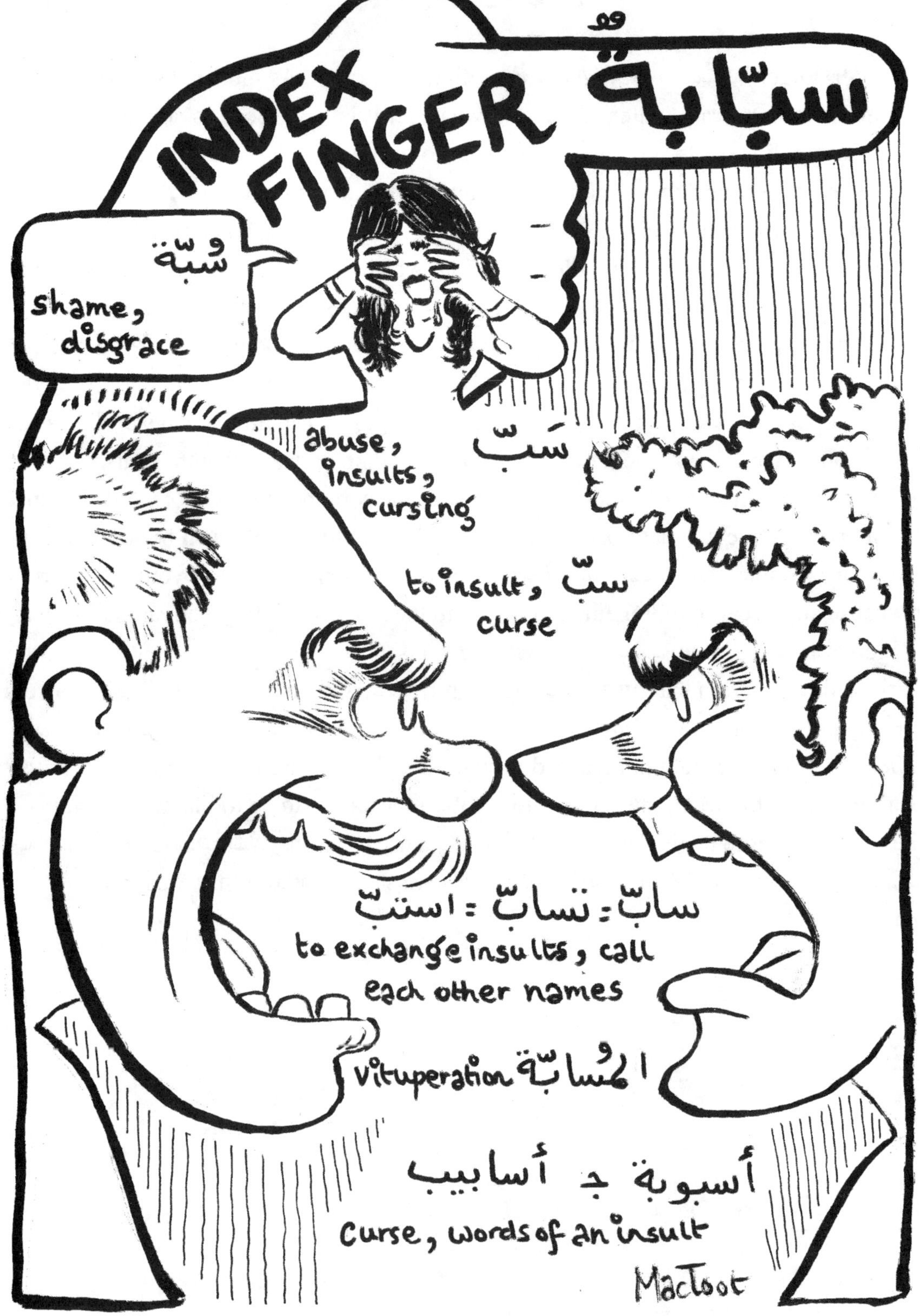
INDEX FINGER سبّابة
سُبّة
shame, disgrace
abuse, insults, cursing سَبّ
to insult, curse سبّ
سابّ = تسابّ = استبّ
to exchange insults, call each other names
vituperation المُسابّة
أسبوبة ج أسابيب
curse, words of an insult
MacToot

85
Index Finger (2) سَبّابة – سَبّابات
Cause; Insult

All the other verbs from the س – ب – ب root form a tight semantic cluster directly linked to the not-so-innocent سبّابة. Forms I سبّ – يسُبّ *sabba*, to insult, curse, or call names, III سابّ, and VIII استبّ are practically synonymous. Form VI تسابّ makes the insulting explicitly mutual. In addition to سَبَب *sabab* and its plural أسباب *asbaab*, in their various meanings, the Form I verb سبّ is used in the Qur'an. Underpinning all of this verbal vituperation is the *maSdar* السّبّ *as-sabb*. To specify just one insult, Arabic adds a *taa marbuuta:* سبّة, *sabba.* A rarer, morphologically more colorful word for an insult, أسبوبة *'usbuuba*, is the product of this root and the pattern أُفْعولة, which is discussed in greater detail in chapter 23. Insults need not entail the use of four-letter words. On the contrary, mockery and derision also qualify. Of particular sensitivity is سبّ الدين, *sabb ad-diin*, insulting religion. A particularly offensive insult—attacking *both* religion and the mother—used widely in the spoken Moroccan register is: لعن الله دين أمّك, God curse your mother's religion! Such an insult is likely to precipitate physical altercations. International, intercultural crises can also stem from visual insults, as happened in 2005 when a Danish newspaper published caricatures of the Prophet Muhammad. This precipitated a decade of escalating insults and attacks between two increasingly hard-line camps, neither of which could bear السُّبّة *as-subba,* the disgrace, shame, and dishonor, of de-escalation.

The noun سبّة, an insult, had other classical meanings, too. Most telling of all, it had a specific anatomical sense, الإست *al-'ist*, the anus, or المؤخّرة *al-mu'akhkhira*, the behind. Furthermore, it had a homonym. One could say: مضت سبّة من الدهر *maDat sabba min ad-dahr*, a (longish) period of time elapsed. Classically, the Arabs noted stretches of uncomfortable weather not as waves, but with this term, سبّة من الحرّ / البرد *sabba min al-Harr / al-bard* a heat / cold wave. Two minimal vowel changes are possible. The word for someone whom everyone insults is سُبّة *subba*, a disgrace. For more on this, see chapter 34 for الجبين, the forehead. Another small change produces the first element of Passion Week: سِبّة الآلام *sibbat al-'aalaam*. This week leading up to Easter, however, is more commonly referred to as أسبوع الآلام *'usbuu' al-'aalaam* or simply, آلام المسيح *'aalaam al-masiiH*, the Passion of Christ. The logical connection of the period of time to the powerful semantic domain of cause and blame is difficult to establish, and may rather be a cognate with the Hebrew for seven (Sabbath).

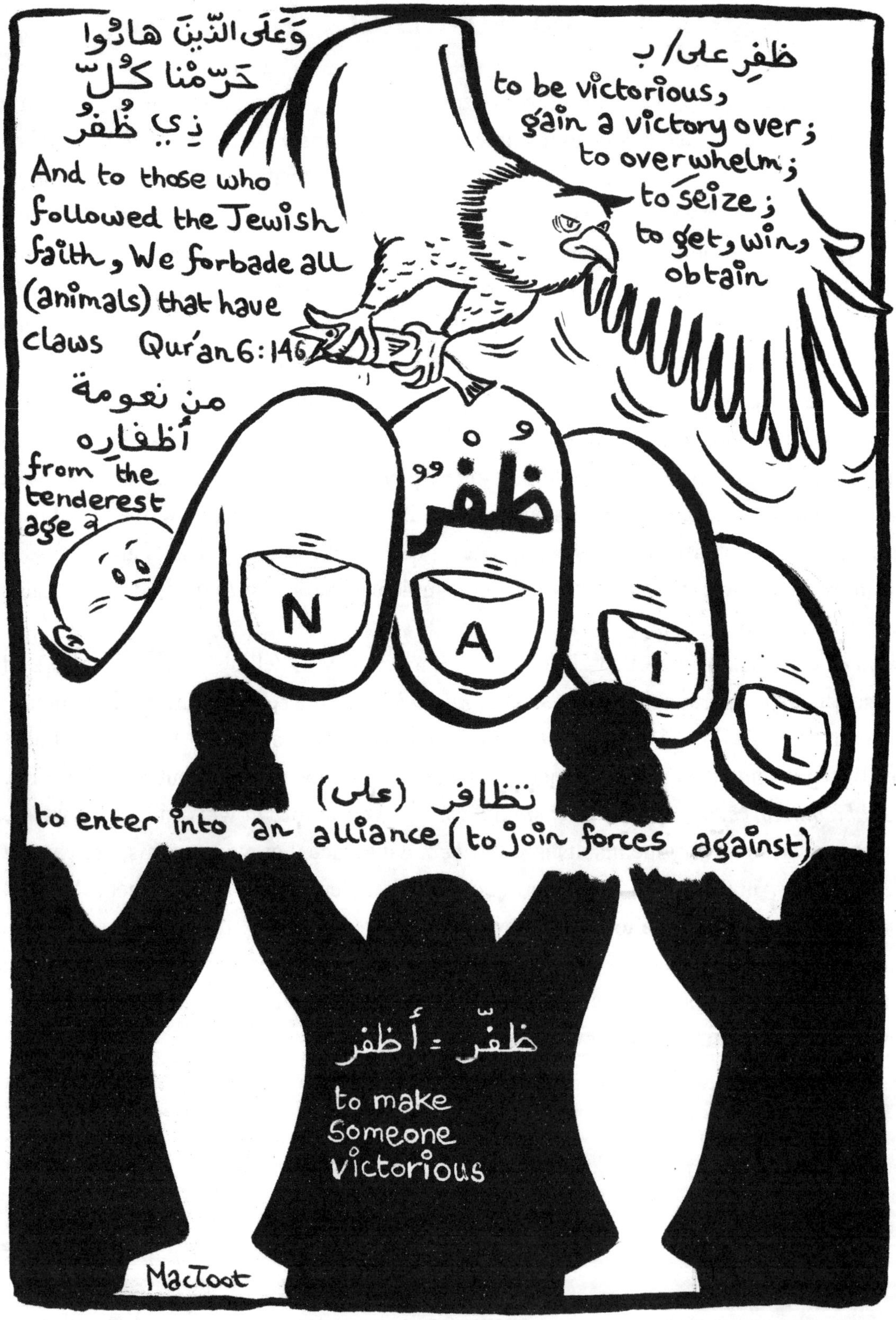
وَعَلَى الَّذِينَ هَادُوا حَرَّمْنَا كُلَّ ذِي ظُفُرٍ
And to those who followed the Jewish faith, We forbade all (animals) that have claws Qur'an 6:146
ظفِر على/ب
to be victorious, gain a victory over; to overwhelm; to seize; to get, win, obtain
من نعومة أظفاره
from the tenderest age
ظُفْرٌ
N A I L
تظافر (على)
to enter into an alliance (to join forces against)
ظفّر = أظفر
to make someone victorious
MacToot

86

Nail ظُفْر – أَظْفار

Seizing Victory

The fingernail and the toenail, الظفر *az-Zufr*, are reminiscent of the claw and the talon, and it is the successful function of the latter in predators that provides the metaphoric cohesion of this root family. Predators must seize and overwhelm their prey to survive and thrive, and the image of triumphant seizure is behind vocabulary from this root. To be successful or victorious is Form I ظفِر – يظفَر بِـ *Zafira bi*. Triumph, itself, is the *maSdar* الظفَر *aZ-Zafar*. Making a parallel between the animal and human domains, the Arabs describe someone who seizes the most plunder or gets the better end of a bargain by saying ظفر بنصيب الأسد *Zafara bi-naSiib al-'asad*, he got the lion's share. To grant victory to or render someone triumphant over someone else is conveyed by either of Arabic's causatives, Form II ظفّر and Form IV أظفر. This latter form is used in the Qur'an in 48:24: مِن بَعْدِ أَنْ أَظْفَرَكُم عَلَيْهِمْ, *After He had made you victors over them*. If mutuality and interaction is to be conveyed, the root avails itself of Form VI تظافر, to enter into an alliance, to join forces. Adding the preposition على allows one to specify against whom the alliance will work.

Among this root's nominal derivatives are a number of historical personages of note. Abu Muhammad az-Zaafir bi-'amr illaah was the twelfth Fatimid caliph. He ruled Egypt from 1149 to 1154, when he was assassinated by his minister Abbas. His name, which begins with his *kunya*, father of Muhammad (Abu Muhammad), is immediately followed by a title, Triumphant by God's Command (az-Zaafir bi-'amr illaah). It is also possible to imply God's agency simply by the use of a passive participle, as in مُظفَّر *muZaffar*, rendered victorious. With a variety of English transliterations, this name has become a particularly popular one in the Muslim East, from Turkey and Iran to Pakistan, India, and Malaysia.

The nail also figures in an endearing idiomatic expression. Observing the soft, pliant nature of a baby's fingernails, the Arabs coined a metaphor to refer to an enduring feature of one's life or character, true since earliest childhood: منذ نُعومة أظفاره *mundhu nu'uumat 'aZfaarihi*, 'since the softness of his fingernails.'

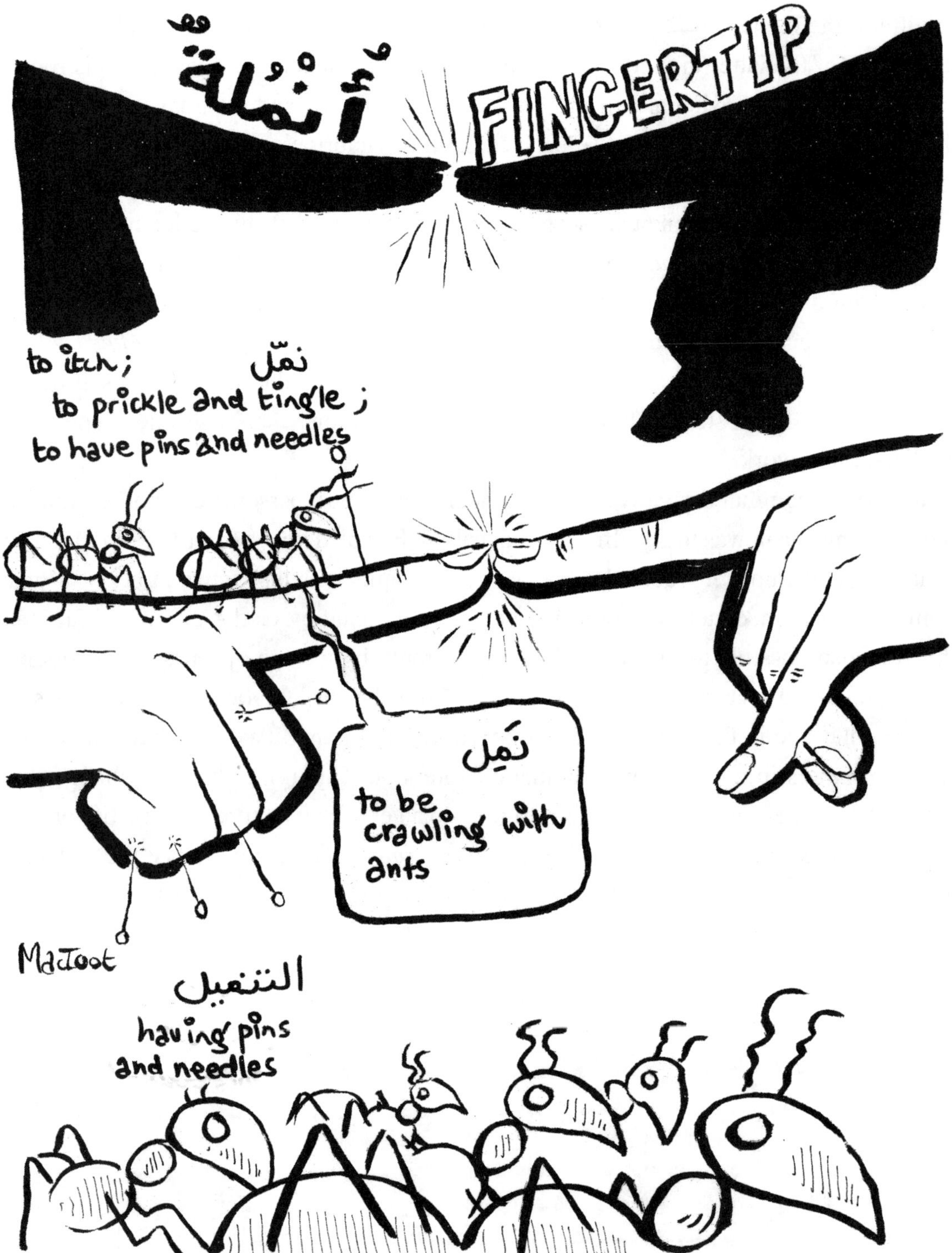

أُنْمُلة
FINGERTIP
نمّل
to itch ;
to prickle and tingle ;
to have pins and needles
نَمِل
to be crawling with ants
التنميل
having pins and needles

87
Fingertip أُنْمُلة – أَنامِل
Tingling

The noun أنامل *'anaamil* is only in common usage in the plural, and its pattern, أفاعِل is not among Arabic's most common. The singular pattern, أُفْعُلة, is particularly unusual. To specify 'a fingertip,' as opposed to many or all of them, speakers may resort to the very classical بنان *banaan*. Alternatively, they may choose an *iDaafa* construction: طرف الإصبع *Taraf al-'iSba'*, the tip of the finger which may also be used in the plural, أطراف الأصابع *'aTraaf al-'aSaabi'*. Returning to the ن – م – ل root, however, and bearing issues of frequency in mind, it is tempting to posit that the Arabs got their inspiration from the natural world when they coined الأنامل. The common, prickly sensation one feels when an ant walks across exposed skin may have suggested the ultra-sensitive fingertips. Although not as prolific as the body, the animal world is another unified semantic field with derivative amplitude. Among insects, the word ants, النمل *an-naml*, ranks 4,738 in the *FDA*. At 5,945, أنامل is considerably rarer. Strengthening the hypothesis that sensitivity is the semantic key to the word for fingertips is the fact that أصابع refers both to fingers and toes, but أنامل refers exclusively to the hypersensitive fingertips. English, as well, has no single word for the tips of the toes, a linguistic fact that may reflect their comparative insensitivity. Both أنامل and أصابع are old words, found in the Qur'an, though only once and twice, respectively.

Giving verbal amplitude to the idea of sensitivity and tingling, the Form I نمِل - ينْمَل *namila* and Form II نمّل both mean to itch, prickle, and tingle, as a limb whose circulation has been impeded tends to do. Its *maSdar*, التنميل *at-tanmiil*, pins and needles in English parlance, is the only noun from the form in common use. The uncommon adjective نَمِل *namil*, means, literally, to be crawling with ants.

CHEST صَدْرٌ
مكان الصَّدارة forefront; position of prestige
صدر الإسلام
The Dawn of Islam
صدر عن/من
to proceed, emanate, arise from; to be published
مَصْدَر
Source
صدّر
to export, dispatch, forward
أصدر
$
to issue (banknotes, passport); to pronounce (a legal sentence); to export; to publish
صُدَيْرِيّ
Vest
تصدّر
to be sent, dispatched; to have a front seat; to preside, head
MacToot

88
Chest صَدْر – صُدور
Front and Center!

The chest is in front, centrally located and prominent. It is no accident that many expressions in which it figures and much of the vocabulary derived from it relate to issues of preeminence. With literal and figurative senses, صدر *Sadr* and its plural صدور *Suduur* occur forty-four times in the Qur'an. The ص – د – ر root is demonstrably one with staying power, too. In modern media, ten of its derivatives figure in the *FDA*, making it a truly prominent body part.

Being at the front can mean being first. Hence the initial phase of anything may include a reference to the chest, as in صدر الإسلام *Sadr al-'islaam* the early days of Islam. In another figurative collocation, الصدر depicts the seat of emotions: انقبض صدره *inqabaDa Sadruhu.* The chest should jut out, but this phrase means his chest constricted. Such departures from the norm signal trouble: he felt distressed, ill at ease, anxious. The chest even has something to add to the sartorial realm. Like صدرة *Sudra*, the diminutive form صُدَيري *Sudayriyy* 'a little chest,' provides a fair portrait of the vest. In the latter instance, it is clearly a garment of reduced proportions.

With its variable present tense voweling and alternative prepositions, the Form I verb صدَر - يصدُر/ يصدِر من /عن *Sadara min / 'an* means to come or go out, to appear, to be published. Each variation suggests movement from a point of origin. Books may do this, as in صدر الكتاب *Sadara al-kitaab*, as well as legal verdicts, صدر الحكمُ *Sadara al-Hukm*. This verb is also the origin of the place noun المَصدَر *al-maSdar*, the starting point or source of something, whether literal or figurative. This word ranks 407 in the *FDA*. What makes it so commonplace? In addition to describing a literal source, المصدر is the technical term used for the all-important grammatical category often called a 'verbal noun.' Like a gerund, it designates an activity and may have the force of a verb. By designating verbal nouns, المصادر *al-maSaadir*, as sources, ancient grammarians underscored how significant they considered them to be. Another important Form I derivative is الصدارة *aS-Sadaara*, forefront, or chairmanship. Used in مكان الصدارة *makaan aS-Sadaara*, it means the position of prestige. Form V تصدّر can mean to be placed in the forefront, or to preside over. This is a verbal version of مكان الصدارة. In fact, semantic links between Forms I and V are not uncommon. The second sense of تصدّر is to be sent or dispatched, a reflexive version of Form II.

The chest has two causative elaborations, Forms II صدّر and IV أصدر. They describe a variety of ways in which to send something forth. Form II exporters, المصدّرون *al-muSaddiruuna*, work in exporting, التصدير *at-taSdiir*. Exports themselves are conveyed by the Form I active participle, الصادرات *aS-Saadiraat*, literally, the things that go forth. The Form IV verb also applies broadly to official contexts and is therefore used with currency, legal sentences, and books, meaning to issue, pronounce, or publish, depending on the object.

The chest's pushy potential is on display in Form III, صادر, a cantankerous verb meaning to throw obstacles in someone's way, or to confiscate land or merchandise. This suggests an aggressive intervention to impede a person's progress, or to dispossess him. Picture a brawny character, chest puffed out, accosting someone and appropriating for himself the other's goods.

قصّ قصصاً على....
to narrate, to tell a story to someone
قصّ
تقصّص
انقصّ
to break up, to be scattered
STERNUM
BREASTBONE
story
قِصّة
MacToot
القِصاص
just retribution
to cut, shear, lop off
قصّ
قصّ أثرَه
to follow someone's tracks
مقصّ
scissors

89

Sternum قَصّ

Cutting off; Narrating

The derivatives of this body part have a wide scope of meaning, one whose metaphoric elaborations call for more than a little speculation. The sternum or breastbone, itself, is not a common word, but both the longevity and the frequency of some of its derivatives are undeniable. The noun قِصّة *qiSSa*, a story, ranks 414 in the *FDA*, and its plural قصص *qaSaS*, though voweled with an initial *fatHa* instead of the modern *kasra,* occurs six times in the Qur'an, and is even the title of Chapter 28, where the story of Moses is recounted over a span of forty-three verses. Logically enough, one of the prime meanings of the Form I verb قصّ - يقُصّ *qaSSa* is to narrate. If one mentions those to whom the account is told, the preposition على *'alaa* is used. However, the phrase قصّ أثَرَه *qaSSa 'atharahu* means to follow someone's tracks. This link is perhaps a simile for the tracker's need to link the smallest details that a trail offers, creating from them a kind of narrative: the person headed this way, camped here, built a fire, and so on.

This same verb has another important sense: to cut, shear, or lop something off. Here, the shape of the sternum offers a vital clue. Located in the middle of the chest, the sternum resembles a vertically aligned dagger, with handle at the top, long flat blade, and tapered, pointed tip. The visual connection to cutting is clear. When it came time to name that very practical cutting tool, المقصّ *al-miqaSS*, scissors, the sternum provided a natural visual metaphor.

There is also an important derivative with special relevance to exacting justice. This is the Form III *maSdar* القِصاص *al-QiSaaS*, just retribution. Used four times in the Qur'an, this juridical term refers to what the family of the victim may demand from someone who has murdered one of its members. As the expression 'an eye for an eye' reminds us, the concept of retribution was shared by more than one society of the ancient Near East. This biblical expression applies to retribution for a variety of injuries, rather than for murder. The use of the term القصاص is still in vogue today in some Islamic circles, and demands for an expedited and religiously legitimized settling of accounts were heard in more than one country during the turbulence of the Arab uprisings when so many lost their lives to the 'opposing side,' however it was defined. But what is the connection of القصاص to cutting and vengeance? It may be that this sanctioned retribution was seen as a way to cut the cycle of relentless vengeance that would otherwise be unleashed by the grim specter of vendetta. It may also be that asking for this retribution necessitated making an account of it, telling its story, as it were.

There are three other derived verbs, Form II, قصّص, an intensive or repetitive version of shearing, and Forms V تقصّص and VII انقصّ, rough equivalents meaning to break up or be scattered, although none is common. One might trace this to the sense of cutting and shearing, which would produce bits and pieces of something that could be so scattered.

ثدي
BREAST
ثديت تثدى
to have or develop large breasts;
to become moist, wet
ثدْياء
buxom
الثديّات
mammals
to nourish ثدّى
MacToot

90
Breast ثدي – أَثْدية / أَثْداء
Nourishment

The Form I verb ثديت – تثدى *thadiyat*, normally conjugated in the feminine, means to have or develop large breasts. A particularly buxom woman can be described as ثدياء, *thadyaa'*, an adjective of the pattern فَعْلاء. This is the feminine version of أفعل, and it is used for the major colors, including hair shades, as in شقراء *shaqraa',* blond, صهباء *Sahbaa',* redhead, and شمطاء *shamTaa',* gray-haired. Quite frequently, it describes physical departures from the ordinary. These are typically defects, as in عمياء *'amyaa'*, blind and خرساء *kharsaa'*, mute, but they may also be positive exceptions to the rule, as in حسناء *Hasnaa'*, beautiful, and هدباء *hadbaa',* long-lashed. This leaves ثدياء open to interpretation: is it critical, or admiring?

No words derived from the ث – د – ي root figure in the Qur'an, but ثدي *thady* and less commonly ثَدًى *thadan*, breast, do make it into the *FDA*, at 4,672. These two singulars, which can be considered grammatically masculine or feminine take the plural forms أثداء *'athdaa'* and أثدية *'athdiya*. They describe male or female anatomy. For medical terminology, الثدي is the designation of choice: سرطان الثدي *saraTaan ath-thady* is breast cancer.

As for ث – د – ي derivatives, one is the very significant zoological term: الثدييات *ath-thadiyiyyaat*. The classification based on the breast is the highest order of vertebrates, mammals. The English term is, in turn, derived from *mamma*, the Latin word for breast and the Italian for mother. It is fascinating to note that while ثدي has no etymological connection to mother in Arabic, *mamma* is quite like the Arabic word for mother, أم *'umm*.

From ancient fertility statuary, through biblical language and classical literature, to modern medical enhancement, breasts have been an enduring subject of esthetic fascination, inspiration, and longing. This word for the breast is not the one Arabic chose to endow with erotic overtones, which tended to be bestowed on النهد *an-nahd*. Instead, the animating metaphor here is size and function. As home of the milk glands and ducts, the breast also has potential problems of overflow. Thus, the Form I verb also means to become wet or damp, a semantic connection nursing mothers would not find surprising. The transitive Form II verb, ثدّى, to nourish, provides further confirmation of the utterly functional connotations of الثدي.

BREAST نَهْد
نهد
ج نُهود
breast, bosom, rise, elevation, hump
نُهَيْد
little breast, little mountain
to be buxom - نهد
to become buxom ينهُد
ناهد
buxom
to heave a sigh تنهّد
MacToot
to distribute shares equally
تناهد

91
Breast نَهْد – نُهود
Buxom

There are two specific words for the breast in Arabic, الثـدي *al-thady* and النهـد *an-nahd*, both of which have some derivative power. A third word, البـز *al-bizz*, is commonly used to designate either the breast or the nipple (see chapter 93).

In one instance, النهـد offers a metaphoric take on the breast's connection to nourishment. However, for the most part, it presents the breast visually. Geography provides a good example of this. Before the mid-twentieth century, a pair of mountains near the east coast of Saudi Arabia was known as النُهَيدين *an-Nuhaydayn*, the two little breasts. However, this bit of old topographic poetry was too suggestive for officials responsible for naming the new town being constructed on the site, and the name was changed to Dhahran: الظهران, 'the two backs.' Dhahran, today, is the commercially vibrant and verbally sanitized petroleum engine of the kingdom. As for naming mountains for their resemblance to breasts, the Bedouin may not have been alone. A large mountain range in western Wyoming in the U.S. is called the Grand Tetons. This name may have been bestowed on them by French-Canadian trappers or their Iroquois scouts. However, it may also refer to a branch of the Teton Sioux nation that inhabited this area.

In another instance of naming, this time of people rather than places and, of course, in the female domain, Arabic offers the quite traditional and flattering ناهد *naahid*, buxom. This name no longer raises any prurient eyebrows, if it ever did. Its straightforward semantic link with the Form I verb نهـد – ينهُـد *nahada* to be or become buxom, of which it is the active participle, has faded from consciousness, or been banished, and now the name Nahid is just appreciated—or not—for its sound.

There are two more verbal derivatives of النهـد. The first is Form V تنهّـد, to heave a sigh. This verb links the movement involved in sighing to the visible rise and fall of the breasts. It is also a prime example of onomatopoeia: in pronouncing *tanahhada*, there is an audible exhalation which engenders this very movement. The second, تناهد, means to distribute shares of something equally with each other. Here is the functional connection to what the breast has to offer. When 'breast' is incorporated into Form VI, one of whose meanings is repetition, it suggests children clamoring for the nourishing breast, and having to share. This latter interpretation is borne out by the meaning of the Egyptian colloquial verbs ناهد and اتناهد, to pester, to nag.

حضن
to hug,
clasp in one's arms,
to raise,
bring up,
to hatch, brood
or incubate (egg's)
BOSOM
حِضْن
حضّانة
an incubator
to hatch
a plot
احتضن
to clasp in
one's embrace;
to bring up,
raise a child,
to harbor a feeling in one's heart
حضانة
nursery school
MacToot
تحاضن
to cling to one another
to nestle against one another
حاضنة
nursemaid who cares for children

92
Bosom حِضْن – أَحْضان
Protective Embrace

A mother's tender embrace of her child or the solicitous brooding of a hen over her eggs is the image invoked by the Form I verb حضن – يحضُن *HaDana*. This is not the nursing that involves nourishment, but rather that of care and affection. Anatomically, الحضن is the part of the body between the outstretched arms, the bosom or breast. By extension, it can mean an armful and an embrace. Bosom and its plural rank a rather high at 3,262 in the *FDA*, and it may be that poetry and love song lyrics have helped them get there. In a line of Umm Kulthum's famous song "Amal hayati" (the hope of my life), we find, in the spoken Egyptian register, "Let me stay by you, في حضن قلبك *fi HuDn 'albak*, in your heart's embrace. . . ."

The locus of an affectionate embrace is the metaphoric source of all three verbs built on this root. Form I is to embrace someone physically, and it is this image that gave rise to its second sense, to raise children. The necessarily transitive Form I almost always involves another person (although it is possible to hug something one is carrying), obviating the need for Form III. However, mutuality still needs specifying, and the go-to form for this is Form VI, تفاعل. The verb تحاضن thus means to cling to one another, to nestle against each other. Here, it is fascinating to contemplate how English metaphorically evokes this same idea. Where do hens brood? In a nest. Their little chicks are the diminutive *nestlings*, and those nestlings *nestle* together. Although the starting point in English is the nest rather than the breast, both languages paint a remarkably similar picture. Related derivatives in the nominal vein in Arabic include the participial حاضِنة *HaaDina*, a nanny who cares for children, as well as the *maSdar*, الحِضانة *al-HiDaana,* bringing up a child, custody. With a minimal change of short vowels, this word is transformed into حَضانة *HaDaana*, a nursery school. Modifying this last word by doubling its second root letter produces حضّانة *HaDDaana*, an incubator. Words of this pattern, with its telltale *shadda*, describe devices or machines that repetitively perform an action. They are usually based on a Form I verb (فتّاحة *fattaaHa*, opener, سيّارة *sayyaara*, automobile, نظّارة *naZZaara*, glasses, ثلّاجة *thallaaja*, refrigerator/freezer) or on a simple noun (ملّاحة *mallaaHa*, salt shaker, صبّانة *Sabbaana*, soap dish/dispenser).

Returning to the root at hand, the Form VIII verb احتضن *iHtaDana* also ranks in the top 5,000, at 4,368. More frequent than Form I, it is often synonymous with it. The little galaxy of associated Form VIII vocabulary includes the *maSdar* الاحتضان *al-iHtiDaan*, as well as the active participle مُحتضِن *muHtaDin*. But احتضن has another metaphoric sense, too: to harbor a feeling in one's heart, and from there, with more explicitly negative implications, to cook up a stratagem, or once again in the fowl domain, to *hatch* a plot.

to snatch, to steal; بزّ
to plunder
to defeat, to outdo
بزّ
BREAST
NIPPLE
ابتزّ
to blackmail;
to pilfer;
to fleece
الابتزاز
blackmail,
extortion
بزّ
to bud
بزبوز ج بزابيز
nozzle, spout
MacToot

93
Breast, Nipple بِزّ – بِزاز / أَبْزاز
Nourishment; Plunder

At least one classical Arabic dictionary, *al-Wasit*, claims that بِـزّ *bizz*, breast/nipple is of Persian origin, but I was unable to confirm this in other sources. Even if it is a borrowing, it is an old one, as there exist classical expressions such as بِـزّ الرجـل لا يُـدرّ لبنًا *bizz ar-rajul laa yadurru labanan*, a man's breast gives no milk, describing men as being naturally disinclined to mercy. As for its proper usage in Arabic, most dictionaries say it means both the nipple and the breast in humans, but can also refer to the nipple in quadrupeds. In pure terms of sonority, this sibilant mono-syllable is more suggestive than الضـرع *aD-Dar'*, the common word for udder, or حلمة *al-Halama* used for the teat of most mammals, or الخِلف *al-khilf*, a rare word for a camel's teat. While the precise anatomical parameters of البِـز may be a bit fluid, the idiomatic expressions in which it is used and the constellation of vocabulary derived from the ب – ز – ز root provide an intriguing degree of metaphoric coherence. That constellation, however, does *not* include the vocabulary having to do with fabric, which seems instead to stem from the Turkish 'bez,' cloth or linen. Consequently, the three words بـزّة *bazza*, a uniform, بـزّاز *bazzaaz*, a cloth merchant or draper, and البـزازة *al-bazaaza*, the cloth trade, may not belong to this Arabic root family.

One meaning of the Form I verb بـزّ – يبَزّ *bazza* is to bud or burgeon. This immediately suggests the nipple, erectile tissue that sprouts, in a manner of speaking, from the breast. Budding seems the likely source word, since Arabic also has حلمة at its disposal for more erotic insinuations. An interesting nominal derivation takes the one-syllable بِـزّ and redoubles it to form بزبـوز *bazbuuz*, a nozzle or spout. This playful bit of acoustic aggrandizement, more common in the spoken register, uses appearance (protuberance) and adds function to it (outlet for liquid) to link a natural or man-made spout to the anatomical nipple.

The breast/nipple also has a near homonym, بَـز *bazz*, and one of its meanings is weapon. This leads us to a second important semantic dimension of the Form I verb: to defeat or outdo someone in a particular field, such as debate. It can also mean to steal in an underhanded way, to snatch. If such snatching is carried out in more systematic fashion, the sense becomes to take booty, as in the proverb مـن عـزّ بـزّ *man 'azza bazza*, he who is powerful plunders. This example reveals the root's underlying associations with conquest and forceful appropriation. How counter-intuitive, given the soft and feminine aura of the breast and nipple! The breast and nipple are the primordial symbols of the nursing, nourishing mother, whose warm embrace provides both security and food. It is the Form VIII verb that shows how the softness of the breast and the violence of plunder are linked: ابتـزّ means to fleece, blackmail, extort. Extortion and blackmail, الابتزاز *al-ibtizaaz*, require the abuser to identify the victim's vulnerable soft spot, and, using the breast analogy, milk it for all it is worth. The blackmailer, المبتـزّ *al-mubtazz*, like an insatiable child, latches onto his victim and doesn't let up, draining him or her right down to the last drop.

حَلَمَة
NIPPLE
to dream .... حلَمَ - يحلُم
a dream(s) ... حُلْم (أحْلام)
حليم
gentle and forebearing
حالم
dreamer
tick, mite حلمة
parasitic حلميّ
الحُلُم
puberty
بلغ الحُلُم
احتلم
attain puberty or sexual maturation
محتلم
pubescent
حلمة الأذن
ear lobe
MacToot

94
Nipple حَلَمة – حَلَمتان – حَلَمات / حَلَم
Dreaming

The م – ل – ح root is an extraordinarily common one, but few native speakers stop to think that dreaminess and mild-mannered patience could be rooted in the body. Morphology shows clearly that both are directly linked to the nursing mother and the dreamily contented aspect of her baby, fondly attached to الحلمة *al-Halama*, the nipple. To dream is the Form I verb حلَم – يحلُم *Halama*, and it may be used with either بـ *bi* or عن *'an* should one go on to specify what one is dreaming of. The noun حُلْم *Hulm*, dream and its plural أحْلام *'aHlaam* rank 637 in the *FDA*, while the verb, at 1,895, is also very frequent. The active participle حالِم *Haalim* can designate a dreamer, or his dreamy state, and the common adjective حليم *Haliim*, gentle and forbearing, also figures among الأسماء الحُسْنى *al-'asmaa' al-Husnaa*, often called God's 'most beautiful' names. The words أحلام and حليم are also used multiple times in the Qur'an.

Physical resemblance to the nipple, essentially just a rounded protuberance, was also an inspiration for related vocabulary. The word حلمة is also used to mean a tick or mite. Consequently, the *nisba* adjective حلميّ *Halamiyy* can refer to either noun, and may mean parasitic, like a tick, or just nipple-shaped. Adding 'ear' to the nipple creates حلمة الأذن *Halamat al-'udhun*, the earlobe. Unlike الرَّحِم *ar-raHim*, the uterus, the derivatives of which are likewise rooted in the mother's body, vocabulary that can be traced back to the nipple may also have a sexually charged meaning. The noun الحُلُم *al-Hulum* means puberty. This word is used twice in the Qur'an, including at 24:58–59: وَإذا بَلَغَ الأَطْفالُ مِنْكُمُ الْحُلُم فَلْيَسْتَأْذِنوا كَما اسْتَأْذَنَ الّذِينَ مِنْ قَبْلِهِم, *When children in your entourage reach puberty, they should ask permission (to enter private chambers), as those before them have done.*

The suggestive phonetic similarity of dream حُلْم *Hulm* and puberty حُلُم *Hulum* is hardly coincidental. As in English, the concept of dreaming is also associated with the erotic. To attain puberty, or sexual maturity, can be expressed by the phrase بلغ الحُلُم *balagha al-Hulum* or simply by the Form VIII verb احتلم. Its active participle produces the adjective محتلم *muHtalim*, pubescent, at one time also considered to mean being of marriageable age.

مريء
ESOPHAGUS
مرؤ to be manly, wholesome
امرأة / المرأة the woman/woman
امْرَء / المرْء the man; man people, one
BON APPÉTIT
مَطْرَح ما يِسْري يمْري wherever it goes, may it be wholesome
استمرأ to find wholesome, relish, enjoy
المُروءة Chivalry, Valor, manliness, sense of honor
MacToot

95
Esophagus مَريء – أمْرِئة / مُروء
Manliness

What possible link could the Arabs have identified between esophagus and manliness? That bulge in the throat known as the Adam's apple in English is technically thyroid cartilage. High levels of testosterone enlarge this cartilage and cause it to protrude. A man امْـرَء *imra'*, therefore, will typically have what is a relatively prominent (upper) esophagus, مـريء *marii'*. In fact, the word for this part of the anatomy is also an adjective, which means manly and virile, as well as healthy and wholesome. The qualities associated with the ideal man (chivalrous, valiant, generous, and honorable) are summed up in the word المُـروءة *al-muruu'a* or, which may also be pronounced with its hamza assimilated to the و of the pattern, المُـرُوّة *al-muruwwa.* In terms of formation, it seems likely that man, امـرء, is the starting point for the vocabulary of this semantic family: the *maSdar* manliness, the adjective manly, and finally, by association, the esophagus. The word for woman simply appended the standard 'ة' to this word, creating امْرَأة *imra'a.* Note the unusual spelling change that occurs when these words are made definite; both lose their initial *alif–kasra* and modify their internal vowels: المَـرْء *al-mar'* and المَرْأة *al-mar'a*. Both man and woman, of course, are high frequency words. However, woman is higher in the list (*FDA* 321 or 1,052, depending on definiteness) than man (2,137), a rather unexpected statistic until one recalls that امـرأة is the only word for woman in the general sense, while امـرء has a very versatile alternative, رَجُـل *rajul*, *FDA* 32.

Along the way, this vocabulary cluster picked up two verbs with a variety of very positive connotations. Form I مـرُؤ – يمْـرُؤ *maru'a*, in reference to a person, means to be manly, and of the climate, to be healthy. In the context of food, it also means to be wholesome and palatable. This sense correlates with the *function* of the esophagus, a conduit for nutrition. Food and vitality have an age-old correlation, something attested to by a famous formula from the spoken register, مطـرح مـا يسـري يمـري *maTraH ma yisrii yimrii*, wherever it goes, may it be healthy. Said by host to guest as or after the latter eats, this wish is like a retroactive 'Bon appétit.' But it is offered in connection to food, not drink, since nourishment is the operative idea. Form X verbs sometimes express the idea of deeming something to be whatever the meaning of Form I is. An excellent example of this is to be found in اسـتمرأ, which means to derive pleasure from something, to find something tasty, or, in the brilliant English trick of turning nouns into verbs, to savor and relish it.

جَنْب
SIDE
جانِبيّ
lateral; marginal; secondary
تجنّب
to avoid, keep away from, steer clear of
جَنْباً إلى جَنْب
side by side
جنب
to avert, ward off; to keep someone from
أجنبيّ
foreigner
جنّب
to avert, ward off; keep (someone) out of the way of, to spare someone or something
جانب = اجتنب
to walk by someone's side, run alongside of; skirt, flank
جنوب
south
MacToot

96

Side جَنْب – جَنْبان – أَجْناب / جُنوب

Away

English expressions often connect the side to movement, and in one of the noteworthy instances where English employs a small spelling change in the way the Arabic derivational system typically does, we have the verb *sidle*. To *sidle up to* someone is to move unobtrusively or surreptitiously toward his or her side. Occasionally one can be said to *sidle away from* someone. The ج – ن - ب root offers a similar take on motion. Forms I جنَب – يجنُب *janaba* and II جنّب are largely synonymous, and can be singly or doubly transitive. Singly, one averts something, sidestepping it, so to speak. These verbs can also mean to keep someone out of the way. Doubly, one spares oneself or someone else something difficult, unpleasant, or dangerous. Form V تجنّب is quite similar to these, with the vague implication of a more sustained effort, and may be translated to avoid or steer clear of. There is another pair of more or less synonymous verbs from this root. Form III جانب and VIII اجتنب mean to walk by someone's side or next to something, or to flank, as trees do a street.

Nominally, the side is quite productive: جنب and six of its derivatives figure in the *FDA*. The ج – ن – ب root is extremely well represented in the Qur'an, too, where eight varieties are used thirty-three times. The word جانب *jaanib* can also be construed as a direction, as when one says من كلّ جانب *min kulli jaanib*, from every side/direction. This is the most frequent of all the words that refer to the side, ranking 208 in the *FDA*. For purposes of comparison, this word for the side is even slightly more common than love (الحب) and university (الجامعة)! It may be from the sense of جانب as a direction that the specific direction of the word جَنوب *januub*, south, evolved. Another derivative found in the Qur'an is جُنُب *junub*, a juridical sense still used in modern times to designate the ritual impurity of not having washed after intercourse, a state that precludes prayer. But this same word in the Qur'an can also mean that which is off to one side, or unrelated, or separate. This is its sense in 28:11, فَبَصُرَتْ بِهِ عَنْ جُنُبٍ, *so she watched him from a distance*. Similarly, in 4:36, reference is made to الجار الجُنُب, the distant neighbor, and/or the neighbor who is not of kin. From here, it is not such a leap to the high-frequency (*FDA* 723) أجنبي *'ajnabiyy*, foreign. Nevertheless, that word does not occur in the Qur'an. In another interesting take on this connotation of distance, the word جَناب *janaab* can be used out of deference, perhaps emphasizing one's social distance from the addressee, as in جناب الوزير *janaab al-waziir*, the right honorable minister.

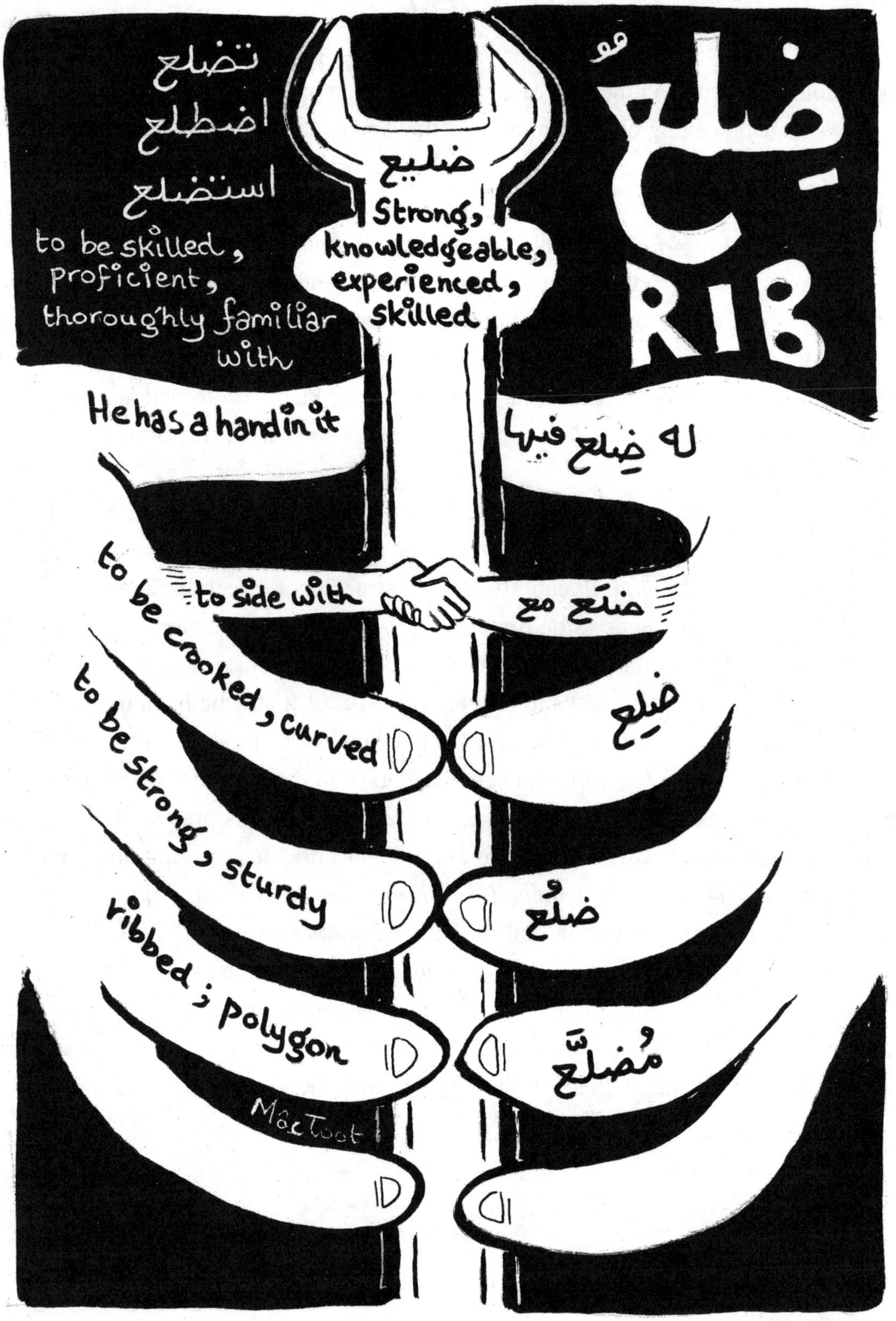
ضِلْع
RIB
تضلع
اضطلع
استضلع
to be skilled, proficient, thoroughly familiar with
ضليع
Strong, knowledgeable, experienced, skilled
He has a hand in it
له ضِلع فيها
to side with
ضلَع مع
to be crooked, curved
ضِلع
to be strong, sturdy
ضلُع
ribbed; polygon
مُضلَّع
MacToot

97

Rib ضِلْع – ضُلوع / أَضْلاع / أَضْلُع

Standing Out; Strength; Involvement

The soft, vital organs of the chest cavity must be protected from harm, and the robust ribs are the just the ones to do it. These sturdy bones are also curved, and the protruding sides of the rib cage make it quite noticeable. The ribs quite literally *stand out*. Such functional and visual characteristics are what animate the Form I verb ضلَع – يضلَع *Dala'a*. In fact, the Arabs endowed its past tense with three different short vowels, each associated with a distinct meaning: ضلَع مع *Dala'a ma'a*, to side with someone; ضلِع *Dali'a*, to be curved; ضلُع *Dalu'a*, to be strong, sturdy, robust. Then, giving this last meaning a clever figurative slant, they created the adjective ضليع *Dalii'*, a person well-versed in something and whose specific abilities stand out. It is interesting to note that Arabic does not associate the ribs with making fun of people. English, however, conceived of a link between the ribs and painful humor. In 'ribbing' and 'poking fun at,' it cleverly embodies the discomfort, often accompanied by pained laughter, of being tickled in the ribs.

All by itself, the rib is used in an interesting idiom. Arabic expresses personal involvement in something in several ways involving the body. One may have a hand in it, له يد فيها *lahu yad fiihaa*, but it is also possible to have a rib in it, له ضلع فيها *lahu Dil' fiihaa*. The person involved can be described with the active participle: هو ضالع فيها *huwa Daali' fiihaa*, he is mixed up in it. In the case of the rib, Arabic seems to be playing on the image of *interiority*. The involvement referred to is perhaps less obvious, more devious than that suggested by the hand.

Since Form I can mean to be curved, the Form II ضلّع may mean to bend something, causing it to be curved. However, it can also be a literal and causative reference to the body part, to give something ribs. In derived forms, one should look to the participles for adjectives, and the passive participle of this Form II is مُضلَّع *muDalla'*, ribbed. As in English, this is a great way to describe the texture of corduroy, a fabric in which the wale protrudes, standing out from the rest of the background warp.

To be very skilled can be conveyed with three different verbs. Forms V and X use the preposition من *min*: تضلّع من، استضلع من. Form VIII prefers the preposition بـ bi-, اضطلع بـ, *iDTala'a*. The unexpected ط in this verb is the result of assimilation: all Form VIII verbs whose first root letter is ض change the standard ت infix to a ط. All three turn the adjective ضليع into an action: to be skilled, proficient, thoroughly familiar with, at home in (a field of knowledge). Here, again, is the idea that the rib is right in the thick of things, well acquainted with the whole area. Form VIII can also mean to take on a difficult task. In that case, the reference is to the strength of the ribs which allow one to shoulder—in English parlance—a burden.

السَّحَر
pre-dawn hours
LUNGS
PULMONARY REGION
سَحْر
Bewitched
مُسَحَّر
ساحِر
ساحِرة
sorcerer, witch
magic = سِحر
sorcery, witchcraft = السِّحْر
to eat تسحَّر
pre-dawn meal
انتفخت مساحره
his chest swelled up
مسحَّراتي
مَسْحور
someone on whom a spell is cast...
ساحِر
enchanting
سحّارة
crate, chest
Ramadan Pre-dawn meal السَّحور
MacToot

98
Lungs; Pulmonary Region سَحْر – مَساحِر
Magic

As a body part, السَحر, *as-saHr* is comparatively obscure. However, its near homophone, السِّحر *as-siHr*, magic, is a very common piece of vocabulary, ranking 2,597 in the *FDA*. Magic is just one of the meanings of السِّحْر; it can also be translated as sorcery and witchcraft. Two other derivatives of the س- ح - ر root also make the top 5,000. Magic, of course, is very ancient vocabulary. Seven distinct forms derived from this root figure in the Qur'an an impressive sixty-three times. Of these, السِّحر, magic, is the most common, appearing in twenty-seven places.

Returning to anatomy, the connection of magic to the lungs is easy to understand. How mysterious the workings of the lungs are! Ancient peoples must have puzzled over the wondrous hidden mechanism that powered breathing. Magical indeed! However, magic is not the source of all the derivatives of this root. Though not so common in and of itself, *saHr* is nevertheless the inspiration for what used to be a common household possession. In a simile based on the physical appearance of a puffed-up chest, Arabic offers the noun سَحّارة *saHHaara*, a crate or *chest*.

The plural form مساحِر *masaaHir* is used in the idiom انتفخت مساحرُه *intafakhat masaaHiruhu*, his lungs swelled or became inflated. This expression does not describe breathing per se but rather the inflated appearance of the rib cage associated with a dramatic emotional state. Someone so described might be puffed up with pride, or very fearful.

This root has three verbal derivatives. Both Form I سحر – يسحَر *saHara* and Form II سحَّر are transitive and mean to cast a spell on, bewitch. People of either gender could do so. It is very interesting to note that the Arabic words show only the typical distinction of gender, ساحِر/ ساحِرة *saaHir/ saaHira*, while their English equivalents, both nominal and verbal, are distinct and gender-biased. A male practitioner of magic is a magician or a sorcerer. A female may be called a sorceress, but is most commonly referred to with the (originally) pejorative witch. This same active participle, ساحِر, can also be used as a common adjective, in which case it has the positive connotations of its English equivalent, enchanting, bewitching. Someone on whom the spell is cast is مَسْحور *masHuur* or, more potently, in Arabic, مُسَحَّر *musaHHar*, bewitched.

Form V is an intransitive verb derived nominally from السَّحَر *as-saHar*, the pre-dawn hours. In Ramadan, the meal taken before the crack of dawn is called السَّحور *as-saHuur* and to eat it is Form V تسحَّر. Lest one drift off to sleep, a مسحّراتي *misaHHaraati* wanders through the streets, banging a drum and calling out a pious phrase that begins, Wake up, sleeper! The noun السَّحَر *as-saHar* is another near-homophone of magic and the lungs, differing from them in only one short vowel. English has some colorful old terms to refer to السَّحَر, too, including the wee hours, and, though not so specific, the witching hour. In *Hamlet*, Shakespeare wrote "Tis now the very witching time of night. . . ." The magical connotations of the dark, mysterious night were clearly not limited to the Arabic worldview.

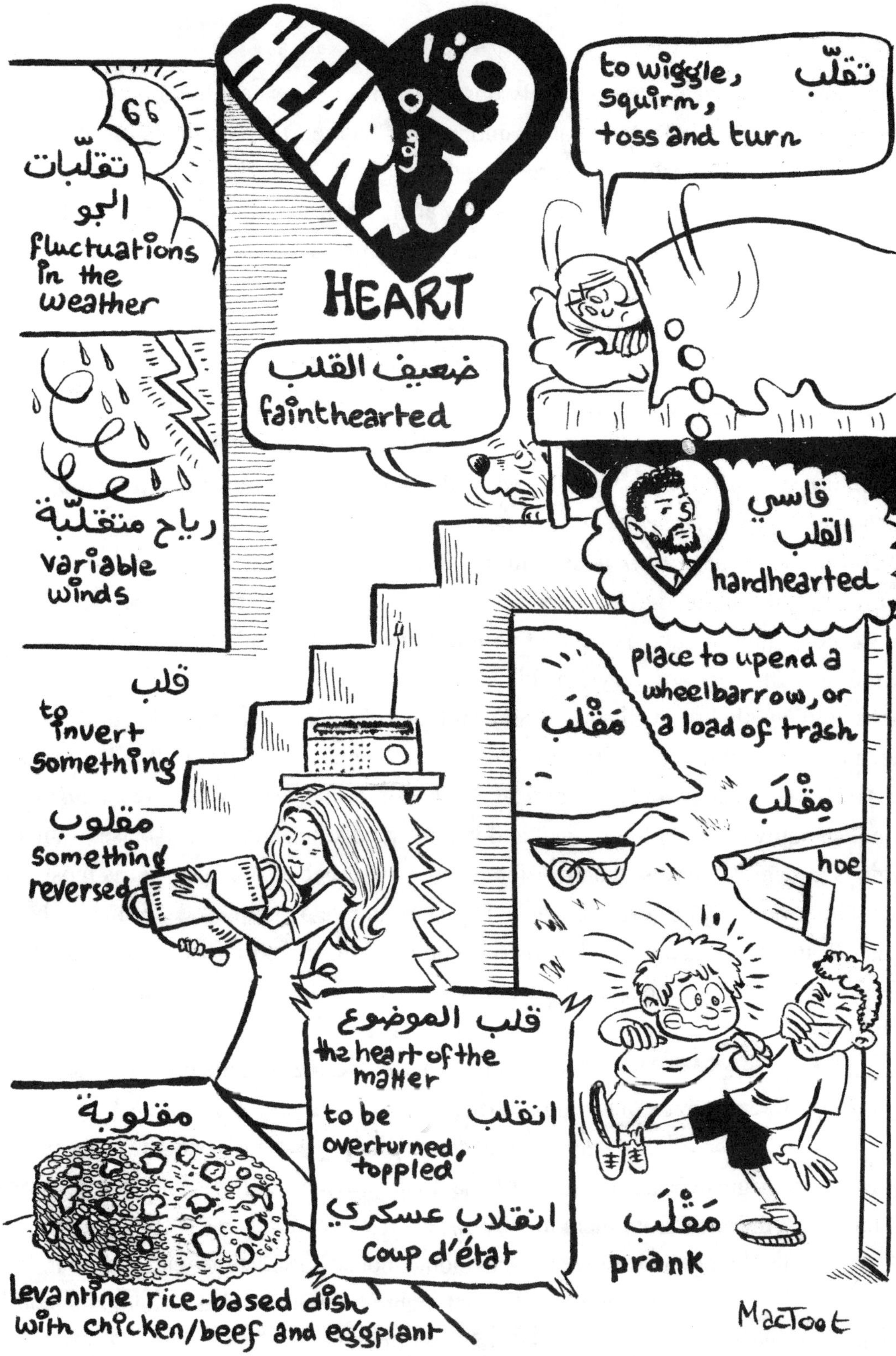
HEART
تقلّب to wiggle, squirm, toss and turn
تقلّبات الجو fluctuations in the weather
ضعيف القلب fainthearted
رياح متقلّبة variable winds
قاسي القلب hardhearted
قلب to invert something
مقلوب something reversed
مَقْلَب place to upend a wheelbarrow, or a load of trash
مِقْلَب hoe
قلب الموضوع the heart of the matter
انقلب to be overturned, toppled
انقلاب عسكري Coup d'état
مقلوبة
Levantine rice-based dish with chicken/beef and eggplant
مَقْلَب prank
MacToot

99
Heart قَلْب – قُلوب
Inconstancy

Arabic has two important words for the heart. As far as القلب *al-qalb* is concerned, English and Arabic agree on a few things. First, both consider this heart to be the seat of bravery, and so the Arabs liked Crusader King Richard's nickname, the Lionheart, well enough to translate it verbatim, قلب الأسد *qalb al-'asad*. Writers of both languages like to offer warm greetings, calling them hearty or heartfelt, تحيات قلبيّة *taHiyyaat qalbiyya*. Someone devoid of tenderness is قاسي القلب *qaasi al-qalb*, hardhearted. Both languages equate heart with essence, as in قلب الموضوع *qalb al-mawDuu'*, the heart of the matter. In the literary domain, Joseph Conrad's masterpiece *The Heart of Darkness* became قلب الظلام, *qalb aZ-Zalaam* in Arabic. Nevertheless, direct parallels between القلب and the heart are fairly limited.

Beyond specifically anatomical references such as heartbeat and heartburn, English derivatives of the heart gravitate toward the semantic domain of sentimentality. One may be heartened, or find a heartthrob, suffer from heartache, be heartsick, or heartbroken. Arabic derivatives of القلب, however, are not nearly so emotive. Instead, astute Arab observers of anatomy noticed that القلب was never still, and they elaborated on its signature flip-flop motion as they put the root through its paces. As for frequency, القلب and its dual and plural are used 133 times in the Qur'an. It remains extraordinarily common in modern usage, too, ranking a heart-stopping 110 in the *FDA*, which makes it the most frequently used body part of all.

The Form I verb قلب – يقلِب *qalaba* means to invert something, turn it upside down, inside out, or outside in. Inverted, therefore, is مقلوب *maqluub*. One use of this passive participle turns up in the culinary domain. The delicious Levantine rice-based dish of chicken or beef with fried cauliflower or eggplant is called المقلوبة *al-maqluuba* due to its signature presentation at table. When the pot is inverted, the turmeric-tinted vegetables cooked first at the bottom of the pot brightly decorate its steaming surface. Form II قلّب is used to convey repetition, as in to turn pages, or to turn multiple things this way and that. The reflexive Form V تقلّب means to get turned over. Possible translations include various types of repetitive movement: to toss and turn, to wriggle, to fluctuate. Meteorology likes Form V, too, as in تقلّبات الجو *taqallubaat al-jaww*, fluctuations in the weather, and رياح متقلّبة *riyaaH mutaqalliba*, variable winds. Form VII, انقلب, a pseudo-passive, typically means to be overturned or toppled. In the political domain, انقلاب عسكريّ *inqilaab 'askariyy* is the ultimate upset, a coup d'état! Adding prepositions introduces some significant changes to the Form VII meaning: the directional إلى yields to turn into or change into (a different state), to become, while the addition of على produces to turn against (someone).

The inversion metaphor is also at work in many common nominal derivatives, such as the hoe المِقْلَب *al-miqlab*, a tool for turning over the earth. A place to upend a wheelbarrow or a load of trash is a dump, مَقْلَب *maqlab*. In Egyptian colloquial, this same noun, *ma'lab*, is a dirty trick, one that might trip you up and send you tumbling. Neologisms have co-opted the root, too: a cement truck that keeps its contents tossing and turning has been dubbed قلّاب *qallaab*.

فأر
to roast or bake in ash (meat, bread)
الفئيد
what has been roasted or baked in ash
فؤاد
emotional understanding
فؤاد
HEART
يا فؤادي لا تسأل أين الهوى ، كان صرحاً من خيالي فهوى
Oh heart, do not ask where love has gone, Twas a castle of my imagination, and has collapsed
Umm Kulthum
Mactoot

100

Heart فُؤاد – أَفْئِدة

Empathic Understanding

This word for the heart has a poetic, emotive ring to it. The celebrated song of lost love "al-Atlal" (the ruins) opens with Umm Kulthum addressing her heart, يا فؤادي *ya fu'aadi*, O, my heart. She commands it not to ask where love has gone, a rhetorical device that then allows for a detailed account of a doomed love. . . . Still popular today, الفؤاد *al-fu'aad* ranks 3,323 in the *FDA*. But it is a very old word, too. Along with its plural أفئدة *'af'ida*, it appears sixteen times in the Qur'an. While القلب *al-qalb* means both the anatomical, beating heart and the more abstract, feeling mind, الفؤاد is strictly the latter. It has strong sentimental and temperamental overtones, and evokes empathic discernment, the emotive side of understanding. Mothers hoping for such a sensitive son may thus be inclined to choose the name Fu'ad.

The Form I verb فأد – يفأد *fa'ada* has a most unexpected and interesting connection with day-to-day Bedouin life. It means to roast meat or bake bread in ashes. In the last few decades, ash pits have become posh features of resorts and select private homes in the West boasting gardens large enough to accommodate them. Cooking in ash and cinders was, of course, a much more plebian feature of seventh-century life. A measure of how common this practice was is suggested by a couple of the verb's other (very classical) derivatives: فئيد *fa'iid*, the term for food that had been roasted or baked this way, and مِفأدة *mif'ada*, the spit or skewer on which it was roasted. The connection would seem to be to the idea of the fire. Emotion typically correlates with heat. But what of understanding? We tend to think of cool reason, but rational analysis only provides a certain type of knowledge, and does not necessarily equate with deep understanding. The transformative power of a cooking fire, which renders something otherwise inedible nutritious, offers further insight into the connection at which الفؤاد may be hinting. There are many ways of cooking raw food, and many ways of coping with and processing the raw data of life experiences. Life often calls on us to make informed emotional judgments, and the empathic faculties of الفؤاد make it the 'organ' of choice. At 16:78, the Qur'an says: وجَعَلَ لَكُمُ السَّمْعَ وَالأَبْصَارَ وَالأَفْئِدَةَ لَعَلَّكُم تَشْكُرون, *And He gave you hearing and sight and minds (*lit., *hearts), so that you might be thankful.*

Interior, heart; center, middle; center of the sky, zenith
كَبِد
LIVER كَبِد
لَقَدْ خَلَقْنا الإنسانَ في كَبَدٍ
Indeed, We have created man for hardship and suffering
Qur'an 90:4
كَبَد
suffering, toiling; hardship
MacToot
كابد
to bear, endure
تكبّد
to bear, endure; to defray (costs)

101
Liver كَبِد – أَكْباد
Suffering/ Centrality

From olden times, the liver الكبد *al-kabid*, has been linked to two basic concepts in Arabic culture. The first of these is centrality. In technical astronomical terms,كبد السماء *kabad / kabid as-samaa'*, was the zenith, the center of the sky, that point directly above the observer's head. To describe the passage of a star through the meridian (a Latin term for the zenith), the Form II verb كبّد could be used. Skillful land and sea navigation permitted the Arabs to successfully engage in long-distance trade, and they became brilliant—and brilliantly imaginative—observers of the stars and their movements. The body of the sky, so to speak, was carefully diagrammed. In this case, its center was metaphorically named after the liver by analogy to the latter's anatomical centrality.

Secondly, the liver had a functional association. Like the skin, it became linked to the idea of suffering. It suggests affliction and distress, and often collocates with خسائر *khasaa'ir*, losses, such as might be incurred in battle, or a bad investment. In fact, the liver has a homonym, *kabad*, meaning hardship and suffering. In the Qur'an, 90:4, this word is chosen to depict an inescapable part of life: لَقَدْ خَلَقْنا الإِنْسانَ في كَبَدٍ, *Indeed, We have created mankind for hardship and suffering.*

Although the liver performs critical functions, it is essentially undetectable until it becomes injured or diseased and ceases to do so. According to Edward William Lane's authoritative *Arabic–English Lexicon* (1885), it is exceedingly rare for names of diseases to be derived from the organ affected, but كُباد, *kubaad*, an ailment of the liver, is one. Inventorying body parts, I have also found النكاف *an-nukaaf*, mumps, an illness which affects النكفة *an-nakafa*, the parotid gland, and الطُّحال *aT-TuHaal*, an inflammation of الطِّحال *aT-TiHaal*, the spleen. The Form I verb كبد – يكبُد / يكبِد *kabada* means to afflict or wear down, and describes what pain, loss, and other adversities may do. The Form II verb كبّد, mentioned above in its technical astronomical application, more commonly refers to suffering: كبّد is doubly transitive, and means to inflict hardship or losses on someone, thus wearing him or her down. However, if one takes hardship upon oneself, both Form III and the reflexive Form V verbs are used, as in كابد / تكبّد خسائر *kaabada / takabbada khasaa'ir*, to sustain losses.

Like the heart, the liver can also be the locus of affection, a fact that may contribute to its high ranking of 3,082 in the *FDA*. In an expression reminiscent of 'the apple of his eye,' but with overtones of dismay, someone may call his own beloved child فلذة كبده *faldhat kabidihi*, literally, a piece of his liver. This classical expression has an echo in the Moroccan spoken register. The exclamation يا كُبيدي, *yaa kubiidi*, 'O, my little liver!' might be translated 'Oh, my poor little darling!' In both registers, the metaphors of suffering and centrality are operative. Another contributor to the frequency of الكبد in the media is an unfortunate medical fact. Liver disease is endemic in Egypt, the Arab world's most populous country, and documentation of أمراض الكبد *'amraaD al-kabid*, liver diseases, التهاب الكبد, *iltihaab al-kabid*, hepatitis, and سرطان الكبد *saraTaan al-kabid*, liver cancer, are all too frequent.

بَطْنٌ
abdomen
هُوَ الأَوَّلُ وَالآخِرُ وَالظَّاهِرُ وَالبَاطِنُ
He is the First and the Last, the Outer and the Inner Qur'an 57:3
to be lined; تبطّن to delve into, to become engrossed in
استبطن to delve into, to try to fathom, to know inside out
بطّن to line a garment
مُبَطَّن lined
SECRET
بطن to be hidden, concealed
to ~ أبطن hide, conceal, harbor
الطّبّ الباطنيّ internal medicine
بَطّانيّة blanket
ventricle بُطَيْن
-Mactoot-

102
Abdomen, Belly بَطْن – بُطون
Interiority

Derivatives of البطـن *al-baTn* are plentiful. Some elaborate on a belly noteworthy for its size, or on things that resemble a belly. Others are extrapolations on the idea of interiority, depicting things not immediately visible or evident. The Form I verb itself suggests this duality. With a medial *Damma*, بطُـن – يبطُـن, *baTuna – yabTunu* means to be or become paunchy. However, with another voweling, بطَـن – يبطُـن *baTana – yabTunu* it means to hide, and to be hidden, or concealed, a meaning it shares with the Form IV verb أبطـن.

A paunchy person can be called بَطِـن *baTin*, and the gluttony that brings this about is البِطْنـة *al-biTna*. Nevertheless, associations with the abdomen are not confined to overeating. Physical shape also served as inspiration for the scientific term for one of the chambers of the heart. Since it is, of course, a dramatically smaller version of this large anatomical feature, the diminutive form فُعَيـل is used, producing البُطَيـن *al-buTayn*, the ventricle. The English word ventricle is, itself, a diminutive of the Latin word for stomach. This auricle / ventricle, أذيـن / بطيـن mirror image cannot have materialized coincidentally, but whether the Latin designations or the Arabic ones are the source is a question for historians of science.

On an utterly prosaic level, another semantic relationship exploited with the abdomen is that of association. What do we use to cover our بطـون *buTuun* on a chilly winter night? The answer, of course, is بَطّانيـة *baTTaaniyya*, a blanket.

For vocabulary that elaborates on the theme of interiority we might start with the *iDaafa* construction for the sole of the foot: بطـن القـدم, *baTn al-qadam*, the foot's least visible part. In analogous fashion, it is possible, though not common to call the palm بطـن اليـد *bAtn al-yad*. Expressions that elaborate on interiority can be very learned or utterly pedestrian. In an example of the former, a crucial duality in philosophy is the contrast between الباطـن *al-baaTin* and الظاهـر *aZ-Zaahir.* While الظاهـر is what is superficial or apparent, الباطـن is what is hidden or intrinsic. Internal medicine is called الطـبّ الباطنـي *aT-Tibb al-baaTiniyy*. Someone afflicted with a gastric or other internal illness in need of a consultation in internal medicine was classically referred to as مَبطـون *mabTuun*. The lining of a garment is its بِطانـة *biTaana*. From this word comes the denominative Form II, بطّـن to line a garment, and its passive participle, مُبطَّـن *mubaTTan*, lined. The Form V verb تبطّن is the reflexive of this Form II, but it also has an abstract meaning, shared by the erudite Form X اسـتبطن to penetrate, to delve into, to know something inside out.

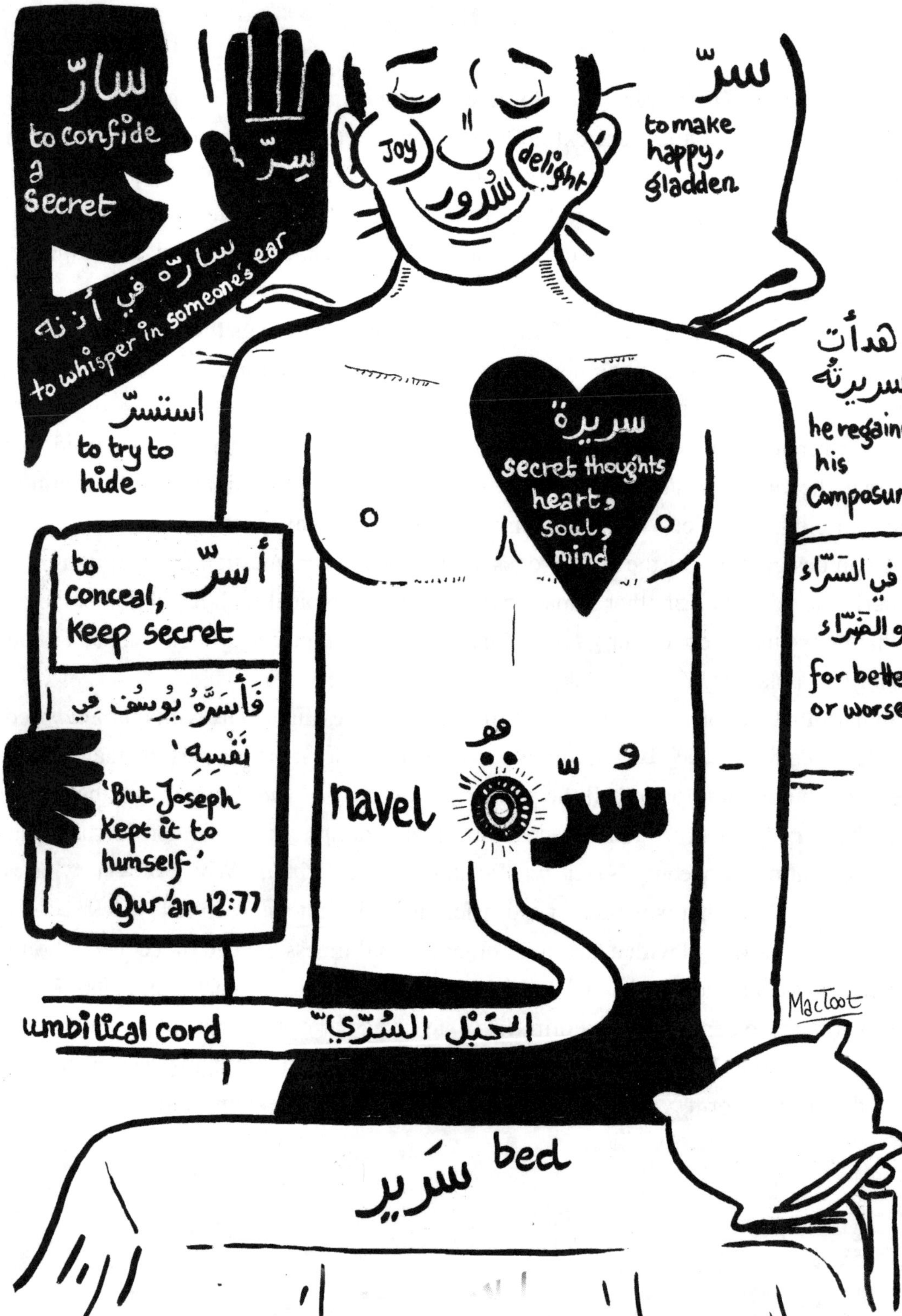

سارّ
to confide a secret
سِرّ
سارّه في أُذنه
to whisper in someone's ear
استسرّ
to try to hide
سرّ
to make happy, gladden
Joy
delight
سُرور
هدأت سريرته
he regained his composure
سريرة
secret thoughts
heart,
soul,
mind
في السرّاء والضرّاء
for better or worse
أسرّ
to conceal, keep secret
'فَأَسَرَّهُ يُوسُفُ فِي نَفْسِهِ'
'But Joseph kept it to himself'
Qur'an 12:77
navel
سُرّة
umbilical cord
الحَبْل السُرّي
MacToot
bed
سَرير

103
Navel سُرّة – سُرَر
Intimacy

The navel, السـرّة *as-surra*, is not without ordinary anatomical associations, foremost among them the medical term, الحبـل السُّـرّيّ *al-Habl as-surriyy*, the umbilical cord. In the vocabulary of food, Egyptian speakers of Arabic, like their English-speaking brethren, say برتقـان بـو سـرّة *burtu'aan bu surra*, navel oranges, taking for inspiration the telltale bulge in the peel so reminiscent of a navel. Labeling that relies on origin or resemblance makes immediate sense, but the connection of the navel to the nouns سـرير *sariir*, bed and سِرّ *sirr*, secret is at first quite mystifying. Still, it is these two words that set the stage for the metaphoric aura of this tiny feature of the anatomy. What they both point to is intimacy. This metaphor is suggestively amplified by other important vocabulary, too, including the common noun السـرور *as-suruur*, joy or pleasure, and the more morphologically unusual السـرّاء *as-sarraa'*, in good times, part of a traditional, formulaic wish for newlyweds echoed in the English 'for better, for worse.'

Although the navel, itself, is not mentioned in the Qur'an, eight of the س – ر – ر root's derivatives are used a noteworthy forty-four times in that text. This is evidence, should we need it, that pleasure and secrets are age-old concerns. In addition, it is a root with modern relevance: five separate words from it figure in the *FDA*.

The vocabulary of joy is, for the most part, specific to Form I سـرّ – يسُـرّ *sarra* and the nouns and adjectives derived from it. The active participle سـارّ *saarr* means delightful, joyous; its passive counterpart, مسـرور *masruur*, delighted. Delight or pleasure appears in the famous and abbreviated polite formula مـن دواعـي سـروري *min dawaa'ii suruuri*, (it would be) among the causes of my delight, I'd be delighted.

The vocabulary of secrets, الأسـرار, is also derived from Form I. The *nisba* adjective سِـرّيّ is quite common and also occurs in the collocation سـري للغاية *sirriyy lil-ghaaya*, top-secret. In another permutation on the theme of secrecy, we find السـريرة *as-sariira*, one's innermost thoughts, commonly translated as 'heart' or 'mind,' as in the expression صفاء السـريرة *Safaa' as-sariira*, peace of mind, or even clearness of conscience.

Four other verb forms flesh out the many possibilities of secrecy. Forms III and VI offer the typical transitive versus reciprocal pairing: سـارّ, to confide a secret to someone, and تسـارّ, to tell each other secrets. Form IV means to conceal something or keep it secret, and Form X, استسرّ, to try to hide something or keep it secret. One of the standard meanings of the Form X verb is to seek whatever is implied in Form I, and as mentioned, many of the derivatives of Form I refer to pleasure as well as to secrecy. In fact, this verb has a very particular medieval meaning, one that is socially and psychologically revelatory. An excellent example of concision, استسـرّ meant to take on a concubine, سـرّيّة *sarriyya*, thus seeking both secrecy and joy.

relief, comfort, release from suffering – CROTCH
فرج
GENITALIA
VULVA
الصبر مفتاح الفَرَج
Patience is the key to relief/release
Patience is the best medicine
to liberate someone, to release from detention أفرج عن
منفرِج
wide open, relaxed
زاوية منفرِجة
obtuse angle
انفرج
to be opened, split apart; to show, reveal; to relax, be relieved
المفرج
relief, relaxation, happy resolution
to show someone something فرّج على
to look at, to watch, observe تفرّج على
فُرْجة
state of happiness; gap, breach, spectacle
MacToot

104

Genitalia; Vulva فَرْج – فُروج

Open; Relieve; Show

Modern Arabic speakers are usually reticent to use the specific vocabulary of the external genitalia. To be sure, some people commonly use coarse words of the spoken register to insulting or erotic effect, but the 'proper' vocabulary of the sexual organs is often rendered by euphemism. As in modern English, a desire for propriety leads to circumlocutions like 'the private parts.' Is this just a modern phenomenon? Undoubtedly not. In fact, الفرج *al-farj*, is an old euphemism.[17]

In modern usage, الفرج is the standard term for the vulva, the opening to the vagina. However, like the word crotch, it also refers somewhat obliquely to the external genitalia of people of either gender and even of animals. In 23:5 of the Qur'an, we find: وَالّذِيـنَ هُـمْ لِفُرُوجِهِـمْ حافِظُـونَ, *Those who guard their chastity* (lit., *sexual organs*). Gender markers in the verse make it a clear reference to men. This word for the genitals has a near homonym in الفَرَج *al-faraj*, relief, comfort, release from suffering, a common noun that figures in the proverb: الصبر مفتاح الفرج *aS-Sabr miftaaH al-faraj*, 'patience is the key to relief/release,' or loosely, 'patience is the best medicine,' Faraj is also a popular man's name. Ordinarily, native speakers give the similarity little thought. Cognitive dissonance keeps the name and what it signifies carefully separated from such impropriety.

Form I فرج – يفرِج *faraja* means to open or split something, as well as to dispel grief or worry. The metaphor that links these two ideas is that an *opening* allows pent up misery to dissipate. Generally speaking, in terms of the body, being open tends to correlate with mental and physical well-being. English and Arabic agree completely on the release involved in زفرة الفرج *zafrat al-faraj*, a sigh of relief. The Form I verb has an interesting *maSdar miimi*, المفرج *al-mafraj*, which mimics the place noun pattern but should be understood to mean relief, relaxation, or a happy resolution. As is usually the case, Form VII offers a pseudo-passive take on all the meanings of Form I. Hence, انفرج *infaraja* can mean to be opened, split apart; to show, reveal; to relax; to be relieved, comforted. This verb's active participle منفرِج *munfarij*, wide-open, relaxed, even has an application in geometry, زاوية منفرجة *zaawiya munfarija*, an obtuse angle.

Form IV أفرج عن means to release someone from detention. Jail capacity around the world is finite, and this verb and its satellites litter the media. The *maSdar* الإفراج عن ranks 3,406 in the *FDA*, as in تـمّ الإفراج عن المعتقل *tamma al-'ifraaj 'an il-mu'taqal*, the prisoner was released. Form II فرّج adds intensity to Form I, to open wide, separate, cleave. With the addition of the preposition عن, it means to comfort or relieve someone. Semantic connections to the anatomy in question are easy to imagine. Changing prepositions, Form II فرّج على means to show (someone) something. It is denominative, based on فُرْجة *furja*, a spectacle. Form II and its Form V reflexive corollary تفرّج على to look at, watch, observe, are particularly suggestive. But who can blame bashful native speakers for not intuiting such an association with this most sheltered part of the body? The idea is entirely counter-intuitive, suggesting, as it may, that the genitalia are destined for show and tell, and matter-of-factly associating them with relief and release.

VULVA بُضْع
بضّع
to carveup, dissect, amputate
تبضّع
to go shopping
بِضع
a few
تبضّع
to be carved up; to be amputated
مِبْضع
scalpel
أبضع
to invest capital
بضاعة
merchandise, goods, wares
to trade استبضع

105
Vulva; Genitalia بُضْع – أَبْضاع
Merchandise; Slash

This word for the vulva, البُضع *al-buD'a*, based on the ب – ض – ع root, is so infrequently used as to be obscure, and one must explore both the nominal and verbal threads of the root to discover its true semantic dimensions. The only two words based on this root to figure in the *FDA* are both nouns. Merchandise, البضاعة *al-biDaa'a*, is the very basis of trade. Goods and commodities are what people have to offer commercially. Even the qualities and attributes with which one is endowed are possible translations of البضاعة. From time immemorial, the importance and universality of trade are difficult to overstate, and trade may also be behind the other common noun based on this root, بِضْع *biD'*, several. Counting and trade go hand in hand, making such a link logical. The commercial angle also finds verbal expression in Form IV, أبضع, to invest capital in an enterprise, and in Form X, استبضع, to trade, literally, seeking goods and commodities. What *is* surprising, however, is the potential link of the vulva to merchandise!

Three other verb forms offer an altogether different—and alarming—association. Instead of the commercial metaphor, the Form I verb بضع – يبضَع *baDa'a* means to cut, slash, or slit open. A near homonym of the vulva is this verb's *maSdar* البَضْع *al-baD'*, amputation. Another small change produces بِضعة *biD'a*, a piece of meat. Should a tool be required, there is مِبْضَع *mibDa'*, scalpel. As is often the case, Form II suggests repetition or intensity, and بضّع can be translated to cut up, carve up, dissect, or amputate. Form V تبضّع conveys the reflexive option, to be carved up or dissected. This confluence of meanings suggests the opening that separates the vulva, as well as the possibility of excision that was sometimes performed on it.

Form III, on the other hand, is the most logical verb associated with the vulva: باضع means to sleep with a woman. This verb joins the many others that use Form III as their morphological conveyance and mean to have sex with someone. Like جامع / ضاجع / عاشر / واقع / باشر and others, Form III suggests acting on another, rather than interacting, semantics with particular relevance to the ب – ض – ع root and its associations of slashing and commodification!

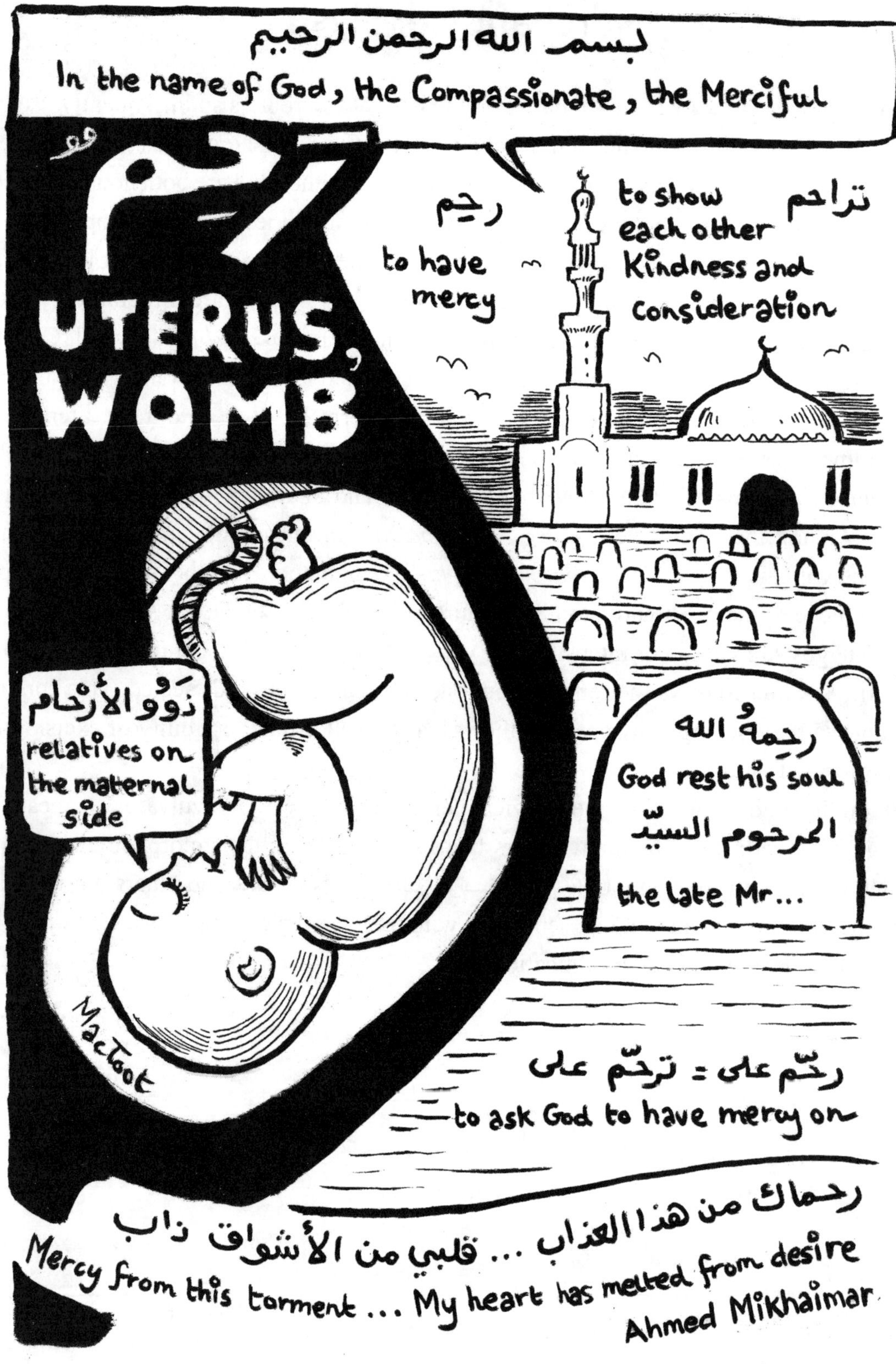

بسم الله الرحمن الرحيم
In the name of God, the Compassionate, the Merciful
رحم
UTERUS, WOMB
رحِم
to have mercy
تراحم
to show each other kindness and consideration
ذَوُو الأرحام
relatives on the maternal side
رحِمهُ الله
God rest his soul
المرحوم السيّد
the late Mr...
رحّم على = ترحّم على
to ask God to have mercy on
رحماك من هذا العذاب ... قلبي من الأشواق ذاب
Mercy from this torment ... My heart has melted from desire
Ahmed Mikhaimar
MacToot

106
Womb رَحِم – أَرْحام
Mercy

What more merciful place could there be in the body than the womb? The gentle miraculous powers of the mother are embodied in this word's many famous and prestigious derivatives. The abstraction mercy الرحمة *ar-raHma* and its much less common *maSdar miimi* alternative المرْحَمة *al-marHama* are themselves derived from this word for the womb. The first of these, الرحمة, is an extraordinarily frequent word in Arabic, ranked 972 in the *FDA*. By comparison, mercy does not even make the top 3,000 in English. In Arabic, it turns up everywhere, from the most sacred to the most secular contexts. Begging for mercy, Egyptian poet Ahmed Mikhaimar (1914–78), gives this noun's feminine ending a sonorous prolongation, echoing common spoken pronunciation, رحماك *RaHmaak*!

The power of men in ancient—and modern—Arab society is well established, but reverence for the mother was paramount, and the language even has important kinship terms to specifically designate maternal kinship: صلة الرحم *Silat ar-raHim*, the tie of the womb, and *dhawuu al-'arHaam* ذوو الأرحام or أولو الأرحام, *'uuluu al-'arHaam* those of the wombs, maternal blood relatives. Appended to the Qur'anic بسملة 113 times, the two most prominent and beloved epithets of God are الرحمن الرحيم, *ar-raHmaan ar-raHiim*, rough synonyms meaning the Most Merciful. Whereas رحيم may identify anyone as merciful, الرحمن is a quality only attributed to God. These adjectives yield the comparative/superlative form أرحم *'arHam*, and God is described in the Qur'an (7:151 and elsewhere) as أَرْحَمُ الرّاحِمِينَ, *the most merciful of those who are merciful or show compassion*. Qur'anically, eleven derivatives of this root occur 342 times, not counting the adjectives appended in formulaic fashion in the بسملة. Also in the adjective domain, this root provides a loving reference to someone who has died, not unlike the English 'the dear departed.' This is / المرحوم المرحومة *al-marHuum* / *al-marHuuma*, depending on the gender of the deceased, on whom, it is hoped, God will have mercy.

A family of verbs referring to acts of compassion and mercy are derived from this root. The Form I verb رحِم – يرحَم *raHima* is a great example of Arabic's interesting optative, a past tense verb to be understood as a wish, as in رحمه الله, *raHimahu Allaah*, May God have mercy on him. Other high-frequency examples of the optative include لا سمح الله *laa samaHa Allaah* God forbid! and بارك الله فيك *baaraka Allaahu fiika* God bless you!, used especially to thank someone.

A special semantic feature of a few Form II verbs offers a marvel of concision well illustrated by this root. Since رحمه الله, is an essential formula of condolence, the Form II رحّم على, all by itself, means to utter that supplication. This can also be expressed by the Form V verb ترحّم على. Another famous example of one of these concise Form II speech acts is كبّر, to say الله أكبر *Allahu 'akbar*, God is great.

Form VI is used to show mutual action or interaction and تراحم therefore means to show each other kindness and consideration. Should one wish to ask for mercy, then the transitive Form X استرحم is used.

PENIS ذَكَر
masculine مُذكّر
نخل ذكر male palm trees
ذكر male
مطر ذكر a hard rain
a strapping fellow رجل ذكر
ذكر proud, haughty, vigorous, hard
شعر ذكر excellent poetry
ذكّر to remind
تَذْكِرة ticket
ذِكر الدَّين I.O.U
شيء (لا) يُذْكَر something (not) worth mentioning
تِذكار memento
مُذكّرات memoranda
to speak ill of a person ذكر

107
Penis (1) ذَكَر – ذُكور
Masculinity; Remembrance

It comes as no surprise that the penis is associated with masculinity. In the singular, the word ذَكَر *dhakar*, a male, is identical with the reproductive organ. Meaning 'male,' it has three common plurals: ذكور *dhukuur*, ذكورة *dhukuura*, and ذكران *dhukraan*, but in the sense of penis, it has just one, *dhukuur.* One of a pair of devices that fit together in anatomical fashion, such as joints and plugs, also shares this designation, and one may say *'unbuub dhakar* أنبوب ذكر / *'unthaa* أنثى , a male / female pipe. The word ذكر can be used adjectivally, too, where its meanings range from manly, proud, haughty, vigorous, and hard, to outstanding and excellent, as in رجل ذكر *rajul dhakar*, a strapping fellow. Anatomically male animals and plants also use it, as in نخل ذكر *nakhl dhakar*, male palm trees. It is even applicable to the inanimate domain, as in مطر ذكر *maTar dhakar*, a hard rain and شعر ذكر *shi'r dhakar*, excellent poetry. Still, all of these important meanings illuminate just one corner of the very significant ر – ك – ذ root.

The Qur'an is a good place to start when studying this root. In fact, one of its alternative names is الذكر *adh-dhikr* or الذكر الحكيم *adh-dhikr al-Hakiim.* This *maSdar* الذكر has multiple meanings, including mentioning and recalling. In an Islamic context, it can refer to the divine revelation as given in the Qur'an and, in some interpretations, in Judaic and Christian scripture. Chapter 21:7 includes a command to those who don't understand an important concept to ask people with a better background in scripture, أَهْلَ الذِّكْرِ *'ahl adh-dhikr.* In another religious application, this same word was chosen to designate the Sufi practice of Dhikr and its meditative technique of chanting a word or formula (God's name, for example) to focus the mind and clear it of everything extraneous. In a social context, الذِكر is what is mentioned about you, so حسن الذكر *Hasan adh-dhikr*, means of good repute. But people like to criticize, andذكر can also mean to speak ill of someone. Financially, ذِكر الدَّين *dhikr ad-dayn* is an IOU. Of the many derivations of the ر – ك – ذ root, nineteen are used in the Qur'an a total of 292 times! *Hans Wehr* lists eight distinct verb forms, all except VII and IX. Of these, Forms I, II, and V make the *FDA*, along with eight other noun and adjective entries. Form IV أذكر is uncommon in modern Arabic. Classically, it could be used to designate a woman who gave birth to a male child. Otherwise, it was synonymous with Form II.

The Form I verb ذكر – يذكُر *dhakara*, which ranks 266 in the *FDA*, has a variety of meanings, somewhat dependent upon context. Central to them are mentioning and keeping in mind. Its passive is often used to describe something (not) worth mentioning, شيءٌ (لا) يُذكَر, *shay'un (laa) yudhkar*. That which has been mentioned or cited is مذكور *madhkuur*. A memory, something to think back on, is ذِكرى *dhikraa*, a word which may also mean anniversary, as in ذكرى رحيله *dhikraa raHiilihi*, the anniversary of his death. Along with its plural, ذكريات *dhikrayaat*, this is the second most common word of the root. There is another kind of memory, our recall capacity; this is الذاكرة *adh-dhaakira*, whether human or machine-based.

ذَكَرَ
الذكر
divine revelation
الذكر
invocation
ذِكر
mentioning and recalling
حسن الذِكر
of good repute
ذِكرى
anniversary
الذاكرة
memory, of man or machine
MacToot

108
Penis (2) ذَكَر – ذُكور
Masculinity; Remembrance

The Form II verb ذكّـر means to remind. It can be doubly transitive, or use the preposition بـ *bi* before the *thing* being mentioned. Classically speaking, the reminder may be an admonishment, with the object understood, but not stated. This is illustrated in 88:21 of the Qur'an, in the imperative form. Muhammad, who laments how much resistance he finds to his preaching, is urged to continue with his task: فَذَكِّـر إِنَّمَا أَنْـتَ مُذَكِّـرٌ, *So warn (them), you are only a warner*. In modern day-to-day contexts, lots of vocabulary is based on Form II and connected to the memory, including تذكرة *tadhkira*, an admission or fare ticket, its plural تذاكر *tadhaakir*, and تـذكار *tidhkaar*, a memento. The latter's *nisba* adjective, commemorative, is تـذكاريّ *tidhkaariyy*. When unassisted memory fails, there's always the handy participial مذكّـرة *mudhakkira* and its plural, مذكّرات *mudhakkiraat*, memoranda.

Form III ذاكر is of some historical and sociocultural interest. Classically, it can mean to confer with someone, but its common modern sense is to review one's lessons. This is a traditional view of studying and learning that prioritizes memorization. The verb takes its inspiration from Form I and its *maSdar* الذِكر *adh-dhikr*, mentioning something out loud, and adds effort to the semantic pot. A formidable memory was highly prized and carefully cultivated in pre-Islamic times, and it remains so down to this day. Epic poetry was the most ancient target of memorization and recitation. Powerful memories were then applied to preserving the Qur'an. Some continue this tradition, an impressive feat requiring years of apprenticeship. It is normally begun in childhood, when much in the text is beyond the child's grasp. Committing to memory also cultivates a personal connection to the text. A deeper and deeper understanding gradually evolves. Some continue to apply recitation to other study tasks, too.

Form V is the very common تذكّر, to remember. Form VIII اذّكر *iddakara* with its noteworthy assimilation—where the 'dh' turns to a 'd' to avoid the lisp-inducing *idhtakara*—is largely synonymous with V, but rare. Finally, there is Form X, استذكر, to recollect, learn by heart, or seek to recall something. One of its signature meanings is the practice of tying a string around one's finger—or someone else's—as a memory aid. However, استذكر دروسه *istadhkara duruusahu* is hardly distinguishable from Form III ذاكر دروسه *dhaakara duruusahu*. Furthermore, استذكر الماضي *istadhkara al-maaDi*, to recall the past, is quite like Form V تذكّر الماضي *tadhakkara al-maaDi*.

Departures from the semantic field of memory are also possible. They take their inspiration from gendered anatomy. The passive participle of Form II provides one of grammar's essential terms, مُذَكَّـر *mudhakkar*, masculine, literally designated as male. Having mentioned النخل الذكر, male palm trees, it makes sense to include a botanical sense of the Form II verb and its *maSdar* التذكير *at-tadhkiir*, to pollinate female blossoms. Egyptian date farmers do so by hand, brushing the blossoms of the male tree over those of the female! In summary, ذ – ك – ر is the locus of intersection between the powers of maleness, memory, and repute. Preventing things from dissolving into oblivion is what's at stake. And that may be the connection, albeit unconscious, with the male organ, itself, which is responsible for procreation, anxious for a good reputation, and surely worth mentioning!

رجّل to comb out one's hair, to let down the hair; to let the hair hang long
الرجولة manhood
رجُل man
مِرْجَل cauldron, boiling pot
ترجّل to dismount; to walk, set out on foot, to behave like a man
رجل to set out on foot
MacToot
LEG
راجِل ج. رجّال ، رجّالة ، رجلان
one who goes out on foot; is walking

109
Leg رِجْل – رِجْلان – أَرْجُل
Walking Man

Animals might walk on all fours, but man—and the human race—evolved into bipeds. The word رِجْل *rijl*, leg, and its near homonym رَجُل *rajul*, man, succinctly suggest this connection. Just that change of short vowels takes you from the leg to the man who walks on it, or vice-versa. The word راجِل *raajil*, with its multiple plurals رَجّالة *rajjaala* / رَجْل *rajl* /رَجّال *rajjaal* /رُجلان *rujlaan*, is one who goes on foot, who is walking. Cairene colloquial, in fact, chose to use راجِل *raagil,* with its plural رِجّالة *riggaala*, exclusively as the word for man. Considering vocabulary that extrapolates on the idea of الرِجْل, we find, among nouns, the old domestic utensil, مِرْجَل *mirjal* a cauldron or a boiler. What is the association? Presumably, as other furnishings may, such a cauldron had legs!

In the verbal domain, Forms I رجِل – يرجَل *rajila* and V ترَجَّل mean to get off (whatever conveyance) and walk. Form V can also be a judgmental comment on condoned gender roles, and may mean to act inappropriately like a man. Form VIII ارتجل expresses a very metaphoric take on the possibilities that legs offer. This verb means to improvise, recite impromptu, extemporize, perhaps from the association of pacing back and forth, like an actor on stage, or as one might do while searching for the perfect turn of phrase. The adjective 'improvised' can be conveyed in two ways, with the passive participle or the *nisba* adjective: مُرتجَل *murtajal* or ارتجاليّ *irtijaaliyy*. Form II, however, is rather mysterious. It seems semantically distinct from all its fellow verbs from the root: رجّل means to comb out one's hair and let it hang loose! Could it be that proper men were wont to do so? A look at pictures of Arabian desert dwellers, especially from the first half of the twentieth century, suggests that this is not such an outlandish interpretation.

The word رَجُل, man, one of Arabic's most frequent words, at 92 in the *FDA*, also has a small constellation of interesting derivatives on the gender theme. The pattern الفُعولة, often associated with significant phases of life and social standing, yields الرجولة *ar-rujuula*, manhood, masculinity, manliness. Verbally, Form X, استرجل, with its implication of seeking, means to try to be like a man, to show oneself to be a man, to act (more) like a man.

to accompany; ساوق
to go along, agree with
to herd (animals), ساق
drive (prisoners);
to drive, pilot
ساق
LEG
سوق
market
سوّق
to market
انساق
to be driven;
to be carried away
تسوّق
to buy and sell
in the market;
to shop
MacToot

110
Leg ساق – سِيقان
Driving (the herd) to market

The economic engine of pastoral nomadic life was buying and selling animals. But for nomadic populations to find a sufficient pool of buyers, they had to ساق – يسوق *saaqa*, drive, Form I, their animals to market السوق *as-suuq*, an enterprise requiring serious legwork. Driving as an activity is the *maSdar* السوق *as-sawq*. Getting to the souk might involve a long and winding trek, whether mounted or on foot, and السائق *as-saa'iq*, the driver, had to pay careful attention to the ever-changing features of the landscape. In Arabic, those literal peregrinations over dune and through wadi are the actual source of the word سياق *siyaaq*, context.

Completely devoid of textual associations at its root, that literal journey nevertheless serves as beautiful inspiration for the metaphoric journey of reading, in which a heightened awareness of the entire milieu has a direct bearing on the value of the whole enterprise. Both ساق and سياق can be used figuratively. With the addition of the preposition إلى one can steer animals or things in a particular direction. One can also steer a conversational journey toward someone or something, ساق الحديث إليه *saaqa al-Hadiith 'ilayhi.* One should, of course, make every effort to follow its thread, an English weaving metaphor.

In 32:27, the Qur'an uses ساق إلى in the sense of directing or channeling water toward barren land. In fact, the eight derivatives of the root س – و – ق which occur in the Qur'an include all of the aforementioned derivatives as well as the *maSdar miimi* المساق *al-masaaq*, the act of driving or herding. In a disquieting depiction of the Day of Judgment, at 75:30, the Qur'an paints a frenetic scene of vast numbers of people being herded along in confusion: إلى رَبِّكَ يَوْمَئِذٍ المَساقُ, *that day, the herding will be toward your Lord.*

The س – و – ق root remains popular in the modern idiom, with a mix of five nouns and verbs ranking in the *FDA*. The Form II transitive verb سوّق, to market something, is a denominative one, with سوق as its source. Form V تسوّق is its reflexive, to trade in the market, go shopping, procure some marketing for oneself. Form III verbs imply the presence of someone else, and this is the case in ساوق, to keep up with someone, or to drive with someone, or try to outdo or outdrive them. Form VI تساوق seems, at first glance, to be quite a detour from the root meaning. It can be translated in a variety of ways, including to draw out; to form a sequence, be continuous; to be coherent; to harmonize. The journey metaphor is still at work, and this form adds the sense of following that journey from start to finish, or weaving the threads of conversation together into a meaningful, connected whole.

Forms VII and VIII complete the verbal panorama with a return to the image of herding animals: انساق means to be driven or carried away, or to drift away, while استاق *istaaqa,* similarly to Form I, means to drive or urge cattle or livestock on.

رُكْبَة
KNEE
مراكبي
boatman, ferryman
تراكيب
linguistic constructions, expressions
مُرَكَّبات
compounds, components
تفضّلوا
عزومة مراكبيّة boat men's invitation (insincere show of generosity)
مركب
boat
راكِب
rider
رَكْب
traveling party, caravan
رَكوب/رِكاب
mount (horse or camel)
ارتكب جريمة
to commit a crime
مَركوب
mount; thing mounted
رُكُب
stirrups
MacToot

111
Knee رُكْبة – رُكَب
Mounting, Riding

The knee is intimately bound to the idea of mounting and riding. As nomads, the ancient Arabs were constantly on the move. Mounting and riding, both conveyed by the same Form I verb, ركِب – يركَب *rakiba*, were therefore primordial considerations, as the Bedouin had to cover considerable distances in their perennial search for water and herbage. It is no simple matter to mount a horse, let alone a camel, and if one's knee, الركبة *ar-rukba,* is not functioning properly, such an endeavor becomes extraordinarily difficult. No wonder, then, that this critical joint and the idea of mounting became linked. Examining the wealth of vocabulary derived from this one root shows how central the idea of mounted travel was to the culture. As the verb ركب is transitive, the passive participle مركوب *markuub* was one way to indicate the thing mounted, a riding animal.

Mounts themselves, رِكاب *rikaab* and رَكوب *rakuub*, referring to horses or camels, are mentioned in the Qur'an. That same noun رِكاب, with the plural رُكَب *rukab*, could also mean stirrups. It is this piece of a rider's equipment on which the expression سار في ركابه *saara fii rikaabihi* is based. To walk in someone's stirrups is an idiom meaning to follow someone loyally, even subserviently. The active participle راكِب *raakib*, rider, most commonly takes the plural رُكّاب *rukkaab*, but another possibility is the collective, رَكْب *rakb*, traveling party, a noun that could refer variously to a caravan, a cavalcade, a group of horsemen, and so on. This collective can also be made plural: رُكبان *rukbaan*. The Qur'an uses seven different words derived from the ر – ك – ب root. In the modern domain, eleven of its derivatives figure in the *FDA*.

Among the idiomatic expressions based on the Form I verb is another with a body equivalent in English, ركب رأسه *rakiba ra'sahu*, to be headstrong. In the nominal domain, مركب *markab* and its plural مَراكِب *maraakib* are used for another essential conveyance, the boat. The long coasts of the Arabian peninsula gave the Arabs easy access to the sea, and they became great sailors and navigators. From the plural, boats, comes the word for boatman or ferryman, مراكبي *maraakibiyy*. Its plural is used in a popular Egyptian expression for an insincere show of generosity, عزومة مراكبية, *'uzuumit mirakbiyya* an invitation of boatmen. As the boat sails by, the crew call out to those ashore to come join them for a meal, an offer they will never have to make good on.

The Form II verb ركّب is causative: to give someone a ride or make them ride. This Form also has extrapolations in the domain of chemistry, where its passive participle مُركّبات means compounds, components, things which have been added to others. In linguistics, a permutation of the typical Form II *maSdar* yields تركيبة *tarkiiba*, a phrase or expression of two or more words.

The Form VI verb تراكب means to overlap, to be laid one on top of another, superimposed. And finally, the most common in the modern media corpus, is Form VIII ارتكب, to commit. As in English, this verb is always used in negative contexts, and collocates especially with a crime, جريمة *jariima*.

FOOT
قدم
1969
GIVE PEACE A CHANCE
القِدم
the old days
قديم
old
استقدم
to summon, to ask people to come
الموقف القادم
the next Stop
التقدّم
progress
2020
تقادم
to age, become old, become antiquated or obsolete
أقدم عليه
to boldly embark on an endeavor
قُدّام
forward
قَدِم
to arrive, to come to a place; to precede
من الرأس حتّى أخمص القدم
from head to toe
MacToot

112
Foot قدَم – قدَمان – أقْدام
Forward Motion

With six verbal and twenty-seven nominal extrapolations, قدم *qadam* and its derivatives take up nearly three pages in *Hans Wehr*. Ten of its forms are used forty-eight times in the Qur'an. In and of itself, the foot occurs in many an idiomatic phrase. One such expression is من الرأس حتّى أخمص القدم *min ar-ra's Hattaa 'akhmaS al-qadam*, literally, from the head to the hollow of the sole of the foot, that is, from head to toe. Its derived metaphoric family is built squarely on directionality. Where does one go on one's feet? Forward, قُدّام *quddaam*! Similarly, القَيدوم *al-qayduum*, the prow of a ship, is an auspiciously dynamic designation.

To arrive or come to a place, or to precede someone else is the Form I قدِم – يقدَم *qadima*. The adjective 'next' is قادم *qaadim*, as in في الموقَف القادِم *fi-l-mawqaf al-qaadim*, at the next stop. One can also ask people to come, or summon them; this is succinctly conveyed by Form X استقدم. When one has made progress, التقدُّم *at-taqaddum*, a Form V *maSdar*, advancing further and further, a glance backward reveals that the time has flown by and the old days, القِدَم *al-qidam*, are far behind. One of the first adjectives elementary students learn is قديم *qadiim*, old, just one of the high-frequency derivatives—499 in the *FDA*—of this ubiquitous root. This adjective also serves as inspiration for the Form VI verb, تقادم, to age, become old, or to become antiquated, obsolete.

Form II قدّم, to physically present something, such as a gift, or submit something, such as a resignation, implies the forward-leaning gesture as the offering is made. The Form II *maSdar*, التقديم *at-taqdiim*, can also be used more abstractly, as in making a presentation to a group of listeners. This is another of the root's frequency stars, ranking 585 in the *FDA*.

More of the positive connotations of forward movement are expressed by the Form IV verb أقدم عليه, *'aqdama 'alayhi* to boldly embark on an endeavor. Its *maSdar*, الإقدام *al-'iqdaam*, audacity and pluck, specifically links moving ahead with boldness. In adjectival form, this character trait found a home in the noteworthy pattern مِفعال. Valiant, daring, and intrepid can all be expressed by مِقدام *miqdaam*. Very few adjectives share this pattern, and all stand out from the ordinary. Examples include مزواج *mizwaaj*, frequently marrying, مطلاق *miTlaaq*, prone to divorcing, مكسال *miksaal*, very lazy, مكثار *mikthaar*, garrulous.

Whether applied to physical action or abstract advancement, the semantics of this root are grounded, as it were, in the physical sense of the proper orientation of the foot. The question is not where the foot is located in the body, nor what it looks like, but where it is going. The body parts considered in the next two chapters address issues of appearance and body placement.

التكعيبيّة
cubism (art)
الكعبة
the Kaaba in Mecca
HEEL-ANKLE
BREASTS-BOSOM
كَعبت البنت
to become buxom
كاعب ج كواعب
a buxom girl
cube
الكعب
متر مُكعّب
cubic meter
الكعب العالي
high heels
MacToot
كعب الشيك
stub of a check

113
كَعب – كعبان – كِعاب / كُعوب / كُعْب
Heel / Ankle / Breasts, Bosom
Cube

Verse 5:6 of the Qur'an has instructions on how to perform ablutions before prayer: وَامْسَحوا بِرُءوسِكُم وأَرْجُلَكُم إِلى الكَعْبَيْنِ, *Wipe off your heads and your feet up to (or including) al-ka'bayni*. Some old commentators interpreted this to mean the heels, and others the ankles, so the ambiguity has persisted. Generally speaking, though, كعب الرجل *ka'b ar-rijl* loosely designates either heel or ankle, and focuses on appearance. The nearly homophonic كعب *ka'b / ku'b* duo makes a very odd couple. Voweled ka'b, and in association with *ar-rijl*, it lumps heel and ankle together. Voweled كُعب *ku'b*, and used alone, it means breasts, or bosom. What a counterintuitive connection! Proximity is clearly irrelevant. Besides, the rough and bony ankle area appears to have little in common with the soft and alluring swell of the breasts. However, a second look reveals a visual link between the non-gendered ankles and the contours of the female upper body. Pablo Picasso, himself, might have found this root inspirational, because it is all about cubes. In fact, *ku'b* is just the plural form of *ka'b*, and *al-ka'b* is the primordial cube. Perhaps in the way that الذراع *adh-dhiraa'*, the forearm, served as an ancient measure of length, the solid block of the heel and ankle offered a simple analogy for builders as they erected large cubic edifices, including what would become Islam's most iconic structure, الكعبة *al-ka'ba*, the Kaaba. Islam appropriated this ancient Meccan pilgrimage site, mentioned in 5:97 of the Qur'an.

What English dubs the stub of a check, Arabic calls its heel, كعب الشيك *ka'b ash-shiik*. Traditionally, sandals and shoes were given heels with some resemblance to the anatomical one until the fashion industry discovered how to market الكعب العالي *al-ka'b al-'aaliyy*, the high heel. Embodiment research in many languages shows that height correlates with social power and prestige. The expression علوّ الكعب *'uluww al-ka'b*, fame and glory, literally the height of the heel, encapsulates just such a correlation. In mathematics, the Form II verb كعّب means to raise to the third power. The passive participle is used in the phrase رقم مكعَّب, *raqam muka''ab*, a cubed number, as well as in measurements of volume, متر مكعَّب *mitr muka''ab*, a cubic meter.

Breasts develop with age, and Form I كَعَب – يكعُب / يكعِب, *ka'aba* means to become full and round. It is the basis for كاعِب *kaa'ib*, a buxom or nubile young woman. In 78:33 of the Qur'an, its plural كواعب *kawaa'ib* appears in a description of the pleasures of paradise, where the blessed will find كَواعِبَ أَتْرابًا *kawaa'iba 'atraaban*, voluptuous companions. Lacking the standard feminine gender indicators, this active participle is morphologically unusual and noteworthy. Since buxomness is deemed an exclusively feminine trait, the grammatical marker is superfluous in the singular and the plural. Some such descriptions are physical, like حوامل *Hawaamil*, pregnant women. Other designations are socially judgmental, like عوانس *'awaanis*, old maids. Note that there is no counterpart for men, deemed marriageable at any age. Social attitudes became embodied in some juridical terms, notably نواشز *nawaashiz*, stubbornly disobedient women. Whereas being buxom and pregnant have their basis in physiology, issues of marriageability and recalcitrance are of a different order. This terminology suggests that, in men, an attribute like recalcitrance was either irrelevant or inconceivable. In any case, it was certainly not legally actionable.

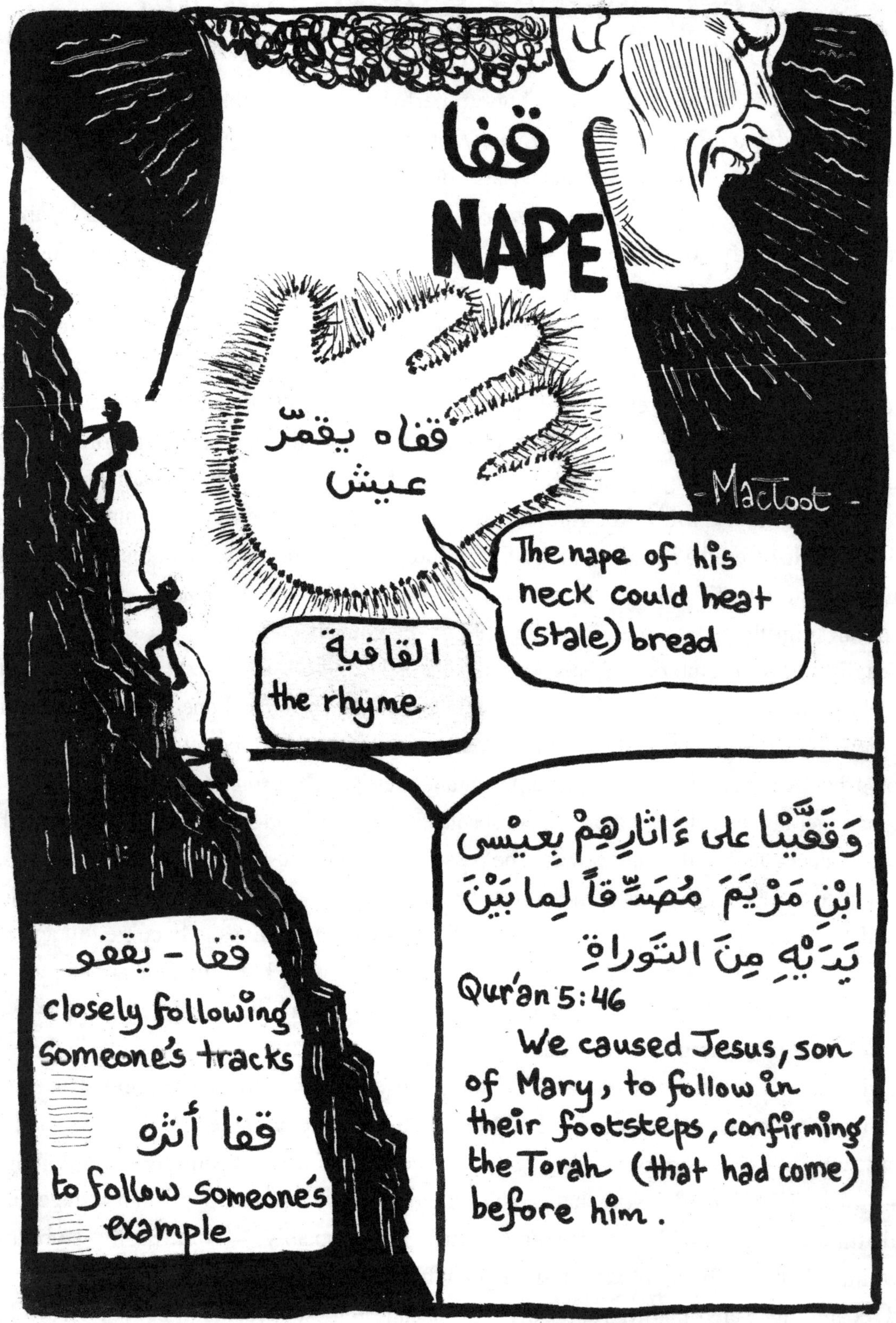
قفا
NAPE
قفاه يقمّر عيش
-MacToot-
The nape of his neck could heat (stale) bread
القافية
the rhyme
وَقَفَّيْنَا على ءَاثارِهِمْ بِعيسَى ابْنِ مَرْيَمَ مُصَدِّقاً لِما بَيْنَ يَدَيْهِ مِنَ التَوراةِ
Qur'an 5:46
We caused Jesus, son of Mary, to follow in their footsteps, confirming the Torah (that had come) before him.
قفا - يقفو
closely following someone's tracks
قفا أثره
to follow someone's example

114
Nape قفا – أَقْفِية / أَقْفاء
Follow, Emulate

As a nomadic people, the Bedouin needed to move through a challenging, even hostile, desert environment with skill and finesse. Because they lived primarily from trade, keeping the caravan together was crucial, so tracking had commercial repercussions. In addition, raiding and plundering were facts of life, which meant that tracking could also have military relevance. On the offensive, the Bedouin had to be able to follow quarry. On the defensive, or under ordinary circumstances, they needed to ensure there were no stragglers. All of these factors combined to prioritize good tracking skills. Among the specific vocabulary that arose for closely following someone's tracks is the Form I قفا – يقفو *qafaa*, a verb directly derived from the nape of the neck, an anatomical feature that someone following closely behind could keep within sight. At some point, the practice of physically tailing others became associated with emulation, and قفا أثره *qafaa 'atharahu,* to follow his track, acquired the figurative meaning of to follow someone's example.

Despite these rather positive verbal associations, the nape of the neck itself became associated with humiliation. In Arab society, a slap on the back of the neck is inflicted not so much to do damage, but rather to demean the victim. In a spoken Egyptian context, قفاه يقمّر عيش *'afaa yi'ammar 'eesh* means 'The nape of his neck could heat (stale) bread,' that is, it looks red-hot, as if he had just received a stinging and humiliating slap. By extension, even the mention of the nape of the neck can be considered impolite, and it is often avoided in polite conversation. It is not surprising that القفا does not figure anywhere in the *FDA*.

However, both Form I قفا and Form II قفّى are used in the Qur'an. A recurring Qur'anic theme is how God repeatedly tried to bring various historical peoples who had gone astray back onto the straight and narrow path. The Qur'an says that He sent prophet after prophet, all of whom delivered their messages, trying to show their fellow men God's will. It is in this sense that Form II is used, causing one prophet to follow another. Among others, Jesus is singled out, in 5:46: وَقَفَّيْنَا عَلَى ءَاثَارِهِمْ بِعِيْسَى ابْنِ مَرْيَمَ مُصَدِّقًا لِمَا بَيْنَ يَدَيْهِ مِنَ التَّوراةِ, *We caused Jesus, son of Mary, to follow in their footsteps, confirming the Torah (that had come) before him.*

The Bedouin Arabs were not only expert traders, trackers, and raiders. They were also masters of the spoken word. Verbal prowess in poetry was held in the highest regard. There were annual regional contests, and winners' fame—and works—spread far and wide. While composing their poetry, the pre-Islamic Arabs also honed their skills at memorizing. Over time, they also developed lots of technical language to describe their poems (like the Greeks with iambic pentameter). Many of these terms were derived from tent structure, but one crucial element, القافية, was taken right from the tracking image. This *qaafiya*, literally *the follower*, became the term for the rhyme, one of those features which helped listeners—most of whom would never see the poem written—to commit it to memory.

الظهيرة
midday
أظهر
to show, divulge, reveal
الظهران
Dhahran, Saudi Arabia
في الظَهر
outwardly
ظاهِر
visible, external
ظهر
to become visible; to come to light, to seem
ظهر على ...
to get the better of, gain the upper hand
ظَهْر
BACK
القشّة التى قصمت ظهرالبعير
the straw that broke the camel's back
MacToot

115
Back (1) ظَهْر - ظهور
Visibility, Backing

This large body part is the basis for the name of an urban center, الظهران, Dhahran, a city in eastern Saudi Arabia a few kilometers from the Persian Gulf. Just a patch of desert in the 1930s, Dhahran is now the very developed home of the petroleum giant Aramco. If transliterated phonetically, the city would be *aZ-Zahraan*. The suffix *-aan* here means two and الظهران actually means 'the two backs,' a reference to two small mountains that are the principal features of the terrain. When navigating desert terrain, physical features visible from a distance merited memorable names. These mountains, however, already had a name, النُّهَيدين *an-Nuhaydayn*, the two little breasts, but officials were apparently reluctant to associate such a suggestive and feminine name with their new settlement. Prudishly settling instead on 'the two backs,' they linguistically veiled those titillatingly named mountains and their fledgling city. Historically, peoples of the Arabian Peninsula were not shy about dubbing geographical features with risqué names derived from the body, but their modern counterparts favor propriety over poetry.

The noun ظهر *Zahr* itself figures in an old proverbial expression an equivalent of which has even made its way into English. For that indispensable beast of burden, the camel, the back is what must support a load. But even the strongest pack animals have limits that must not be exceeded. Hence القشّة التي قصمت ظهر البعير *al-qashsha allatii qaSamat Zahr al-ba'iir*, the straw that broke the camel's back. Here, instead of the all-purpose الجمل *al-jamal*, we find البعير *al-ba'iir*, a powerful male camel, perhaps analogous to stallion. The collocation قصم الظهر refers not to 'back-breaking' in the sense of wearying, but in the sense of inflicting a mortal wound.

Metaphorically speaking, derivatives of the noun ظهر show that it is closely associated with visibility, as well as with backing and support. It seems puzzling that visibility should be associated with the back. However, one can easily conceal—and protect—one's front, whereas the back is exposed. It is especially exposed to anyone stalking up from behind, a worrisome fact that may well have inspired the military term الظهير *aZ-Zahiir*, the rear guard, someone marching behind to offer protection. This same military usage was then applied to the soccer domain, where الظهير is the back, a position that likewise offers protection to the forwards.

The back and eleven of its derivatives are used fifty-nine times in the Qur'an, but the prominence of this root in usage is not confined to the classical sphere. The back ranks 1,373 in the *FDA*, and twelve of its derivatives figure in Arabic's most frequent 5,000 words. Two significant ones, thematically, are الظُّهر *aZ-Zuhr* and الظهيرة *aZ-Zahiira*, noon and midday, when visibility is at its height.

مُتظاهِرون
demonstrators
public demonstrations مُظاهَرات
ظهّر
to endorse (a check, by writing on the back)
to pretend; to make a public demonstration تظاهر
ظاهر
to help, assist, support someone
أظهر على ...
to render victorious
تظاهر على
to back each other, make common cause, gang up against
MacToot
BACK ظَهْر

116
Back (2) ظَهْر – ظُهور
Visibility, Backing

The Form I verb ظهـر – يظهَـر *Zahara*, *FDA* 611, means to appear, become visible, be perceptible. On a playful note, from the spoken idiom, comes a rhyming formulaic appeal to a genie. It offers indemnity if the genie will just come out of hiding. اِظهَـر وبـان عليـك الأمـان *iZhar wi baan 'aleek il-'amaan*! Appear, and show yourself; safety will be yours!

The place pattern yields مَظْهَـر *maZhar*, external appearance or guise. When appearance means the act of coming into view, Arabic uses the *maSdar*, الظُّهـور *aZ-Zuhuur*. In philosophy, a fundamental conceptual dichotomy is الظاهِر *aZ-Zaahir* and الباطِن *al-baaTin*, the superficial or apparent and the hidden or intrinsic. The addition of a *taa marbuuta* to this Form I active participle creates another rather learned word, ظاهـرة *Zaahira*, phenomenon, with the surprisingly high frequency ranking of 1,057.

Adding the preposition لِـ to the Form I verb ظهر – يظهَر *Zahara* allows the introduction of a personal object: to be evident *to someone*, to seem *to someone*. The causative version of this is the domain of the Form IV verb, أظهـر, *FDA* 1,024, to *make* something visible, to divulge it. Adding the preposition علـى (itself based on the root for 'height') to the Form I verb creates a new idiom, to get the upper hand over someone. Adding this same preposition to the Form IV verb is doubly useful. As expected, it creates the causative of Form I, to give someone the upper hand, to render him or her victorious. It can also mean to make someone aware of something, or to enlighten someone on a topic, exposing that information and rendering it visible.

The Form II verb from this root, ظهّر, rather than exploiting its causative potential, is denominative. It has a practical physical meaning, one with an echo in English. Endorsing a check entails signing it on the back. Without having studied Latin, it is difficult to guess that 'dors-' is a body referent, although we may grasp it more clearly in a shark's 'dorsal fin.' 'Endorse' is a good example of English's penchant for choosing Latin roots for more technical or erudite vocabulary. In Arabic, ظهّـر الشـيك *Zahhara ash-shiik* is this same action, to 'back' it, that is, to add one's signature on the back. In Arabic, the term is a high-frequency body part in a high-frequency pattern, easily understood.

Form III ظاهـر offers an excellent example of how the pattern فاعـل implies the presence of another person. This necessarily transitive verb means to support someone, to back him or her up. Its reciprocal counterpart Form VI, تظاهـر, means to back each other up, offer each other mutual support. It can also mean to make common cause against a third party, and thus may be used in the sense of ganging up against others. However, both of these verbs have a second, more common meaning, to participate in a demonstration. In this sense, تظاهـر embodies the metaphor of visibility: making one's position on an issue visible. The Form III *maSdar*, مظاهـرة *muZaahara*, is most commonly used for a demonstration or rally, while the active participle of VI متظاهر *mutaZaahir*, is a demonstrator. The use of Form VI clarifies that such a person is normally not alone.

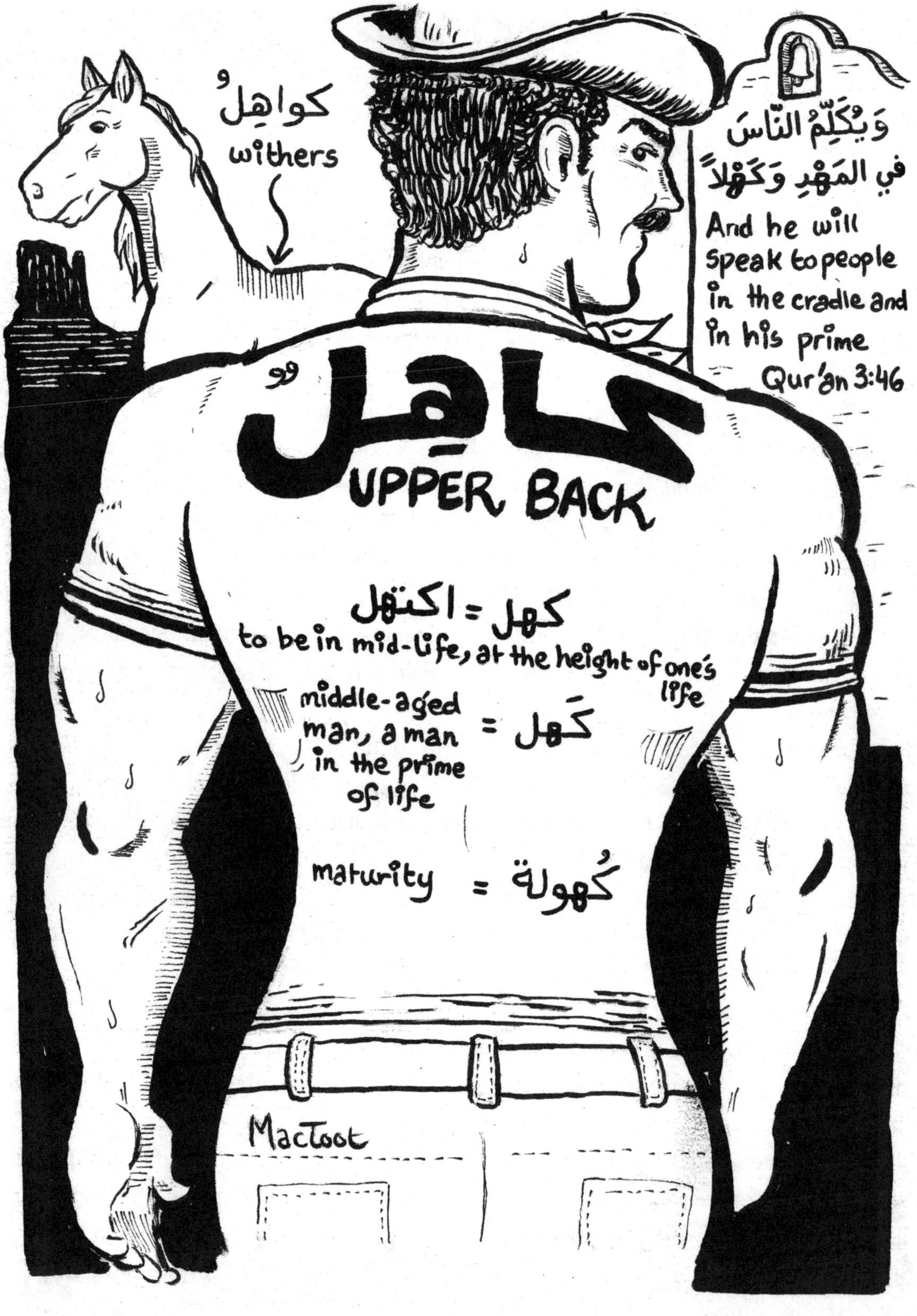

كواهِلُ
withers
وَيُكَلِّمُ النَّاسَ
في المَهْدِ وَكَهْلاً
And he will speak to people in the cradle and in his prime
Qur'an 3:46
كاهِلٌ
UPPER BACK
كهل = اكتهل
to be in mid-life, at the height of one's life
middle-aged man, a man in the prime of life = كَهل
maturity = كُهولة
MacToot

117
Upper Back كاهِل – كَواهِل
Strength

The broad area of a person's upper back is called الكاهِل *al-kaahil*, and in the plural, it is used to describe that same region in a horse, the withers, كواهل الفرس *kawaahil al-faras*. This is the part of the body used to shoulder a burden, and it collocates with words like حِمل *Himl*, a load, and عِبء *'ib'*, a burden. The Arabic expression أثقل كاهلَه بالديون *'athqala kaahilahu bi-d-duyuun*, means he has weighed down his back with debts. This has an echo in an English idiom that also evokes a horse's back: 'he is saddled with debt.' The very fact that man and horse share this anatomical feature is another allusion to strength. Therefore, شديد الكاهل *shadiid al-kaahil*, means strong and courageous. In the same vein, a classical metaphor for the man looked to for support in times of difficulty was كاهل قومه *kaahil qawmihi*, what one might loosely call in English his people's or tribe's backbone.

The use of the pattern فاعِل for this word for the back reveals that it is not the source vocabulary word. Instead, one must look for a shorter source. There are only a few other derivatives of the ك – ه – ل root, all of which refer to the prime of life, typically but loosely described as being between the early thirties and fifty. The Form I and Form VIII verbs, كَهَل – يكهَل *kahala* and اكتهل both mean to attain one's prime, to be at the height of one's powers. Specifically, the period of الشباب, youth, is over, and old age has not arrived. Classical descriptions also make reference to the fact that a man of this age may well have some gray in his hair. Maturity is thus termed الكُهولة *al-kuhuula*. The individual who has attained it, a mature man, is called كَهل *kahl*. Neither the person so designated nor the body part is common enough to be ranked in the *FDA*. However, كهل figures twice in the Qur'an, including a reference to Jesus in 3:46: وَيُكَلِّمُ النَّاسَ فِي الْمَهْدِ وَكَهْلاً, *And he will speak to people in the cradle and in his prime*. The singular pattern فَعْل is not a common one in reference to people, and perhaps for this reason, 'mature man' has an altogether impressive array of broken plurals: كُهَّل *kuhhal* / كِهال *kihaal* / كُهول *kuhuul* / كُهْلان *kuhlaan*.

fortitude المتانة
on board ... على مَتْن
مَتُن
يمْتُن
to be firm
strong
sturdy
على مَتْن الهواء
on an air current
مَتْن
BACK
to fortify مَتّن
to make stronger
MacToot

118
Back مَتْن – مُتون
Solidity

As we have seen, Arabic has two other common words for the back. This third one, المتـن *al-matn*, is more general. It can be used to refer to an animal's back, especially the back of a beast of burden, but it may also refer to humans. One such reference occurs in a famous short poem by Egyptian poet Ismail Sabri Pasha (1854–1923) that opens with a light-hearted play on the homophony of 'my back wearied' and 'she spoke to me.' طرقـتُ البـابَ حتّـى كلّ متنـي ولمّـا كَلّ متني كلّمتْنـي *Taraqtu l-baaba Hattaa kalla matni, wa lamma kalla matni kallamatni*, I beat on the door until my back wearied, and when my back wearied, she spoke to me. This word for the back also has figurative applications. In each case, its little band of derivatives reveals metaphoric associations with strength.

Using the image of an animal's back, the phrase علـى مَتْـنِ *'alaa matn* means "on board." English bases its idiom on the image of a ship and the material from which it was traditionally constructed. Arabic, on the other hand, chose to compare any conveyance one may ride to the sturdy back of a four-legged mount. The utility of this practical expression makes متـن the most frequent derivative of the م – ت – ن root in contemporary media usage, ranking 3,694 in the *FDA*. In a much more poetic vein, علـى متـن الهـواء *'alaa matn al-hawaa'* depicts the air currents that a bird may ride as another such back, albeit an invisible one. Great observers of nature, and with a serious flair for poetry, the Bedouin coined this term long before the modern domain of aviation co-opted it.

The Form I verb متـن – يمْتُـن *maTuna* means to be firm, strong, or sturdy. Its chief derivative is the adjective مَتين *matiin*, strong, sturdy. This is the only other commonly occurring derivative of the root, just barely squeaking in under the frequency wire at 4,992. Nevertheless, the Form I *maSdar* المتانـة *al-mataana*, strength, is a familiar word, as well. In addition to physical strength, it may also convey fortitude. A body image from English that suggests fortitude is 'backbone,' from the same region. The Form I verb has a causative and transitive counterpart, the Form II متّـن *mattana*, to make strong, fortify.

Finally, Islamic jurisprudence uses the word for the anatomical back, المَتن, as a crucial term in rating the authenticity of a Hadith, a deed or saying of the Prophet Muhammad or his companions. The Hadith are also known as Prophetic traditions. Many early religious and legal concepts were handed down orally, and with the rapid expansion of the empire, it became increasingly important to weed out possible corruptions of the original oral text, and also to check if the attribution claimed was credible. The saying itself was called المتن because the solidity of the message, so to speak, was essential. The chain of transmitters also needed careful checking; this chain was called الإسـناد, the isnad.

دبر
BACKREAR
دبّر to make arrangements, manage something well
تدبّر في .. carefully reflect on, ponder, contemplate
دابر الزمن Bygone days
بالأمس الدابر the past
الدّبور west wind
قطع دابره to uproot something
المدبّر ringleader of a plot
Mactoot
الدّبّور hornet
BANK PLAN
تدبّر to be carefully planned

119
Back of the Body, Rear, Hindquarters دُبُر – أَدْبار
Turn away; Plot

Like much of the vocabulary referring to the posterior in Arabic, derivatives of this particular body part occur in the most ancient texts, dating even from the pre-Islamic period. In an oft-cited line from one of the oldest extant epic poems, collectively termed *al-Mu'allaqaat*, the famed Imru' al-Qays paints a picture of a horse in the heat of battle, frenetically galloping this way and that. The horse's retreat is conveyed by a Form IV active participle, used adverbially, مُدْبِرًا *mudbiran*, turning tail. The past tense of this same verb form is used to dramatic and poetic effect in the Qur'an (74:33): وَاللَّيْلِ إِذا أَدْبَرَ, *By the night, when it slips away!* The body part itself plays a crucial role in verse 27 of the Qur'anic chapter named for Yusuf: وَإِنْ كانَ قَمِيصُهُ قُدَّ مِنْ دُبُرٍ, *But if his shirt has been torn from the back.* In fact, eleven different forms of this root appear forty-four times in the Qur'an.

Like Form IV, the Form I verb دبر - يدبُر *dabara* also conveys the physical movement of turning one's back. Furthermore, it has a temporal sense. The elapsing of time can be expressed with the image of time having receded, turned away. Thus, دابِر الزمن *daabir az-zaman* means bygone days. Another indefinite reference to the past is بالأمس الدابِر *bi-l-'amsi ad-daabir*, sometime in the past. It is also possible to refer to the end of something as دابره *daabiruhu*, and therefore, قطع دابره *qaTa'a daabirahu* means to uproot something and eradicate it. While Form I refers to the action of an individual, Form V تدابر confers mutuality on the scene: to stand back to back, face in opposite directions, as duelists might while pacing away from each other. This may also be construed abstractly, and mean to hold opposite opinions, to be incompatible.

The most common form in modern usage is Form II دبّر, to make arrangements, manage (something) well, ranking 3,645 in the *FDA*. It may also suggest clever strategizing, as would be called for in hatching a plot. Someone who manages a complicated undertaking can therefore be termed المُدبِّر, a word which figures in the collocation العقل المدبّر *al-'aql al-mudabbir*, the mastermind. The connection to the back seems to lie in the image of carefully keeping one's plans out of view or close to one's chest, to use a body idiom from English. Plotting and scheming tends to happen behind others' backs, not out in the open. Form V تدبّر, is the reflexive of this. For example, in the expression تدبّر الأمر *tadabbara al-'amr*, a matter is described as having been seen to, taken care of, with the implication of careful planning and management. With the addition of the preposition في, it means to carefully reflect on, ponder, or contemplate, and it may have the added sense of treating something potentially problematic with care and circumspection.

In the nominal domain, there are two intriguing derivatives of دبر, the west wind, الدَّبور *ad-dabuur*, and the hornet, الدَّبّور *ad-dabbuur*. One might be smart to turn one's back on a strong desert wind, whose sting could be painful, though not so sharp as a hornet's, as that telltale *shadda* suggests.

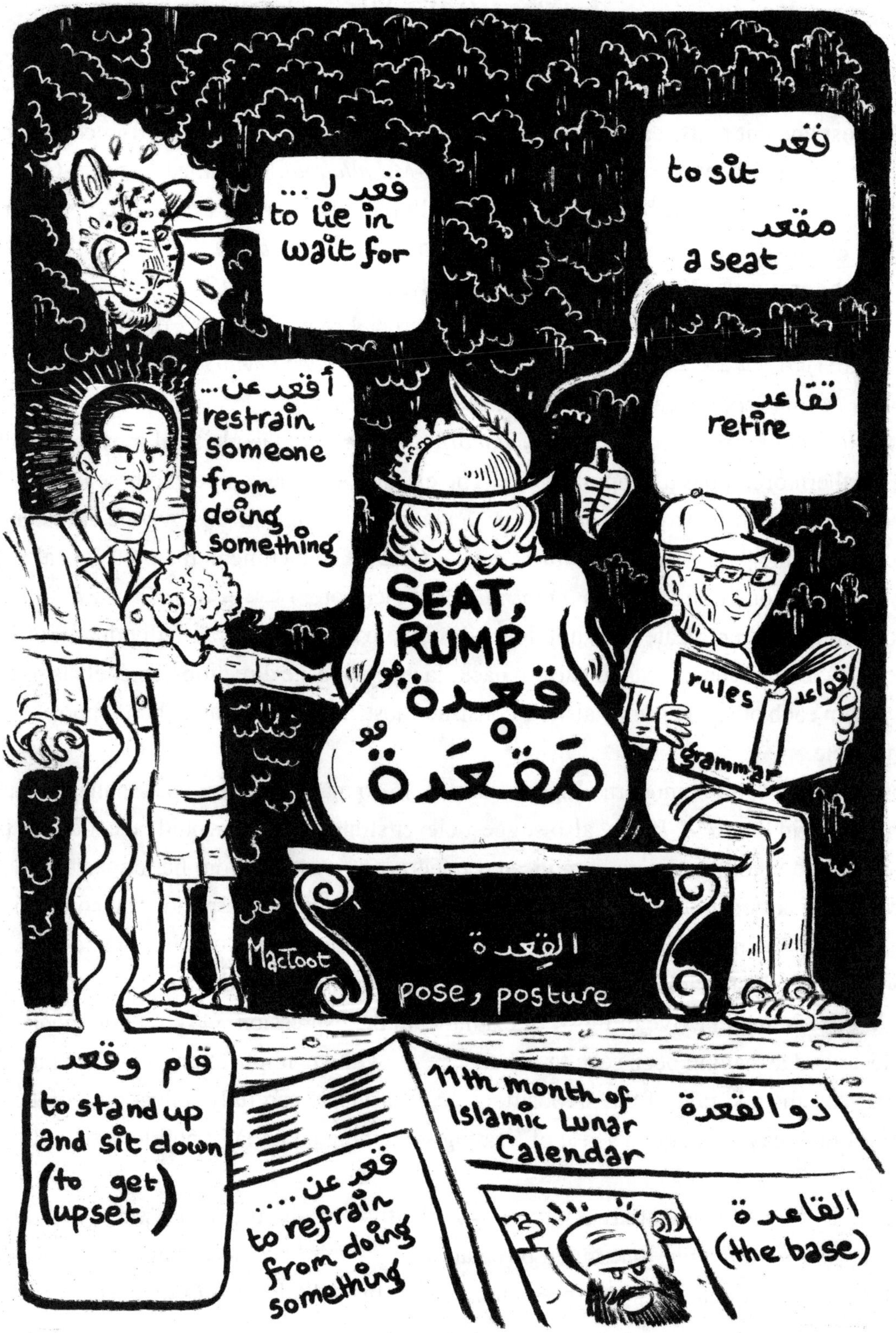

قعد لـ ...
to lie in wait for
قعد
to sit
مقعد
a seat
أقعد عن...
restrain someone from doing something
تقاعد
retire
SEAT, RUMP
قعدة
مقعدة
قواعد
rules
grammar
MacToot
القِعدة
pose, posture
قام وقعد
to stand up and sit down (to get upset)
قعد عن....
to refrain from doing something
11th month of Islamic Lunar Calendar
ذو القعدة
القاعدة
(the base)

120

Seat / Rump مَقْعَدة – مَقاعِد

Foundation, Base

Arabic has a wealth of expressions for the anatomical posterior, and this one, المَقْعَدة *al-maq'ada*, is a place pattern, and has a close equivalent in English's 'seat.' A near replica of the anatomical seat is المقعد *al-maq'ad*, a place to sit, whether designed as furniture or simply a convenient perch. Deciding whether the Form I verb قعد – يقعُد *qa'ada*, to sit, came first, or whether the physical rump did is like trying to solve the riddle of the chicken and the egg. The *maSdar* of قعد is القُعود *al-qu'uud*. This Form I derivative is utterly unfamiliar in English, but the same verb's active participle القاعِدة *al-qaa'ida*, is now a common—and commonly mispronounced—word in the news, Al-Qaeda. This organization's name means the base, suggesting a foundation and a base of operations. In the plural, قاعدة produces قواعد *qawaa'id*, a word which also means rules, principles, and, in the language domain, grammar.

Other derivatives of the Form I verb include القعدة, voweled *al-qi'da* and *al-qa'da*. The first is a way of sitting, a pose or a posture. The second is an 'instance noun,' an action done once, taking a seat. This forms the basis of the name of the eleventh month in the Islamic lunar calendar, ذو القعدة, Dhu l-Qa'da, The Month of Sitting. This month is the first of four in which fighting among Muslims was prohibited, hence a time of sitting. The link suggested between sitting and inaction is spelled out very clearly in the Form VI verb تقاعد, to retire. While Form VI most commonly expresses reciprocity, it has other semantic parameters, too. With this root, it describes doing the Form I action more and more. Form VI verbs like this depict things that happen incrementally, rather than in one fell swoop. In modern employment contexts, retirement may be sudden and decisive, but the original sense is a more gradual, progressive one. The English word retirement suggests withdrawal and seclusion; Arabic offers an image of someone becoming more and more sedentary.

The Form I verb is used in two important and very different verb–preposition idioms, قعد لِـ and قعد عن. In the first, the directional preposition لِـ *li*, toward, describes nefarious intentions that English conveys not with sitting, but rather *lying* in wait. With this choice of preposition, the subject's intentions are clearly directed *toward* the potential prey. In the second, we find عن *'an*, away from, and the resulting idiom indicates renunciation, waiving something one might have a right to, refraining from an action. Another idiom uses verbal contrast rather than directional prepositions to convey its sense of motion: قام وقعد *qaama wa qa'ada*, literally to stand up and sit down, means to become quite agitated, or to get upset, reminiscent of the idiom to be hopping mad.

This root creates one other verb form, the causative Form IV أقعد. English and Arabic morphology work in nice parallel here. The transformation from *sitting* to *seating* is akin to that of قعد to أقعد. Other examples where English makes a small phonological change to an intransitive verb to create a transitive one include to fall – to fell (a tree); to rise – to raise. The verb أقعد can also be used with the second prepositional idiom available to Form I, yielding أقعد عن, to restrain someone from doing something, to make someone renounce a course of action.

BUTT عَجُزٌ عَجِيزَةٌ
عَجَزَ to be weak, lack strength; be incapable of, unable to; to age, grow old
فَاعْلَمُوا أَنَّكُمْ غَيْرُ مُعْجِزِي اللَّهِ
Know that you cannot outdo God
Qur'an 9:3
عَجَّزَ to weaken; to hamstring, cripple, paralyze
مُعْجِزَة
miracle
أعجز
to weaken; to hamstring, cripple, paralyze; to outdo
إِعْجاز القرآن
the inimitability of the Qur'an
عَجوز old woman
MacToot

121
Butt, Bottom عجيزة / عَجُز – أعجاز
Incapacity

English has an impressive gallery of words for the butt, as we have seen, but none of them evoke the associations inherent in العجيزة *al-'ajiiza*. This word conveys inability of one sort or another: weakness, crippling, advanced age. Form I عجز – يعجِز *'ajaza* means to be weak, lack strength; its active participle عاجز *'aajiz* means incapable. This same verb can also mean to age, grow old. The associated noun عجوز *'ajuuz*, though apparently masculine in form, means an old woman, specifically coupling the idea of old age in women with weakness or incapacitation. With the addition of the preposition عن, the verb means to be incapable of doing something. Another noun in the Form I galaxy has important implications for economics: العَجْز *al-'ajz* is the technical term for deficit.

Form II عجّز and occasionally Form IV أعجز are causative versions of this: to weaken, cripple, paralyze. Usage is often figurative, denoting general disability, but a literal meaning is at the source. The derivation of these verbs from the buttocks is reminiscent of one of English's anatomically inspired choices for conveying incapacity, the verb to hamstring. The ع – ج – ز root also makes use of one of the interesting parameters available to Form X. The transitive استعجز means to consider someone incapable.

However, Form IV, أعجز deserves a closer look. Although to weaken is a possible translation, it has another more common meaning, one that is quite surprising, given the root's associations with weakness and incapacity. This second meaning is to outdo, to be so wonderfully capable as to be unsurpassable. Linked to inability, this verb nevertheless expresses a reverse image of it, so to speak. Someone capable of great feats renders others weak by comparison. Nominally, it is often applied to God's works, in particular, the Qur'an: إعجاز القُرآن. The Qur'an is thus portrayed as speech that outdoes any other, speech that is inimitable. Form IV is used participially at 9:3, where God's invincibility is spelled out: فَاعْلَمُوا أَنَّكُمْ غَيْرُ مُعْجِزِي اللهِ, *know that you cannot outdo God.* The Form IV verb's active participle, معجزة *mu'jiza*, is Arabic's most common word for miracle.

رِدْفٌ
RUMP
REAR
ردف
to come next
أَنِّي مُمِدُّكُم بِأَلْفٍ مِّنَ الْمَلَائِكَةِ مُرْدِفِينَ
I will reinforce you with a thousand angels bringing up the rear
Qur'an 8:9
الرِداف
riding animal's rump
رادف
to ride behind someone
ترادف
to follow one another, come in succession; to be synonymous
مترادفات
Synonyms
MacToot

122
Rump, Rear, Buttock رِدْف – أرْداف
Replacement

Inspiration from animal mounts lends some color to الـردف *ar-ridf*, variously translated as rump or rear or buttock in English. When used of people, the plural الأرداف *al-'ardaaf* is commonly used for buttocks, although the dual الردفان *ar-ridfaan* is more classically correct.

When speaking of a riding animal, something the mobile Bedouin had ample opportunity to do, الـرِّداف *ar-ridaaf* is often used for its rump. This piece of anatomy gave rise to four different verbs. All four elaborate on the visual and functional aspects of the body part. Form I, ردِف – يردَف *radifa*, to come next, come immediately after, and Form VI تـرادف, to follow one another or come in succession. Both suggest trekking along in single file, like camels in a caravan, or mules in a mule train. The verb can apply to such a literal and physical succession, as well as to events. In its literal sense, Form III رادف means to ride behind someone on the same mount. More figuratively, it means to substitute for or replace someone. Form IV أردف offers the causative sense, to seat someone behind someone else on a mount, or to make someone or something follow someone or something else. In this sense, we find the Qur'anic usage at 8:9: أنّـي مُمِدُّكُـمْ بألْـفٍ مِـن المَلائِكَـةِ مُرْدِفيـنَ, *I will reinforce you with a thousand angels bringing up the rear.* Derivatives of the ر- د- ف root occur three times in the Qur'an, but none figure in the *FDA* top 5,000.

Beyond the semantic domain of riding animals, Form III رادف also has an unexpected linguistic and literary sense: to be synonymous. This abstraction offers a humorously suggestive take on the visual rump, specifically the symmetry of one buttock to the other. In addition, it is a reminder of the common Arabic stylistic device of using synonymous words back-to-back, one after the other. Both Form III and Form VI can be used in this sense, making مرادفات *muraadifaat* and مترادفات *mutaraadifaat* synonymous as well.

BACKSIDE
HINDQUARTERS
كَفَل
تكافل
to vouch for each other, back each other up
كفل بـ ...
to foster, take responsibility for a child
كفل
to feed, support, provide for...
كافِل
breadwinner, supporter, legal guardian
كفيل
answerable; sponsor, legal guardian
كفيل
bail, pledge, collateral
كافل
to conclude an agreement; to make a contract with
تكفّل لِـ ...
بِـ ...
to pledge to someone to do something
MacToot

123
Backside, Hindquarters كَفَل – أَكْفال
Backup; Guaranteeing

The backside depicted by الكفل *al-kafal* is one you can rely on, one that supports you, one that backs you up. This word is also the croup or rump of a horse or other quadruped. The Form I verb كفل - يكفل has every possible internal voweling, most commonly *kafala – yakfulu*. Its meanings include to feed or provide for (a family), to post bail for someone, and to sponsor, act as legal guardian. These meanings are denominative, semantic outgrowths of the nouns and adjectives based on the root. The noun كَفْل *kafl* means a guarantee, or a pledge. Used as an adjective, كفيل *kafiil* means liable; as a noun, bailsman, sponsor, legal guardian. That guarantor may be a person or an institution. Where there is a guarantor, something should be guaranteed. This is the passive participle مكفول *makfuul*. When speaking of constitutional guarantees, one may say حقّ مكفول *haqq makfuul*, a guaranteed right. In financial contexts, مكفول means 'covered,' used for banknotes in circulation that are backed up by the authority of the central bank. The ك – ف – ل root has another noteworthy derivative, الكفالة *al-kafaala*, financial collateral and bail.

Form II كفّل is denominative as well. Depending on the context, it can mean to vouch for someone, be or become a legal sponsor or guardian, or post bail. Form II and Form IV أكفل are also used causatively to mean designating or appointing someone else as a guardian, or as responsible for bail. The *implied* contractual sense in those verbs is actually spelled out in Form III, كافل *kaafala*, which means to conclude a legal agreement or make a contract with someone, thus making responsibilities clear.

As sometimes happens, Form I كفل and Form V تكفّل are nearly synonymous. Form V takes prepositional objects: تكفّل له بـ means to vouch for someone to do something, or to be answerable for someone to a third party. The last of the verbs derived from this root is the reciprocal Form VI, تكافل, to vouch for each other, to guarantee each other, to back each other up.

Three of these words rank in the *FDA* top 5,000, the most frequent being كفيل, at 3,081. The word كفيل appears in the Qur'an once, and five other derivatives of the root occur there nine times. The most common of them is the Form I verb. In 3:44, reference is made to the Virgin Mary, whose father had died, and thus needed a guardian: وَما كُنْتَ لَدَيْهِم إِذْ يُلْقُونَ أقلامَهُمْ أَيُّهُمْ يَكْفُلُ مَرْيَمَ, *And you were not present among them when they cast lots (to decide) which of them might become guardian of Mary.*

In a more modern social-media context, كفيل appears in a tweet (تغريدة *taghriida*, from birdsong, like the original English) by Egyptian journalist Maha Matbuli, celebrating the launch of an annual film festival in El Gouna, a resort town on the Red Sea.[18]

to be late
تأخّر
أخّر
to make late, to delay
تأخير
obstruction; delay; deferment
الآخِرة
the hereafter
مُؤخّرة
DERRIÈRE
BEHIND
MacToot
آخِر
last, ultimate; end, conclusion, last part
آخَر/أُخْرى
other, another, one more

124
Derrière, Behind مُؤَخّرة – مُؤَخّرات
Lateness

The أ - خ - ر root engendered three verb forms; only two of them are in common modern use. As a consequence, one might not expect to encounter vocabulary from the root too often. But, in fact, nine of the fourteen derivatives of it listed in *Hans Wehr* are to be found in the *FDA*. Form II أخّر and Form V تأخّر provide an array of meanings, all of which align neatly with the elegant French 'derrière' and the familiar English 'behind.' Form II, naturally, is the transitive item of the pair; it must have an object. These objects sometimes collocate with specific English verbs. To select a few, أخّر can mean to delay (a meeting), to defer (a decision), to impede (an investigation), to hold (someone) back, to shelve (a resolution), and to set (a watch) back. Form V تأخّر, its intransitive counterpart, means to lag behind, to be behind schedule, delayed, impeded. It can mean to hesitate, or to be *in arrears*, a like-minded English locution in terms of anatomical inspiration! As for the verbs' *maSaadir*, Form II yields التأخير *at-ta'khiir*, delaying (something), while Form V produces التأخّر *at-ta'akhkhur*, delay, hesitation, tardiness, under-development. Form X استأخر is *largely* synonymous with Form V, to hold (oneself) back, remain behind, and is only common in Qur'anic usage.

In terms of structure, المؤخّرة *al-mu'akhkhira* is a Form II feminine active participle. Changing it to the passive participle and removing its feminine ة yields المؤخّر *al-mu'akhkhar*. This word can be the rear part of many things, including the stern of a ship, but not of the human body. But المؤخّر also has an important legal meaning. It is a variable sum of money to be paid to a woman should her husband ever divorce her. Since the sum is agreed upon at the time of drawing up the marriage contract, its eventual payment, should the marriage fail, is necessarily delayed. With the addition of the grammatical *fatH al-tanwiin*, this noun can be transformed into an adverb,مؤخّرًا *mu'akhkharan*, lately, recently.

Although no Form I verb is extant, its feminine active participle, الآخرة does exist. This is a word loaded with religious significance. Typically used in contrast to الدنيا *ad-dunyaa*, الآخِرة *al-'aakhira* signifies the hereafter, that life which can only come *after* we have lived this one. This noun occurs a stunning 115 times in the Qur'an. Its masculine counterpart, آخِر *'aakhir,* is a common adjective meaning last, ultimate, extreme. As always, one must pay careful attention to the short vowel on the second root letter. Changing it to a *fatHa* yields آخَر *'aakhar*, other, another. Gender is also of paramount consideration with this word which is actually of the pattern أفعل, and therefore takes the feminine form أُخرى *'ukhraa*. This masculine/feminine pair is the most frequent of all the root's derivatives, ranking at 38. One more adjective is also in very common use: أخير *'akhiir*, last, latest, the second (of two). When الأوّل is paired with الأخير, the former and the latter is a good translation. As we have seen above with the المؤخّر / مؤخّرًا duo above, this adjective can also be turned into an adverb by the addition of *fatH at-tanwiin*: أخيرًا *'akhiiran*, finally.

to alternate, عاقب take turns with; to punish
عَقَبة steep path; obstacle
خليج العقبة Gulf of Aqaba
to compromise, show up; to review critically عقّب على
to follow(s come after, عقب ensue
عُقب، عاقبة end, outcome, consequence
HEEL
عُقب end, butt, stub
عِقاب عُقوبة punishment
to trail تعقّب
MacToot
to be consecutive, follow one after the other تعاقب

125

Heel عَقِب – عَقِبان – أَعْقاب

End; Repercussion; Punishment

The end! The physical placement of the heel, العقب *al-'aqib*, is the key to its metaphoric functions. The heel falls at the end of the body's vertical axis and at the back of the foot's horizontal one. *Everything* stops at the heel, no matter which direction it is coming from. Many of the heel's derivatives depict this end-of-the-line relationship. The tail end of a number of things, like the stub (of a pencil) or the butt (of a cigarette) is called العُقب *al-'uqb*. Bodily orientation is important in terms of the heel, too. Heads should be high, but heels, الأعقاب *al-'a'qaab* (as opposed to الكعاب *al-ki'aab*), should not. Consequently, when one takes a tumble and proper bodily position is inverted, Arabic and English use an almost identical idiom, رأسا على عقب *ra'san 'alaa 'aqib*, head over heel(s).

The heel seems a rather modest body part, and yet a famous geographical feature owes its name to its derivative power. Like ن – د – ب, the root for the word scar, ع – ق – ب lends its name to a large body of water, خليج العقبة *khaliij al-'aqaba*, the Gulf of Aqaba. A city of the same name falls at the 'heel,' so to speak, of this long, narrow gulf. Archaeological research shows that a settlement has existed on this same spot for thousands of years. As a common noun, العقبة means an obstacle, a steep road or track, especially one in the mountains. Al-Aqaba and its gulf are in fact surrounded by mountains with steep, narrow passes, ones on which pursuit would have been difficult.

Setting the semantic parameters for all of this root's verbs, Form I عقب – يعقُب *'aqaba* means to happen afterwards, or alternatively, to follow someone. That latter sense is reminiscent of قفا أثره *qafaa 'atharahu*, to track, inspired by the nape of the neck, but the lowly heel is *never* metaphorically linked to emulation. It does, however, carry a temporal load, and is even the source of an explicit adverb of time, عَقِبَ *'aqiba*, immediately after. At 1,423, it is the top derivative of the root in the *FDA*. Form II عقّب على *'aqqaba 'alaa* and its *maSdar* التعقيب على *at-ta'qiib 'alaa* mean to pursue. This may be a verbal pursuit, as well: to follow up with a remark or a critique. Form V تعقّب, to track, is echoed by the catchy English heat metaphor, to be hot on (his) heels.

One meaning of Form III عاقب is to take turns with. Form VI تعاقب, therefore, means to take turns with each other. For sequential actions, to be consecutive is a fair translation, but again, English has a perfect metaphoric equivalent. One may say تعاقبت العواصف *ta'aaqabat al-'awaaSif*, the storms came on each others' heels. In addition to taking turns, Form III عاقب has another crucial meaning, to punish, a verb all about repercussions. Punishment, العِقاب *al-'iqaab*, is the expected outcome or consequence, العاقبة *al-'aaqiba*, of a reprehensible action. In both temporal and logical terms, consequences and punishment *follow* an action. Such outcomes are never anodyne, as shown by the collocation, عواقب وخيمة *'awaaqib wakhiima*, dire consequences. One can almost imagine a wagging سبّابة, pointing out the blameworthy agent. Form III has an alternative *maSdar*, too, المعاقبة *al-mu'aaqaba*, which conveys either sense of the verb, taking turns with, or punishing. Besides the term for political or economic sanctions العقوبات *al-'uquubaat*, the second most frequent derivative of this root in the media, and the adverb of time, seven other derivatives figure in the *FDA*. All of this shows that the heel gave the ع – ق - ب root the last word!

Appendix 1 Multiple Designations

This appendix consists of a list of forty-two parts or areas of the body for which Arabic has multiple—between two and seven—and nearly synonymous designations. Slang terms are not considered in either Arabic or English. The list is not exhaustive, but it does include body parts not discussed in this book and offers a reasonable basis for comparison. These forty-two parts or areas produce sixty-two designations in English, but 110 in Arabic! Four of them have three or more designations in English, while seventeen do in Arabic. The English clusters (two words or more) total nine, less than 25 percent of those on offer in Arabic. It is interesting to note, however, that in two categories—excrescences and the ineffable and the back of the body—English is almost as productive as Arabic.

For quick reference, the number of English words in each of the five categories is indicated on its left, with one asterisk, and the corresponding number of Arabic words appears on its right, with two. A key at the end of the table clarifies this.

*7 'Body' and Here, There, and Everywhere **15

1 Body جسم – جسد – بدن

2 Limb(s) / Extremities جوارح – أطراف – إرب / آراب

3 Skin جلد – أديم – بشرة

4 Corpse جثة – جثمان

5 Vein عرق – وريد

6 Birthmark وحم – شامة

*5 Excrescences and the Ineffable **6

7 Drool / Spittle / Slobber لعاب – ريال / ريالة

8 Mind عقل – ذهن

9 Brain مخّ – دماغ

*19 Front Upper Body (Head and Shoulders) and Arm **41

10 Face / Visage / Countenance / Mien وجه – مُحَيَّا – طلعة

11 Eyelashes أهداب – رموش

12 Eye عين – مقلة – ناظر

13 Pupil حدقة – بؤبؤ

14 Dimple غمّازة – نونة

15 Nose أنف – خشم – مَعطِس

16 Throat / Gullet (internal) حلق – زور

17 Jaw فكّ – شدق

18 Neck رقبة – عنق – جيد

19 Throat / Neck (external) مزرد – نحر / منحر – خناق / مخنق

20 Shoulder كتف – منكب – عاتق

21 Forearm زَنْد – ذراع – ساعد

22 Elbow كوع – مرفق

23 Wrist معصم – رُسْغ

24 Palm كفّ – راحة

25 Fingertips أنامل – بَنان

*19 Trunk and Lower Body, from the Front **34

26 Breast / Bosom ثدي – نهد – كُعب – حضن

27 Nipple / Teat بزّ – حلمة

28 Side / Flank عطف – جنب – كنف

29 Pericardium شغاف – تأمور

30 Heart قلب – فؤاد

31 Waist كشح – خاصرة

32 Intestines / Guts / Bowels أحشاء – أمعاء – مصارين

33 Vulva فرج – بُضع

34 Vagina غِمد – مَهْبَل

35 Penis أَير – ذكر – قضيب

36 Foreskin غلفة – قلفة

37 Pudenda عورات – سوءات

38 Leg رجل – ساق

39 Heel كعب – عقب – كاحل

*11 Back, Top to Bottom **14

40 Back ظهر – كاهل – متن

41 Backside / Bottom / Butt / Buttocks / Derriere / Hindquarters / Rear-end / Posterior / Seat ألية / إلية – ردف – دبر – عجيزة / عجز – مؤخرة – مقعدة – كفل – سافلة

42 Anus شرج – إست

** = total number of English terms; ** = total number of Arabic terms*

Appendix 2 Frequency of Body Patterns

Sections A and B of this appendix list all thirty-eight singular patterns of the body vocabulary, including but not limited to body parts treated in *Rooted in the Body*. Roughly 70 percent of these common singular words are based on sixteen *simple* patterns not augmented by additional long vowels or non–root consonants. Section C provides sixteen broken plural patterns. This is a representative sample, not an exhaustive one, because many singulars take multiple plurals, some of which are rare. Two of these sixteen broken plural patterns emerge as extremely common. They house almost as much vocabulary as the other fourteen patterns combined. This is, of course, related to the fact that so many body singulars are based on simple, unaugmented patterns that have an affinity for those two plural patterns. Furthermore, only five of those other fourteen plural patterns have significant amounts of vocabulary. Taken together, this information should give students more confidence in identifying roots and patterns, and should also help them make increasingly educated guesses as they work to recognize and produce plurals.

A. Simple Singulars and Collectives (16)

٢٩فَعْل: عظم – شعر – لحم – عضل – نفس – عقل – رأس – وجه – عين – أنف – حلق – زور – فكّ – لحي – نحر – كفّ – صدر – قصّ – ثدي – نهد – جنب – سحر – قلب – بطن – فرج – ساق – كعب – ظهر – متن

١٤فِعْل: إرب – جسم – جلد – عرق – ريق – جفن – شدق – سنّ – حضن – بزّ – ضلع – غمد – رجل – ردف

١٣فَعَل: جسد – بدن – ندب – عصب – عرق – نفس – حنك – شغف – كشح – ذكر – قدم – قفا – كفل

٦ فُعْلة: ركبة – سرّة – قلفة – غلفة – عقلة – جثّة

٦ فُعْل: روح – مخّ – هدب – كوع – ظفر – بضع

٤ فَعْلة: طلعة – راحة – وحمة – شامة

٤فَعِل: كتف – كبد – رحم – عقب

٤فُعُل: قبل – أذن – عنق – دبر

٣ فَعَلة: حدقة – رقبة – حلمة

٣فَعْ: دم – يد – فم

٢ فُعْلة: مقلة – عقلة

١ فَعُل: عجز ١ فَعِل: كبد ١ فِعْلة: لحية ١ فِعَة : شفة ١ فُعْ : فو

B. Augmented Singulars (22)

٦فاعِل: حاجب – شارب – عاتق – جانب – ساعد – كاهل

٦فِعال: رباط – ريال – دماغ – لسان – خناق – ذراع

٣فَعيل: وريد– جبين – مريء

٣ مَفعَل / مَفْعِل: مخنق – منحر / مفصل

٢ مِفْعَل: مرفق – معصم

٢ فُعال: لعاب – فؤاد

٢ فَعّالة: غمّازة – سبّابة

١ فَعِيلة: عجيزة

١ فاعِلة: خاصرة

١مِفْعال: منخار

١ مَفْعال: مسامّ

١ فَعْليّة: قرنية

١ إفْعَل: إصبع

١ أُفْعُلة: أنملة

١ مُفعِّلة : مؤخّرة

١ مَفْعَل: مهبل

١ مَفْعِل: منكب

١ إفْعال: إبهام

١ مُفَعَّل: مُحَيًّا

١ فِعْلان: شريان

١ فُعْلان: جثمان

١ تَفْعول: تأمور

C. Broken Plurals (a selection, for a relative sense of frequency)

٣٠ أَفْعال: أبدان – أجسام – أجساد – آراب – أطراف – أرواح – أنفاس – أمخاخ – أذهان – أهداب – أحداق – أسنان – أشداق – أعناق – أحلاق – أزوار – أجياد – أكتاف – أرساغ – أعطاف – أجناب– أثداء – أحضان – أرحام – أرداف – أدبار – أعجاز – أكفال – أشراج – أعقاب

٢١ فُعول: ندوب – عروق – نفوس – عقول – رؤوس– وجوه – رموش – عيون – أنوف – فكوك – حلوق – نحور – كفوف – صدور – نهود – قلوب – فروج – بضوع – أيور – ظهور – متون

٩ مَفاعِل: مفاصل – معاطس – مناحر – مخانق – مزارد – مناكب – عواتق – معاصم – مقاع

٩ أَفْعِلة: أربطة – أوردة – أدمغة – أمرئة – أجبنة – ألسنة – أشغفة – أفئدة – أقفية

٨ فَواعِل: جوارح – حواجب – نواظر – شوارب – سواعد – كواهل – كواحل – سوافل

٨ فُعَل: جثث – عقل – مقل – لحًى – سرر – غلف – قلف – ركب

٧ فِعال: عظام – شفاه – رقاب – زناد – قصاص – بزاز – كعاب

٣ أَفاعِل: أنامل – أيادٍ – أصابع

٢ فَعالِين: شرايين – جثامين

٢ فِعْلان: كيعان – سيقان

٢ أَفْعُل: أذرع – أرجل

١ فُعْلان: قضبان

١ مَفاعِيل: مناخير

١ تَفاعِيل: تآمير

١ فُعْل: كعب

١ فَعْل: راح

Endnotes

1 George Lakoff and Mark Johnson, *Metaphors We Live By* (Chicago: University of Chicago Press, 1980); Mark Johnson, *The Body in the Mind: The Bodily Basis of Meaning, Imagination, and Reason* (Chicago: University of Chicago Press, 1987).

2 W. Wright, *A Grammar of the Arabic Language*, 3rd ed. (London, New York, Melbourne: Cambridge University Press, 1896–98, 1932).

3 A few body parts are not 'productive' in this derivative sense. Some of them appear in appendix 1, which lists multiple words for a single part of anatomy, but they are not further addressed in this book.

4 Tom Buckwalter and Dilworth Parkinson, *A Frequency Dictionary of Arabic* (London and New York: Routledge, 2011).

5 J.M. Cowan, ed., *Arabic-English Dictionary: The Hans Wehr Dictionary of Modern Written Arabic* (3rd ed., Ithaca, NY: Spoken Language Services, Inc., 1976).

6 Munir Baalbaki and Rohi Baalbaki, *al-Mawrid* (9th ed., Beirut: Dar al-'Ilm li-l-Malayin, 2005); *The Oxford English–Arabic Dictionary of Current Usage* (1972; repr., Oxford: Oxford University Press, 1978).

7 Elsaid M. Badawi and Muhammad Abdel Haleem, *Arabic–English Dictionary of Qur'anic Usage* (Leiden and Boston: Brill, 2008).

8 El-Said Badawi and Martin Hinds, *Dictionary of Egyptian Arabic* (Beirut: Librarie du Liban, 1986).

9 Zouheir Maalej, "Figurative Language in Anger Expressions in Tunisian Arabic: An Extended View of Embodiment" in *Metaphor and Symbol*, (2004): 51–75; Zouheir Maalej, "The Embodiment of Fear Expressions in Tunisian Arabic: Theoretical and Practical Implications," in *Applied Cultural Linguistics: Implica-*

tions for Second Language Learning and Intercultural Communication, edited by Farzad Sharifian and Gary B. Palmer (Amsterdam, Philadelphia: John Benjamins Publishing Company, 2007), 87–104; Zouheir Maalej, "The Heart and Cultural Embodiment," in *Culture, Body, and Language: Conceptualization of Internal Body Organs Across Cultures and Languages*, edited by Farzad Sharifian, René Dirven, Ning Yu, and Susanne Niemeier (Mouton de Gruyter, 2008), 395–428; Zouheir Maalej, "Figurative dimensions of 3ayn 'eye' in Tunisian Arabic," in *Embodiment via Body Parts*, edited by Zouheir Maalej and Ning Yu, (Amsterdam, Philadelphia: John Benjamins Publishing Company, 2011), 213–40.

10 *Online Etymology Dictionary*, www.etymonline.com.

11 Wilfred G.E. Watson, "Notes on the Gender of Nouns in Semitic," *Aula Orientalis* 26 (2008): 195–209.

12 This Hadith chain goes from at-Tarmudhi to Anas ibn Malik to the Prophet.

13 Retrieved from almaany.com.

14 Gibran Khalil Gibran, "Khalil al-kafir," in *al-Arwah al-mutamarrida* (Beirut: Mu'assasat Nawfal, 1981), 111. Quotation translated by Lisa White.

15 Mohssen Esseesy, *Grammaticalization of Arabic Prepositions and Subordinators* (Leiden: Brill, 2010), 40, 257.

16 This phrase is sung by Fadia Al Haj in the song *'Ayyuhaa as-saaqi* (O, wine steward). It is attributed to Ibn Zuhr al-Hafiid, a poet–physician who was born and died in Seville. Exact birth and death dates are contested, but it is generally agreed that he lived a very long life beginning in the second decade of the twelfth century.

17 Elsaid M. Badawi and Muhammad Abdel Haleem, *Arabic–English Dictionary of Qur'anic Usage* (Leiden and Boston: Brill, 2008), 698.

18 Maha Matbuli, September 3, 2017.

Note on Citations

A number of translations from the Qur'an are taken from Elsaid M. Badawi and Muhammad Abdel Haleem, Arabic–English Dictionary of Qur'anic Usage (Leiden and Boston: Brill, 2008).

Additionally, in two cases, for عاتق on page 155 and for أهل الذكر on page 229, rather than a translation, there is a short discussion taken from this same reference.
The page numbers of the translations taken from Badawi and Abdel Haleem are listed below:

25 (5:4), 41 (49:12), 43 (2:232), 69 (3:30), 87 (58:8, 33:44), 99 (34:13), 113 (14:49), 115 (104:1, 83:30), 121 (2:93), 153 (23:74), 155 (22:29), 167 (12:32), 175 (5:11), 187 (48:24), 207 (28:11, 4:36), 215 (16:78), 217 (90:4), 218 (57:3), 223 (23:5), 227 (7:151), 231 (88:21), 243 (5:46), 253 (12:27), 261 (3:44)

All other translations from the Qur'an are by Lisa White.

Index by Arabic Root